NEWCASTLE/BLOODAXE POETRY SERIES: 13

PAUL BATCHELOR:
READING BARRY MacSWEENEY

NEWCASTLE/BLOODAXE POETRY SERIES

NEWCASTLE/BLOODAXE POETRY SERIES: 13

Reading Barry MacSweeney

EDITED BY

PAUL BATCHELOR

BLOODAXE BOOKS

ISBN: 978 1 85224 988 5

First published 2013 by
Newcastle Centre for the Literary Arts,
Newcastle University,
Newcastle upon Tyne NE1 7RU,
in association with
Bloodaxe Books Ltd,
Highgreen,
Tarset,
Northumberland NE48 1RP.

www.bloodaxebooks.com
For further information about Bloodaxe titles
please visit our website or write to
the above address for a catalogue.

Supported by
**ARTS COUNCIL
ENGLAND**

Cover design: Neil Astley & Pamela Robertson-Pearce.

Printed in Great Britain by Bell & Bain Limited, Glasgow, Scotland, on
acid-free paper sourced from mills with FSC chain of custody certification.

CONTENTS

A Note on the Text

Where possible, all references to Barry MacSweeney's poetry throughout this book are to *Wolf Tongue: Selected Poems 1965-2000* (Tarset, Northumberland: Bloodaxe Books, 2003), and page numbers are given parenthetically in the main text.

PAUL BATCHELOR

Introduction

The last full-length collection that Barry MacSweeney lived to see published was *The Book of Demons* (Bloodaxe Books, 1997). Many of the most impressive aspects of this volume – the intricate symbology, the vertiginous swoop of registers, the unsparing wit, the complexity of characterisation, the syntactical resourcefulness – had been earned over a lifetime of restless self-testing; but this same restlessness simultaneously gives the book the kind of daring, hubristic, allusive, raw dazzle usually associated with a precocious first collection. The book draws its power from such contradictions: a chronicle of failure, it has a swaggering confidence; a departure, it felt to many like a homecoming.

The homecoming aspect is partly a matter of literary history. MacSweeney's first book, *The Boy from the Green Cabaret Tells of His Mother* (Hutchinson, 1968), sold thousands of copies on the back of an ill-judged publicity stunt that saw the nineteen-year-old poet nominated for the Oxford Chair of Poetry. Derided in the press when he received only three votes, MacSweeney was quickly dropped by Hutchinson. He subsequently embraced small-press publishing, spurning "official" literary culture for three decades. The warm reception afforded *The Book of Demons* (it received a Paul Hamlyn Award and a Poetry Book Society Recommendation: unusual accolades for this poet) raised MacSweeney's profile once again, and a reading tour brought him into contact with the biggest audience he had reached since the success of his début. More obviously, the book felt like a homecoming because of its auto-biographical subject matter and framework: the title sequence charts MacSweeney's nightmarish struggle with alcoholism in contemporary Newcastle, but it is preceded by *Pearl*, a sequence of contemplative lyrics about his rural Northumbrian upbringing and his childhood love for a mute girl whom he taught to read and write.

It is a demon's business to tempt, and *The Book of Demons* tempts us to read it as the final word on MacSweeney, presenting itself as the culmination of his life and career and frequently striking a summative and doom-laden note. The blurb opens by yoking poetry and alcoholism together in a Mephistophelian non sequitur: 'Barry MacSweeney wrote his first poem at the age of seven – 42 years ago – and has been an alcoholic since he was 16.' But this only makes explicit the argument of the poems themselves, which present the speaker not simply as an alcoholic but as an alcoholic poet ('Just look, I snarled my lute / in waspish worsement, claggy gob / clipped claptight shut') and look back wistfully, or ruefully, on a childhood 'before poetry was written, long before harm // and its broods of violence' (p.221; p.278). The city in which the speaker often appears trapped is a *paysage intérieur*, with many of the invented locations named after disordered mental states, or physical ailments: 'Do-lalley Drive…Cirrhosis Street / and Wrecked Head Road' or even the 'Department Store of Sighs' (p.222; p.268). Other locations are named after natural disasters, in an outrageous projection of the poet's sense of guilt: 'Earthquake Street…Richter Scale Prospekt', 'Tumble Down Town', 'Nixville' and 'Snowville' (p.244; p.263; p.240; p.266). The poet is imprisoned inside his own construction, and this relates to his attempt to "cast out" the demons of his earlier selves and styles: he wishes to escape from himself. And, of course, this story is itself a construction.

The accompanying sequence *Pearl* is equally personal and equally theatrical. In the repeated assertion 'I am Pearl' we hear a mute girl's satisfaction in finally being able to declare herself a subject, and her pride in outflanking the poet's attempts at containing her; but we also hear MacSweeney telling us something so directly we are liable to miss it: he *is* Pearl. Pearl's only utterance is 'a-a-a-a-a-a', a kinetic rhythm incapable of figurative or conceptual function, having stalled at the beginning of the alphabet; but the voice MacSweeney creates for her is highly articulate, and even her declarations of muteness are strikingly verbose: 'I do not emit articulate sound' (p.196). Pearl's voice and persona are fruitfully paradoxical: she is both mute and articulate; illiterate and yet able to make literary allusion; lost in the past and yet looking back from the present-day; a victim of bad government and yet a prophetic political commentator. The sequence's significance extends far beyond any actual relationship MacSweeney might have once had. Pearl functions as a political symbol, because the image of two innocents helping one another is essentially a symbol of co-operation and solidarity; and Pearl's return as a ghostly presence in the immediate aftermath of Thatcherism testifies to the vanquishing of those ideals. Her silence is also symbolic of personal distress, for MacSweeney endured a depressive six-year silence prior to writing these poems: after 'Finnbar's Lament' in 1986, he wrote little and published nothing until *Hellhound Memos* (The Many Press, 1993), in which the figure of Pearl begins to emerge.

Dying is always a risky career move. Coming as it did just three years after *The Book of Demons* appeared, MacSweeney's death seemed to confirm a narrative in which his life had been a quest that culminated in writing that final book, as though its style and poetic procedures were somehow more authentically his own, and the small-press years could stay forgotten... This narrative is a trap, and while it is easy to disparage those who fall for it, we should not overlook the part MacSweeney played in setting it. The man liked telling stories about himself, and many of his poems project a partial version of himself, treat his earlier work cavalierly, and employ a quest-like narrative structure. Had he died soon after writing *Ranter* (Slow Dancer, 1985) or *Hellhound Memos*, they too would have appeared to conclude his career arc, and to eerily predict his imminent demise. MacSweeney could not have foreseen how successful the story he told in *The Book of Demons* would be, and at times in those last three years even he seems to have worried whether he would be able to write his way out of that style and persona and into another. He took extreme measures, blending his voice with that of child killer Mary Bell, and even Adolf Hitler. Such part-identifications were perfunctory and unconvincing, but perhaps succeeded in freeing him from his demonic incarnation, allowing a more successful persona to emerge. The posthumously-published *Horses in Boiling Blood* (Equipage, 2004) finds the poet at large in a new country, a new time and a new language: that of Apollinaire's France. The collection is billed as 'a collaboration, a celebration' rather than a translation, and although most of it is based on original poems by Apollinaire, the central figure is a hybrid – 'Gwillam Mad MacSweeney' as he is called in 'Miss the Mississippi and Thee' – who can move freely between 1990s Newcastle and the trenches of the First World War. Had MacSweeney lived longer, further self-inventions would surely have followed.

The ultimate refutation of a too-simplistic view of MacSweeney's life and work is found in the range and ambition of the poems themselves. At the time of his death, MacSweeney was in the early stages of preparing a selected edition, *Wolf Tongue*, which was eventually published posthumously by Bloodaxe Books in 2003. The volume brought much of MacSweeney's poetry back into print, and demonstrated the vast sweep of his work. We can only speculate as to the effect it might have had on MacSweeney to see it published.

Critical interest in MacSweeney has been growing steadily for some years. The first important piece of sustained criticism on the poet was John Wilkinson's review-essay of *The Tempers of Hazard* (an anthology of three poets' work, though Wilkinson focussed solely on MacSweeney), which appeared in 1995, in *Angel Exhaust* No.11, and was subsequently reprinted in his book *The Lyric Touch* (Salt, 2007). Wilkinson offers an extended reading of 'The Last Bud', 'Jury Vet' and 'Wild Knitting', praising MacSweeney's recklessness, his principled restlessness, and his self-interrogative honesty. Marianne Morris's essay 'The Abused Become the Abusers', which appeared in *Quid* 14 (October 2004), also centres on MacSweeney's political writing, praising its courageous refusal of nostalgia and sentiment, and paying particular attention to 'Colonel B', a poem Wilkinson dismisses. After reviewing many of MacSweeney's individual books over a number of years, Andrew Duncan produced an overview of MacSweeney's career, 'The mythical history of Northumbria; or, feathered slave to unreasonable demands', which was published in the first issue of *Poetry Salzburg* (Spring 2001). Clive Bush's somewhat lengthier overview can be found in the chapter-essay 'Parts in the Weal of Kynde', from *Out of Dissent: A Study of Five Contemporary British Poets*. Bush's study is valuable not least for its consideration of MacSweeney's lesser-known publications, such as *Flames on the Beach at Viareggio* (Blacksuede Boot Press, 1970), *Our Mutual Scarlet Boulevard* (Fulcrum, 1971), and *Black Torch* (London Pride Editions, 1978). In *Three Lyric Poets* (Northcote House Publishers, 2009), William Walton Rowe considers MacSweeney's poetry alongside that of

Lee Harwood and Chris Torrance. Peter Barry devotes a chapter of his book *Contemporary British Poetry and the City* (Manchester University Press, 2000) to *Hellhound Memos*, praising the sequence for the way it dramatises poetic and political radicalism in terms of a contemporary urban environment, rather than relying on more traditional, rural tropes. Matthew Jarvis considers the same sequence in 'Presenting the Past: Barry MacSweeney's Cultural Memory' (*Pretexts: literary and cultural studies*, Vol. 11, No.2, 2002), and focuses on MacSweeney's subsequent volume, *Pearl*, in his essay 'Barry MacSweeney's Moorland Romance' in *Culture, Creativity and Environment: New Environmentalist Criticism* (Rodopi, 2007). *Pearl* is also examined in Harriet Tarlo's essay 'Radical Landscapes: Contemporary Poetry in the Bunting Tradition', collected in *The Star You Steer By: Basil Bunting and British Modernism* (Rodopi, 2000); while the question of whether Bunting was a formative influence on MacSweeney is re-opened by Rebecca A. Smith's provocative essay in *Jacket* No.35 (Spring 2008), 'Barry MacSweeney and the Bunting Influence: a key figure in his literary universe?'.

Other recent publications illuminate the contexts in which some of MacSweeney's work was written. Peter Barry's fascinating account of the Poetry Society takeover in *Poetry Wars: British Poetry of the 1970s and the Battle of Earls Court* (Salt, 2006) offers insights into the man behind the poetry, as MacSweeney played an important role in the Poetry Wars and, as Chairman of the Poetry Society, led the mass walk-out on 26 March 1977. *Certain Prose of 'The English Intelligencer'* (Mountain Press, 2012) brings back into print prose selections from the eponymous magazine that ran from 1966 to 1968, featuring MacSweeney alongside Jeremy Prynne, Andrew Crozier, John James, Peter Riley and others. One of the editors of this volume, Luke Roberts, is also a MacSweeney scholar.

In May 2001, Newcastle University acquired the Barry Mac-Sweeney archive, which is now housed in the Special Collections department in the Robinson Library. The papers were given to the university by the poet's family, and further material has been donated to the archive by Robert Sheppard, Nate Dorward and Peter Riley. The archive consists of draft manuscripts and corres-pondence, as well as the poet's personal library of books, pamphlets, magazines and vinyl. The fact that MacSweeney frequently dated and annotated the books he was reading makes it possible to chart his enthusiasms closely. The first PhD studies to draw on the MacSweeney papers were completed in 2007 and 2008, by Rebecca A. Smith and myself.

This book, the first collection of essays to be dedicated to Mac-Sweeney's work, is the natural next step. A diverse range of writers – academics, poets, journalists and friends of MacSweeney – have been brought together to offer perspectives on this most protean, prolific, and contradictory of poets. As will be seen, they are far from reaching a consensus: many offer overviews of MacSweeney's career, but, convincing as they are, these overviews frequently contradict one another.

We begin with Harriet Tarlo, who feels that 'critical readings have suffered from over-indulgence in the personal, failing to recognise that MacSweeney's personae are always characters in his work, just as the characters are always poets'. Instead, Tarlo focuses on the image of the poet that MacSweeney presents, and on Mac-Sweeney's need to construct a poetic lineage from which to speak; an approach that allows her to draw together many disparate strands of the poet's oeuvre. Tarlo also offers a sensitive reading of Mac-Sweeney's attitude to place, and shows that the poet's work engages with all of England, not just the North-East in which he lived for much of his life: 'from his deeply-rooted locality... MacSweeney finds a place to speak for the country as a whole'. However, in a fruitful point of disagreement, the North-East is very much the focus of Matthew Jarvis's essay, which scutinises the way Mac-Sweeney experiences place both physically and culturally. Bringing an environmentalist perspective to bear on the poet, Jarvis argues that MacSweeney's work questions the human/nature dualism that underwrites so many artistic encounters with the natural world (in the Western tradition anyway), in favour of an 'intertwining of human and non-human which is seemingly integral to MacSweeney's poetics of place'.

Andrew Duncan's focus is not so much the poetics of place as the politics of place: he is the first of three critics here to deal with MacSweeney's more overtly political writing of the late 70s and early 80s. Duncan offers a re-evaluation of a volume frequently dismissed by MacSweeney's critics, and indeed by the poet himself: *Black Torch*. This book concerns coal-miners' working conditions and strike action in the nineteenth and twentieth centuries, and

Duncan reads it in terms of a 'social drama' that investigates and reveals the underlying principles of social structure. William Rowe focuses on the ways in which MacSweeney's concerns with poetic identity and the isolation of an individual in *Brother Wolf* and *Odes* become politicised in 'Wild Knitting', as the poet turns his attention to the breakdown and loss of communities under Thatcherism. John Wilkinson considers MacSweeney's political poetry alongside contemporaneous work by Martin Amis and Elvis Costello, reading the work of all three in terms of male panic occasioned by Margaret Thatcher's term as Prime Minister, and as a series of attempts to register the three great shocks of the Falklands War, the miners' strike and financial deregulation.

Peter Riley sees this phase of MacSweeney's career in very different terms: 'The violent and obscene poems of the early 1980s are for me the central disaster in Barry's career'. Riley places *Pearl* at the centre of MacSweeney's achievement. After opening with an inspired close-reading of a single three-line passage from that sequence, Riley argues that Pearl's importance lies in the way she symbolised redemption, and the way she redeemed the poet and his writing: 'Through her it became possible [for MacSweeney] to bestow unmitigated praise on someone who was not a sexual object and not a model hero or suicidal alter-ego'.

My own essay looks at MacSweeney's relationship to father figures in his poetry, in particular Basil Bunting. I begin by considering two of MacSweeney's earliest successful poems, 'The Last Bud' and *Brother Wolf*, both of which reject Bunting while tellingly displaying his influence. I then consider *Ranter*, the poem in which Mac-Sweeney most clearly presents himself as a follower of Bunting, and demonstrate that the poem does not, in fact, follow Bunting as closely as it might seem. W.N. Herbert also investigates what he calls 'the demons of influence', arguing that 'MacSweeney was neither/both mainstream nor/and experimental, a writer who had to find his own position almost in despite of these categories'. As Herbert demonstrates, MacSweeney's genius lay in 'swerving away from what he perceived was expected of him', and nowhere is this more true than in *Pearl* and *The Book of Demons*, collections in which we see MacSweeney most clearly and characteristically in moments of wild oscillation 'between town and countryside, between real, remembered, imaginary and hallucinated landscapes'.

The book closes with two pieces that offer more intimate perspectives on the poet. Terry Kelly was a close friend of MacSweeney's, and his colleague at the *South Shields Gazette*. In 'Not Dark Yet', he looks at MacSweeney's use of popular music, in particular his lifelong love of Bob Dylan's work. Finally, the concluding piece by S.J. Litherland, MacSweeney's former partner, offers invaluable insights into both the poet and the man: his vulnerabilities, but also his enthusiasms, and his readiness to take up crusades against injustices large and small. In particular, Litherland demonstrates how important MacSweeney's career in journalism was to him, describing him as a man who 'carried around the excitement of the newsroom'.

Appreciation of MacSweeney's achievement will grow in tandem with our understanding of the considerable challenges he faced: his was a Romantic sensibility, and yet he was drawn to Modernist poetics; he remained committed to his social and regional origins, but addressed all of England in his poems, some of which he described as 'state of the nation bulletins'; he demanded directness of utterance, but was also devoted to avant-garde art; he was hungry for recognition but given to disguise, being equally fascinated and repelled by the notion of fame; and much of his poetry was fuelled by his often turbulent life, and yet, with the exception of some of his last poems, it eschewed confessional appeals or other simplifications. His finest work holds such oppositions in charged proximity with each other, and the reader must do something similar: a purely autobiographical reading of MacSweeney's work would be as misleading as one that avoided autobiography altogether; and to describe him as a follower of, say, Basil Bunting would be as disingenuous as to deny Bunting's influence out of hand. A more integrated personality might have resolved some of these conflicts sooner; indeed, might never have come to understand himself in such oppositional terms in the first place – but MacSweeney's was a polemical, polarising imagination, and the reader must work harder to appreciate the coherence of his vision. MacSweeney dares us to ask as much of poetry as he did; to be as eclectic and adventurous; not to align ourselves with a particular school or movement; to join him in the risk.

HARRIET TARLO

Brother MacSweeney and the new-old English Poet

Language is a steady stick

More than ten years after Barry MacSweeney's death, the dust is settling and, as the publication of this volume illustrates, the time has come to consider the work in all seriousness, in particular without undue emphasis on MacSweeney's alcoholism and the manner of his death. However, MacSweeney's poetry was not only at times self-consciously confessional, but was also deeply caught up with the role of the poet in terms of both poetics and politics. In this essay, I am not interested in excavating autobiographical or biographical references to MacSweeney's life and loves. In truth, I feel that critical readings have suffered from over-indulgence in the personal, failing to recognise that MacSweeney's personae are always characters in his work, just as the characters are always poets.[1] It is the image of the poet MacSweeney presents that interests me, in particular the English poet in relation to the land of his origins, the English oak 'which used to be a sign of / strength, but now is only a sign of age / and decadence' (p.16). I shall argue that MacSweeney reaches beyond the self, into the history of English culture and poetry, to find his own poetics. Ultimately, I shall conclude, he is concerned with finding a new-old role for the English poet.

Readers might be surprised by my use of the word 'English' here, rather than the more common appellation applied to him: 'North-East', 'Geordie' or 'Northern'. One of the arguments I wish to make is that it is precisely from his deeply-rooted locality that MacSweeney finds a place to speak for the country as a whole or, in other words, why should not a Northerner, particularly one who garners his forces from the gamut of English poetry, speak

15

for England? The fact that MacSweeney's poetry was marginalised for much of his lifetime, that he would not have been perceived as a national poet by the largely Southern-dominated press and literati, is irrelevant. To speak *to* the times is not to be *of* the times. The two are often incompatible, an idea that MacSweeney explored in his own reading of the life of the eighteenth-century poet, Thomas Chatterton, an important figure in this essay. In the early long poems, *Brother Wolf* and 'Wolf Tongue: a Chatterton ode', MacSweeney builds the mythology of Chatterton as a 'brother', as he confirmed in interview.[2] Chatterton is also the subject of a prose essay *Elegy for January* (1970). Shortly before his death, MacSweeney chose the title *Wolf Tongue* for his selected poems and included all his Chatterton poems in the selection.

As a young working-class poet with strong local links to his place of origin in Bristol, Chatterton was lauded as a youthful talent, lured to London and then betrayed by his poetry "friends", in particular Horace Walpole, dying of arsenic poisoning in a poverty-stricken and friendless state. MacSweeney felt some of his own experiences with London society and publishers were not dissimilar. Whilst Chatterton's rejection at the hands of Walpole in the 1780s was largely on the grounds of his humble origins, MacSweeney, as a working class lad from the provinces in the 1970s, might have made a go of it had he been willing to fulfil that role. Fêted in 1967-68 as the young bright hope of British poetry, he faded rapidly from the mainstream literary scene. He refused to compromise, to temper his work for mainstream publishers, to be 'something like a Geordie answer to the 'Liverpool poets': consumable, "regional"'.[3] Although he identified himself as Northern, he wanted to be more than this. He wanted freedom of form, freedom of expression, and freedom to talk about English politics.

In an invaluable interview with Eric Mottram, MacSweeney explained his break with his publisher on the grounds that they 'were forcing me to edit poems...take out the dirty words and all that'.[4] As Marianne Morris explains:

> This experience drove him to start up his own Blacksuede Boot Press in 1970, an act of rebellion that meant he could publish whatever he liked, without fear of being edited or otherwise humiliated. MacSweeney's dissatisfaction in this case drives towards a poetic persona that comes to represent rebellious and anarchistic disgust that views all forms of arbitrary control and authority as its enemy, preparing the way for the

poet who, ten years later, reacts with such violent glee and disgust to
the Thatcher government.[5]

Jennifer Keith, an eighteenth-century scholar, reflects on how
Chatterton was left alienated by 'the increasing commodification
of art and artist' and hence impeded in his attempts to 'negotiate
or defy the vagaries of the literary marketplace'.[6] He wrote on
regardless from a position of 'isolation' thus risking 'estranging the
reader'.[7] Her words ring equally true for MacSweeney two hundred
years later. As John Wilkinson, drawing the parallel with Chatterton,
writes, MacSweeney's 'wolfish streak impels him to give offence to
any possible welcoming constituency'.[8] MacSweeney did indeed
become an isolated figure for much of his life, largely unsupported
by British institutions. He estranged readers too of all poetic creeds,
often by being "too much": too radical, too traditional, too lyrical,
too confessional, too misogynistic, too mercurial. It is this very
wolfishness that enabled him to develop such a formally and
politically challenging poetics. I shall draw from all periods of
MacSweeney's poetry to elucidate these points in an attempt to
draw parallels across his oeuvre.[9] I shall consider place, politics
and language in my journey to some final conclusions about the
poet's role in MacSweeney's work.

Place

In the brief 'autobiography' which opens MacSweeney's first book,
The Boy from the Green Cabaret Tells of His Mother (1968), the poet
talks about his place of origin:

> Open to the city and the country. You can walk out of Newcastle for
> half an hour and be in greenery. The city gave words a harshness, like
> the steel or coal. Then I wd flit off to [sic] little stone cottage on the fells
> and fish for trout, and pick mushrooms. & swim in the freshwater lakes.

Place is important in MacSweeney's work, but place here is not
singular but plural, 'the city and the country'. The same exposure
to the urban and the rural, and, just as significantly, the places in
between, is made in discussion with Mottram. MacSweeney presents
himself as naive about the literary world, growing up in a 'working-
class background...in a close community on a housing estate'.[10] He

emphasises how the estate was close to the Roman wall, near the edge of the city where you could just walk out into the country. But he also refers to the stimulation of the thriving art scene in Newcastle, as well as the cottage at Allenheads in Northumberland where he was partly brought up. As Clive Bush notes in his reading of the early poems, 'issues of home and locality are seen neither as definitive or stable'.[11] The plurality and instability of 'home' in the broadest sense contributes to MacSweeney's ability to criticise the homeland, to find it lacking.

However, this diverse homeland also gave his work a realist kick. Although he presents himself as a teenager growing up in a marginal position, not knowing 'what the hell was going on' certainly with regards to the London-dominated literary scene, MacSweeney knew plenty of what was going on in the wider country. He was exposed to the sort of places where most English people lived: cities (he started life in a flat in the shipyards), new housing estates sprawling out into the mud outside cities, and rural cottages with beautiful views but not much opportunity to earn a living, as farming, mining and other rural industries slid into decline. Andrew Crozier, the poet and friend of MacSweeney who visited Sparty Lea for the renowned poetry festival of 1967, reflects the importance and diversity of the region in his obituary of the poet: 'both the moorland landscape around Allendale and its derelict industrial sites and communities inadequately redeveloped – remained a constant frame of reference for MacSweeney'.[12]

The early Chatterton poem, *Brother Wolf*, presents the rural Allendale aspect of MacSweeney's Northern origins through a series of natural images simultaneously mythic and gritty, images which will find their culmination in the poems of *Pearl*. Although mythologised, they are not idealised (p.25):

> At Sparty Lea the trees don't want Orpheus
> to invoke any magic
> they dance by themselves.

Here MacSweeney overtly rejects the need for gods and myths to translate landscape into poetry. Yet, these independent dancing trees become their own neo-pantheistic myth and the landscape is celebrated as a direct source of inspiration to the 'young poet' (p.24):

A young poet's life burns
Presses
(july wind on Hartfell)
taking our hearts (and poetry) higher...

Certain words and images, the dancing trees, the rain, the black geese (a Northumbrian name for the Brent Goose) are repeated in endless permutations throughout MacSweeney's work, a mantra to place, to the specific place and to the *idea* of locality and Englishness.[13] There is a sense in MacSweeney that for the English poet the place of origin remains central; identity is based in locality. When Chatterton left St Mary Redcliffe Church in Bristol for 'cowarde Londonne' in search of fame and fortune, it led ultimately to his suicide. Engagement with one's own place brings one's own form. The space of the land, 'so much *land*', seems to equate to MacSweeney's sense of space on page, his long, rangy lines, full of rhythm, movement as the wind moves through trees and the gaps too in his lines, the open form structure he employs. Here we see Olsonian poetics enacted in English places. Yet he also equates poetic form with the urban in his 'autobiography': 'The city gave words a harshness, like the steel or coal'.

It is so easy to construct the poet one desires out of a writer's oeuvre. MacSweeney can be presented as a local rural poet or as a local urban poet, yet neither the emphasis on locality or on one particular place is adequate. Perhaps I have been guilty of this myself, discussing his 'radical landscape poetry' in an earlier essay. Similarly, MacSweeney is singled out by Peter Barry, in his book on *Contemporary British Poetry and the City* as one of the few poets bucking the trend of portraying poetry-writing as a rural craft. Barry notes his unusual use of an 'urban implement', an oxyacetylene torch, as a metaphor for the act of writing in *Hellhound Memos* and goes on to offer a valuable reading of that work.[14] In truth, Barry and I are both right about MacSweeney: he wrote powerfully out of both city and country.

It is also notable that neither urban nor rural places are valorised or demonised in MacSweeney's work. I think Matthew Jarvis rather falls into this trap when he reads the poet as being in 'hell with the demons' in *The Book of Demons* and 'in heaven with "Pearl"' in his 'moorland romance' of the same name.[15] Jarvis goes on to analyse how 'alcoholic suffering' is embedded in the 'built environment' in *The Book of Demons* so that 'the built, the urban, or the human-colonised is nothing less than the generic locus of suffering'.[16] He argues, convincingly enough, that being cut off from the 'organic environment' is deeply problematic for 'the MacSweeney character'.[17] He goes on to select passages from *Pearl* which demonstrate the rural scene of *Pearl* as one of ecstasy and, making reference to the medieval *Pearl*, heavenliness, virtue and salvation, even from alcoholism.[18] I am in sympathy with Jarvis's eco-ethical motivation for this reading of MacSweeney; he concludes with the argument that MacSweeney advocates the value of wild or natural space in the human economy just as it is.[19] Yet, I think it is a restrictive reading of place in MacSweeney's work, largely because it is focused too intensively on the poetic protagonist/ persona of the poet.

In fact, both *Pearl* and *The Book of Demons* dwell in places real and imagined, albeit places that are exemplary of England's hotchpotch landscapes and cityscapes. As Jarvis himself notes, *Pearl* is shot through with a deep-seated critique of the economic poverty and legacy of lead mining in the area.[20] Even *The Book of Demons* (1997), which does indeed, as Jarvis states, evoke a bleak urban landscape, is by no means a purely urban poem, nor is the urban a wholly negative space. The poem is saturated with realist and allegorical references to place, constantly panning back and forth between the rural and the urban North-East and beyond and between. Perhaps the most striking example of this is the final stanza of the very first poem of the sequence which begins in eroticism, but soon moves into other territory (p.219):

> And then there is the pure transmission of kissing you, when
> solar winds seethe in amber wonder through the most invisible wisps
>   and strands in a tender half-lit prairie sometimes, caught in
> light which is not quite light, but as if the entire world was drenched slate,
>   or reflected thereof, in the soon to be handsome dawn of a reckless
> damp November, with the gunmetal heavens plated quite beautifully
>   in goldleaf of fallen nature already so readily ready for the rising
> sap of a dearest darling spring when we will start again and the curtains
>   will not be drawn at dawn beneath the monumental viaduct of the
> great engineer. The truly great span of the legs above the city, spread
>   and wide, rodded north and south and electrified by power passing
> through beneath the novas and planets and starres. Magnetised!

In these twelve sibilant lines, MacSweeney encompasses the natural and the urban as fused, both through the imagery (the world shining like 'drenched slate', the 'gunmetal heavens') and the sense of spring in the city. The first nine-and-a-bit lines of this extract flow through from the lover's kiss to the 'monumental viaduct'. After the caesura, the perspective opens right out and up, becoming far less personal and indeed local. Characteristically the viaduct is linked to its industrial past, its 'great' maker, and then on to the outside world. Perceived as a physical being, its legs spread both North and South, encompassing the country as a whole and its position too in the wider universe, beneath the 'starres', their timeless status and cultural significance emphasised by MacSweeney's customary spelling. For Jarvis, this is a transformation of the city 'if it is understood within the larger environmental context of the non-human', the winds, planets and stars for instance.[21] For me, the final one word sentence or declaration 'Magnetised!' is multifunctional, referring back to the lover's kiss and outwards to both the electrification of the railway line (the literal wires that run above the viaduct) and the magnetic effects of solar winds and planets. In other words, to the natural and the man-made, to the country and the city, to the North and the South. Here then is the Northern poet reaching out beyond the fixed point of Durham City's viaduct.[22]

A further illustration of a localised image gaining in symbolic power and significance is that of the falling rain which recurs incessantly in MacSweeney's work. We first find it in Northumberland scenes, particularly the Chatterton poems set in 'a land of black geese / & rain' (p.68). The poet emerges from this wateriness (p.23):

There is so much *land* in Northumberland. The sea
Taught me to sing
          the river to hold my nose. When
it rains, it rains glue.

But, again, it is too easy to assume that the rain is a blessing in the country and a curse in the city. When the 'High hearts' of Hartfell are 'wrecked', the poem rushes towards its end, replaying its own language and motifs in an increasingly fractured and disjointed manner including (p.30):

Rain
     hurt
with its own

density
dies. The sun
too.

The poems of *Pearl* teem with rain, the 'rain-soaked law', the landscape shaped by 'years of rain sweeping over the cairns' and the love of 'gentle' rain recurring.[23] Yet, particularly in the poem 'Fever', the rain is harsh too, the land 'lashed by rain', rain pouring into Pearl's dumb mouth 'acting like a gutter or a gargoyle', but not granting her speech (p.203). Rain can be cleansing in the cityscape of *Hellhound Memos*, yet it is also 'dismal, scum-filled rain'.[24] Rain, no longer natural but lethal, 'acid rain', is referenced in *Hellhound Memos* and *The Book of Demons* (pp.19, 282). Yet, as Barry argues, urbanism in MacSweeney is not an abnegation of nature: rain falls from an urban sky as lines of writing in *Hellhound Memos*.[25]

It is an obvious national truth that rain falls throughout our land as it does in MacSweeney's poetry, veering from benediction to curse to being simply present. Just as the wolf featured as a totemic animal for MacSweeney, so rain becomes a condition of writing. Ranter writes 'Recording on a slate in the rain' and the same image recurs in *Pearl* (see pp.165, 196, 208). Blessing or curse, poet and rain often fuse into one as in the harsh 1980s world of 'Liz Hard' (p.128):

Rain snaps
the burning quiet,
&
all
the
piss-filled clouds

gather brimming at my brow.

Similarly in the *Hellhound Memos* of the 1990s, the protagonist declares, 'I come down like slate-grey rain' (p.187). Ultimately, MacSweeney's rain spreads through the land, becoming emblematic of the English poet in the English scene.

Of recent critical material, only Rebecca A. Smith acknowledges the breadth of MacSweeney's place of origins:

Taking as his early focus the province's modern 'capital' Newcastle, MacSweeney addressed all aspects of his realm and saw, in the multi-faceted textures of the existing North-East region, an analogy for the divergent elements of his composite identity.[26]

Smith is right about the poet's 'composite identity', but this vision of the North-East is also intrinsic to MacSweeney's vision of England, not just his own identity. He is not, as Smith seems to imply in her discussion of *Pearl*, a rather parochial poet. She reads the poem as autobiographical, a 'personal mythology', as 'subjective rather than objective', the valued world being only that which 'lies within his fundamental sphere "up here on the rim of the planet"'.[27] Smith rightly acknowledges MacSweeney's home-grown 'social ethics' and consciousness of rural issues, but a study of his whole oeuvre sees him extending these ideas much further out into the world.[28] Her comments come in the context of a comparative discussion of Bunting and MacSweeney in which she contrasts Bunting's classical and international references with MacSweeney's local ones. I agree that *Pearl*, which experiments with children's voices, does exhibit 'an ingenuousness which contributes to its authenticity'. However, the references she cites, the Woolworths' clip, Co-op coat, sheep bones and crisps are ubiquitous to English life, not just the 'rural North-East' as she implies. It is the desire to distinguish between Bunting and MacSweeney that leads Smith to exaggerate the latter's associations with the local and the contemporary, also perceiving Bunting's stance as archaic and MacSweeney's as anarchic.[29] Yet, anarchic as he may be, MacSweeney is also archaic. Indeed, *Pearl* itself is written in collusion with the medieval English work, *Pearl* and, as I shall argue below, MacSweeney revisits earlier English poetry to construct a poetic lineage from which to speak. I think it is also inaccurate to see MacSweeney as lacking in international reference. It is less relevant to my argument here, but there is a wide range of reference to largely European revolutionaries and avant-gardes throughout his work from Voznesensky and Rimbaud at the start to Malevich and Apollinaire at the close of his writing life.

The reality is a far less parochial or indeed personal affair than previous readings of MacSweeney have implied. It is notable that, having made his comments about Newcastle and its environs in his introductory 'autobiography' to *The Boy from the Green Cabaret Tells of His Mother*, MacSweeney goes on to explain in the very next paragraph that, despite his feelings of alienation in this 'synthetic new town', he actually wrote the poems themselves while at Harlow Technical College in Essex. Already, MacSweeney's vision, his 'eye, my colour/sluice' was moving outwards, becoming 'a funnel'. He did not live in the North-east all his life, residing in London, Kent and Bradford at different times. But more important to this essay than where he lived, is what he saw the poet's role as being in relation to his nation. In this respect, the American poet, Charles Olson, was a significant influence. Nearly ten years after *The Boy from the Green Cabaret Tells of His Mother*, MacSweeney was to tell Mottram about discovering Olson via Jeremy Prynne who played the 'OLSON AT BERKELEY' tape at the Sparty Lea Poetry Festival. This was, for him, about 'flinging language out beyond the self...not using sentences, breaking up, working with the breath, which I'd never realised'. A little later, he says:

> It wasn't until then that suddenly a massive vista opened up, projective verse, and I studied it for a long time and read all the Olson I could get hold of, and read about Black Mountain. 'The figure of the outward' is a phrase, but for me it means like taking a language outside of the ego, the self, one's own personal relationships, and suddenly realising that all that land is out there.[30]

These testimonies to Olson relate inextricably to MacSweeney's unearthing of his own *form* and his own *role* as a poet, in relation to his locality and his ethical, political position. The odes he goes on to write clearly demonstrate Olsonian projective verse in action. The revelation that 'all the land is out there', that he could from 'the local, the centre, which was my energy, what I am', find it possible to 'write about politics, my geographical, historical and social heritage, background, history' is rooted in his reading of Olson.

Politics and Form

So MacSweeney emerges into a life's work of formal innovation and social critique, beginning close to home and broadening out to all England. In form these interventions range from avant-garde 'nodal' poems through fractured narratives to overtly realist interventions. Hope for MacSweeney lies in international socialism and communal action, hence his fascination with miners' strikes and revolutions. He sees little enough of it, but grasps it where he finds it. In early texts such as *Flames on the Beach at Viareggio* (1970) England is a 'faded outlaw', 'withered and stooped', a nation that needs to deepen its colours into the flame colours of Shelley's death and of socialism: 'may the modal / English green deepen to scarlet as the sun sets why not'. 'Black Torch Sunrise' is set against the action of the Sorbonne students viewed against the British government's failure to live up to socialist ideals. *Far Cliff Babylon* (1978) foreshadows the imminent dominance of Conservatism and death of society which was to be associated with Margaret Thatcher's era. In first publication, the cover showed protesters being beaten down in the street and includes a note describing it as a 'political poem' and a 'little reggae piece'. The Rastafarian connection, manifest in the title, beat and references to racism in this piece, suggests a profound alienation from a corrupt and consumerist society: Albion become Babylon. The line, 'I represent no people', confirms this and foreshadows Thatcher's notorious rejection of the idea of society.

In the 1970s, MacSweeney worked on *Black Torch*, a 'long... work drawing on the socio-political activities of the Northumbrian and Durham miners'.[31] It drew on original sources from records of strikes to Baptist ministers' (or Ranters') texts. The plan was to include 'tape recordings with residents of Sparty Lea and the Allen Valley'. The first part, *Black Torch* (1978) is best described as poetry as witness in which close engagement with social history and authentic sources enables the poet to tell the tale of coal and iron which 'came from the north to feed you'.[32] The sequence employs a variety of forms from ballad, dramatic monologue in the voice of pit owners and miners and polemical interventions including the one page declaration 'it is slavery'.[33] There are some powerfully voiced poems, such as this one in the voice of a striking miner when the bailiffs enter the house:

> fa godsake hav yis not done enough
> ya fuckin getsyi bastads
> aal fuck you aal fuck you
> its alreet pet its alreeet   (to bairns)[34]

The second part, *Blackbird* (1980) is a more condensed, less transparent, 'elegy for William Gordon Calvert', MacSweeney's grandfather. At the heart of the piece is an angry critique of the class system through an elegy for the working man and his antecedents, the 'ghosts of miners on the fell / shadowy poachers armed with snares' (p.85). The poignant reprieve, 'melt & make no noise' (itself a line from the Metaphysical poet, John Donne), speaks to the whole culture, past and present, not just the dead man. In 'Black Lamp Strike', the penultimate poem of *Black Torch*, MacSweeney spreads his in-depth insight back into the past and geographically outward, with references to Luddism's end 'on the scaffold', to Blackburn spinners and to Welsh miners.[35] Once again, he is working outward from Geordie concerns to a position where he feels able to critique the whole system.

MacSweeney's mid-career, particularly the period from late 1970s to the mid-1980s, was dominated by satirical critiques of all-England of a far less transparent nature than *Black Torch*. Uncomfortable to read, couched as they are in aggressively sexualised, even fetishistic, terms, they are not MacSweeney's most popular works, although recent valuable analysis by Morris and Wilkinson will perhaps help to mitigate this. Yet 'Colonel B'; 'Liz Hard'; 'Liz Hard II'; 'Jury Vet' and 'Wild Knitting' are both witty and brilliant in their brutal exposure of an increasingly consumerist society. MacSweeney draws language samples from all over the culture, particularly popular fashion, food, and journalism writing, only to deploy them against themselves in acts of aggressive pastiche. 'Colonel B' and 'Jury Vet' both gain their titles from political scandals in which even that bastion of British identity, the law, was shown to be corrupt. But these poems are more than political, in that 'Jury Vet' in particular savagely removes the human consolations of love and the body, now 'ULTRA REAL', courtesy of the culture (p.121):

> UP in tampon pools. Yr sanguine theses
>   prick a bra. Brown Cuban heels
>   on Karen, plain satin Nehru troos
>   on Viv – slack trax to the
> EVER OPEN DOOR FROM YOU

The idea of a feminine principle, embodied in 'Liz Hard' (based on an immigration officer MacSweeney met), is mocked and corrupted, by the Thatcherite presence and politics.[36] Images of endlessly exploited, fundamentally artificial images of femininity are thrust repeatedly at us (p.99):

> Trigger me, I'm hotter than a cartridge, wooed voodoo Liz.
>   Let me dead a victim or I can't come.
>
> Fill my chambers. Pump me redhot. Blast
>   each lipstick quimtrick.

We are battered by the repetition of 'Liz Hard' in all her manifestations, a sexualised phallic creature, yet a meaningless modern mantra too.[37] Morris argues convincingly that these are poems 'of negative mourning…cherishing abjections, and manipulating these abjections in order to create a linguistic energy that becomes the driving force of the poems'.[38] The juxtaposition of this contemporary language with references to archaic touchstones in MacSweeney, such as 'Perle' and 'Breve' adds to this feeling of something valuable lost. Throughout this work, and indeed his oeuvre, he favours the oldest known name for England, Albion. In this, there is a tribute to the Romantics, Blake in particular who, in 'A Little Boy Lost' asks, 'Are such things done on Albion's shore?'. MacSweeney echoes such lines in 'Colonel B' and 'Wild Knitting' with 'Albion, to be repealed', 'redundant Albion Mills (idle)' and 'Arcadia defunct, Albion / sucking up to the calamity, wrenched from harmony' (pp.93, 132, 135). These are 'state of the nation' poems, a phrase MacSweeney himself uses about 'Colonel B' and 'Wild Knitting'. *Hellhound Memos* takes up the critique for the 1990s.

Even in *The Book of Demons*, ostensibly MacSweeney's most confessional sequence (peppered as it is with references to the American confessionals, Sexton and Plath), there is a similar thread about the deterioration of England. The cleaning up of the fitting alcoholic is set right beside 'Albion…distressed upon her hardened knees' (p.224) or 'badly / bruised' (p.245). The collapse of poet and nation is a parallel process: 'And that's the nation of me too: each of us / in very separate parts brought to our knees' (p.245). The poem is threaded through with disgust at the Tory party and disillusionment with the Labour Party, the 'clowns of conceit' who have made this 'ugly nation' (p.245, see also p.238). Its references to dole queues, bus cuts, public toilets and government initiatives such as Health Trusts and the National Lottery build a bleak picture of the nation (see pp.246, 266, 281).

Pearl and *The Book of Demons* both feature characters, one rural and one urban, on whom the state of the nation impacts. Crozier wrote in his obituary for MacSweeney, 'More than he detested the destruction of communities witnessed in the last two decades, he loathed its impact on individual lives, whose vulnerability he already understood'. Pearl is significant not only as a lost childhood love but as a marginalised representative of the rural poor. MacSweeney's first Pearl poem in *Black Torch* portrays a tragic victimised life and ends:

> then aa heard
> ya mam died
> & you were put
> inside [39]

Tom in *The Book of Demons* embodies the urban drunk. 'Tom in the Market Square Outside Boots' and 'John Bunyan to Johnny Rotten' conjure up the poverty and isolation of the old mining villages in County Durham, complete with 'underground ghosts' (p.283) and ever-increasing environmental pollution (p.282):

> Tom you're away from a haunt but furled in a toil
> Tom, there's a spoil heap in every village without a colliery
>   there's a gorse bush on top you can hide in naked
> but you can't escape the molten golden rays of the sky
> bleaching the leukemia lonnens of ICI Bone Marrow City
> Tom out here on the A19 the long September shadows of England
> stretch from Wingate all the way to Station Town....

The deep disillusionment of *The Book of Demons* was not new in MacSweeney. We find it in 'The Last Bud', written when he was only twenty one. It is here that he first refers to the English oak 'which used to be a sign of / strength, but now is only a sign of age / and decadence...' (p.16). Here too he first refers to 'the Gates of Dis', most obviously a reference to the Roman underworld or Hell. In MacSweeney it comes to signify negation, acting as it does as a prefix of negation or reversal as in disillusionment; disbelief; discontent; dishearten; disown. It is also of course part of the word 'Dissent'. The poet figure toys with the demonic: is it the only way to assert effective revolutionary power or will it ultimately lead to nihilism and despair? Like many motifs from early poems, Dis and the demonic run through MacSweeney's work. In *Brother Wolf*, the Keatsian bee-sucking lips become dismembered lips, the path to Dis is 'always the same red road' and the heroic medieval sword is a 'Dis-/-honoured sword' (pp.29-30, see also p.92). *Hellhound Memos* pursues the legend of Robert Johnson selling his soul to the devil, but, most notably, Hell is right here in 1990s inner city England at the Gallowgate Crossroads and the hellhounds are 'carping and crapping / all over the cairn and the law' (p.190). In *The Book of Demons*, the demons are of course representative of alcoholic cravings, but they are also destructive of English culture. Poems such as 'Himself Bright Starre Northern Within' and 'Strappe Down in Snowville' rival 'The Last Bud' for sheer impassioned disillusionment. In the first of these, MacSweeney enters his poetic history, 'deleting' all elements (p.258-61):

I say delete midnight, midnight lawstarres, Pearlwords,
the Mojo moon, no executed kings tonight, never enough,
delete kisses, poutlips, fast breasts, all the once-couple talk. [...]

Delete the brightbairn, the laughing lad, the happy son, the singer of songs,
the larker outlarking the breast-high larks, out in the mad spring meadow.

Delete being under the hellhounds' paws, padding over thee,
right on your chestbreast, think yourself an upright man do you?

This selection of revolutionary poetic figures from MacSweeney's own work – the young poet lad, the hellhound, the 'upright man' – have failed, between them, to see through the revolutionary English impulse that the execution of Charles embodies. The sequence is full of references to the 'executed king' and to the nineteenth-century miners' brief moments of revolutionary action memorialised in *Black Torch* (p.267, see also pp.276, 277, 285):

We did not burn enough magistrates' houses. We executed
one king but did not drag out enough Tories, and hang them
from the greenwood tree.
These forever here in the snow-laden urinal are my hysterical
historical regrets....

...I DIE HARD, Pookah Swoony
Sweeney swan Ludlunatic, revelling Leveller....

Despite the brief uprising of a 'Fight for your rights for the rest of your days' (p.277), and the fleeting, bedraggled appearances of Cromwell, Milton and Blake 'looking for the dreams of Albion' (p.285), the overall conclusion of this poem comes in two bald definitive statements: 'Nothing left in England now. / One king only not enough' (p.284).

The ending of the final poem of *The Book of Demons*, 'John Bunyan to Johnny Rotten' consists of the large-format exclamation, *'!GOD SAVE THE QUEEN!'*, a reference to the Sex Pistols' famous alternative Queen's Jubilee single. The song's use of the repeated lines, 'There is no future / In England's dreaming' and its remorseless chorus 'no future' is in keeping with the mood of

The Book of Demons. At first glance, Bunyan and John Lydon's notorious punk persona, Johnny Rotten, may not have much in common, but Bunyan was first and foremost a folk-poet, interested in oral history, and Johnny Rotten's vernacular performance was an expression of popular dissent. Bunyan also served in the Parliamentarian side in the Civil War whilst Rotten is perhaps the closest MacSweeney can come to an anti-monarchist for the twentieth century. Like Jim Morrison, as described in MacSweeney's interview with Mottram, the Sex Pistols were 'tearing down old idols'.[40] This, for MacSweeney, was optimistic and hopeful. Bunyan and Rotten both spoke in the language of their own times to the common people of their time. They wrote and performed out of a sense of crisis, not just personal but national:

> England shakes and totters already, by reason of the burden that Mr Badman and his Friends have wickedly laid upon it. Yea, our earth reels and staggereth to and fro like a drunkard, the transgression thereof is heavy upon it.[41]

Thus writes Bunyan in *The Life and Death of Mr Badman* (1680). His outrage is directed most obviously at personal immorality, yet, as Richard Greaves has argued, it was also political. In selecting Bunyan and Rotten for this poem, MacSweeney is celebrating and declaring himself as part of the dissenting tradition in poetry and performance. He is also mourning England's lost ages of radicalism, so often maintained by those outside the educational elite, the autodidacts in search of their own authentic history.

Many of MacSweeney's poems, in all their diverse forms, are rants. The mid-career sequence, *Ranter* (1985), although peppered with Northern references, follows the ranting radical all over England or the 'dear green land' (p.147). It is the nation Ranter engages with or, rather, rants about (p.144):

> Dear God
> what kind of country is this
> reduced and reduced

Ranter, both the persona and the poem, is 'armed with centuries of anger', threatening direct and violent action particularly in the poem 'Ranter's Reel' (p.168). This anger is also on behalf of the land itself, 'sheepwire stapling / her fells and fields / wild Northumberland / hemmed in, stitched up' (p.165). Ranter and the land itself fuse speech in protest (p.166):

> My heart a harvest
> keep your threshers at bay.
> I won't have Massey Ferguson's [sic]
> rolling over me.

The sense of a land that has been hijacked runs right through MacSweeney's poetry and is not just relevant to the countryside. In *Hellhound Memos*, the urban rebels 'swank delirious with gallons of snakebite / on what common ground's left'.[42]

Language

The history of MacSweeney's poetic language reflects the same process as his interrogation of locality and land. Beginning with his local, native speech, he began to look into the roots of English speech and poetry in search of a new-old English poetics. In interview with Mottram, MacSweeney does see himself as part of a 'poetry revolution', but not a flash-in-the-pan contemporary affair with no basis: 'You can't bring up hundreds of years of language, all this refinement, this cutting down, and just lay it on people overnight'.[43] MacSweeney was excited by his contemporaries. Wilkinson has noted the diversity of influences in MacSweeney's very early work, citing the presence of a diverse series of contemporary poets from the Liverpool poets to Frank O'Hara to J.H. Prynne. Wilkinson seems torn about how to regard these, bandying around terms such as 'fake', 'rip-off' and 'shamelessness', yet claiming that 'in this shamelessness lies the strength of the most interesting poems in the collection'.[44] The work Wilkinson dislikes is that which is caught up in authenticity and sentimentality, 'the lyric persona implicated with a *faux-naif* restitution of the Edenic Real Me'. MacSweeney himself described his earliest work as 'complete and bad imitations of an echo I'd caught from Carlos Williams...bad little lyrical-erotic stuff'.[45] There is the same creative tension with his immediate predecessors, particularly Bunting.

Ultimately however, MacSweeney was interested in taking the quest further back. Chatterton again proves an important figure. *Elegy for January* confirms that MacSweeney came to Chatterton via the Romantics and in this way he picked up a poetic and

31

ideological thread running through late eighteenth-century poetry and into the Romantic age. Eighteenth-century scholars have noted the mid-century 'vogue of the past',[46] fuelled by a desire for 'primitive poetry'[47] or 'native traditions that would revivify their own work'.[48] 'Macpherson's supposed translation of the ancient Gaelic epic bard Ossian…and Chatterton's brief career of forging medieval verse'[49] are examples usually cited, sometimes linked to the Gothic Revival of the same period. In the Romantic period, this trend continued and John Keats saw Chatterton as an important conduit for a language of English poetry. *Endymion: A Poetic Romance* is 'Inscribed to the memory of Thomas Chatterton' and the fourth and final book opens with an invocation to a specifically English muse:

> MUSE of my native land! loftiest Muse!
> O first-born on the mountains! by the hues
> Of Heaven on the spiritual air begot!
> Long didst thou sit alone in northern grot,
> While yet our England was a wolfish den;
> Before our forests heard the talk of men;
> Before the first of Druids was a child; –
> Long didst thou sit amid our regions wild
> Rapt in a deep prophetic solitude.[50]

This, Bloom argues, is 'in effect the muse of Thomas Chatterton, of British native genius, of deep prophetic solitude and Druidic rhapsodisings'.[51] The 'wolfish den' would have appealed to Mac-Sweeney of course, but also the 'northern grot' from where Keats's spirit of English poetry arises. Various spirits of poetry from Hebrew, Greek and Italian sources attempt to awaken this patient muse, but he resists, sticking to his 'native hopes' for a 'full accomplishment', an English poetry of which Keats hopes to be one of the servants. It is through Keats's loyalty to the native muse that MacSweeney unearths the idea of Chatterton's language as 'entirely Northern'. Here is MacSweeney's citation of Keats in situ *Elegy for January* in situ:

> *The purest English I think – or what ought to be the purest – is Chatter-*
> *ton's – The language had existed long enough to be entirely uncorrupted of*
> *Chaucer's gallicisms, and still the old words are used. Chatterton's language*
> *is entirely northern. I prefer the native music of it to Milton's cut to feet.*
> *That isn't chauvinism.*[52]

The Keats text is from a letter Keats wrote to his brother and sister-in-law about learning foreign languages (French, Italian and Latin) and comparing Chatterton's 'pure' English to Milton's which is, though 'remarkable', a 'corruption of our Language'. The sentences quoted by MacSweeney immediately follow Keats' description of Milton's 'northern dialect accommodating itself to greek [sic] and latin [sic] inversions and intonations'.[53] MacSweeney also cites a further quotation in which Keats compares Chaucer's use of French idiom and particles with Chatterton's 'genuine English idiom in English words'.[54] This is echoed directly in Mac-Sweeney's 'Ode: Resolution' (p.56):

French words dominated
Chaucer's day.
     They ate away
the oak and the rose.

The adamant final line of 'Wolf Tongue', 'I eat no Latin bread', confirms this wholesale rejection of the ornate linguistic influences that entered English via Chaucer and Milton (p.72 and see p.56). It is notable that many of the phrases parodying fashion language in 'Liz Hard' are absurdly and pretentiously Frenchified: 'CERISE DRAGONETTE', 'CHARTREUSE blanquette' or even 'LOVE-DOLE BEANOS FUCK SUCH PRUDERIE ANGLAISE' (pp.102, 107, 118).

As this context demonstrates, Keats's 'entirely Northern' language is the original Northern European English, not the dialect of Northern England, although he, like MacSweeney, may have believed that English was less diluted in the North.[55] For Mac-Sweeney, this 'Northern language' is the closest it is possible to get to a genuine *English* language: 'It's very English...longer lasting, it's durable, it's harder, it's springier, it's more elemental, it comes out of all sorts of historical, geographical and social conflicts'.[56] The much-cited 'absolute commitment / to a language going north / without maps' in 'Wolf Tongue', reflects the idea of heading back into an older English language *and* heading back into his own linguistic origins in the North-East. Hence the reference to Harry Hotspur, the impulsive fourteenth-century Northumbrian hero of Shakespearean and Chattertonian fame. Here is a historical figure who encapsulates both processes: 'brondeous Hotspur's rural *rrr*', a reference to the Northumbrian burr *and* to a powerful, even brondeous (furious) Northern language.

All this gives substance to the view that a Northern writer can represent England, and that MacSweeney is a less local, or parochial, writer than he is often perceived. Lastly, it makes sense of MacSweeney's persistent, some would say puzzling portrayal of the West Country Chatterton as Northern. MacSweeney's North is a bigger North than his region of birth. There is a difference between the Northern language and the use of North-East dialect in his work, although there is overlap between the two. Where MacSweeney uses more specifically North-East language, he tends to use the term 'Northumbrian dialect' or to refer to a 'burr',[57] as in 'Newcastle's kindest / harshest burr' (p.83). However, 'Northern language' is more than this. An apposite example of this micro/macro Northern dialect/language is MacSweeney's use of the word 'lad' to describe Chatterton in both *Elegy for January* and *Brother Wolf*. 'Lad' is a word more commonly associated with Northern England and Scotland than the South, but originally it was a Middle English term for a boy used widely from the Fourteenth Century onwards. As such, it is wholly appropriate for Chatterton and is precisely the sort of 'pure' English word that MacSweeney can revive as suitable for all speakers of the language, not just poets and not just Northerners. It also of course emphasises Chatterton's pitiful youth at the time of his death.

The influence of Chatterton on MacSweeney is not just a matter of biography then, but also one of language and poetics as his praise of Chatterton's work in its own right demonstrates. He more than once uses the term 'genius' about him.[58] The alliterative tendency in old English verse, which we see in Chatterton, is prevalent in MacSweeney whole oeuvre and range from 'Jury Vet' to *Pearl* and, as Paul Batchelor has noted, we still find 'Chatterton-esque kenning' in MacSweeney's posthumous collection, *Horses in Boiling Blood* (2005).[59] MacSweeney's archaic spellings no longer seem quite so eccentric or even pretentious as they might have done before. For instance the use of 'starres', mentioned above, references starres as linguistic and cultural essences in a history of poetry. It also connects MacSweeney to other users of archaisms, Chatterton and Hopkins (whom Sears mentions in passing) being perhaps the best known, as well as contemporaries such as Maggie O'Sullivan who also employs archaisms.

At one level, MacSweeney's Northern voice is fake or, as Wilkinson puts it, is 'a concoction'[60] of Rowleyan language and Northern dialect. Yet it is also authentic, strange though it may seem to evoke such a concept about a poet often classed as avant-garde or post-modern. MacSweeney is closer to MacDiarmid than Bunting in this respect; he heard MacDiarmid read and refers to him as 'the one person'[61] who both writes and reads his poetry in dialect. When Mottram perceives a 'gap' between MacSweeney's page and his Geordie accent in performance, MacSweeney goes on to say that he *has* in fact written phonetically in dialect and he goes on to do so in *Black Torch* of course.[62] But MacSweeney's Northern language, like MacDiarmid's synthetic Scots was more than dialect, drawing as it did on historical sources and being full of archaisms and neologisms. The protagonist of MacDiarmid's *A Drunk Man Looks at the Thistle*, a serio-comic persona-poet who claims to speak for the nation as he rambles over the moor half-cut, is not dissimilar to several of MacSweeney's 'heroes'.

There are further insights to be gained from analyses of Chatterton's 'fake authenticity' by eighteenth-century specialists. Jennifer Keith remarks that 'Paradoxically the more these works were forgeries, the more original they were'.[63] She goes on to explore the experience of reading Chatterton as follows:

> The work's increased use of Rowleyan language makes the act of reading unavoidably self-conscious as we can no longer rely on our usual ways of making sense of poetry. Language reveals itself as matter with an obstructing consistency: language is no longer the dress of thought, as the Augustans saw it, but a quasi-opaque body. Chatterton's language is singularly isolated and isolating. ...[His] Rowleyan diction has no existing community that shares its language.[64]

Keith draws attention to Chatterton's description of the 'principle' of the fifteenth-century language he half-emulates, half-creates as 'lawlessness'. As a result, 'Chatterton's Rowley poetry is at once supremely elitist and democratic: its community must be made with each reader entering into Chatterton's language on an equal footing...'.[65] Many of the terms Keith uses to describe Chatterton could just as easily be found in accounts of modernist poetry; they are reminiscent of the old arguments over whether modernism is an elitist or democratic practice, or, as Keith suggests, both. It is of course always educational for a twentieth-century specialist to remember that innovation in language has been a continuous, revolutionary affair between poet and reader through the ages. Even more relevant to MacSweeney is the idea that it is through his archaic imagination, his 'lawless' invention of a new-old language that Chatterton is innovative. The word, 'lawless' seems especially resonant here, given MacSweeney's profound horror of rules, groups and institutions, whether literary or societal. MacSweeney's hybrid medieval-modernist language pays tribute to Chatterton, but ultimately contributes to the development of a whole series of individualistic forms of his own. MacSweeney, as he says of Chatterton in *Brother Wolf*, 'was no lemming' (p.23).

The Poet's Role

Having established that MacSweeney's poetry engages with all England and does so through a carefully researched and constructed poetic language, the final section of this essay considers his conception of the poet's role in the light of this. The blurb for *The Boy from the Green Cabaret Tells of His Mother* promotes MacSweeney as the 'kind of poet' who is 'relatively new in this country', but who also recalls 'the lives and the spirits of the medieval troubadours, travelling from town to town with their songs'. He is extolled for his newness, youth and brightness while being linked with a 'restatement of old truths that have fallen out of currency'. This is of course a piece of promotion, an idealised and romanticised picture of the youthful poet. But there is some validity to it, if not in its reflection of who MacSweeney was, but certainly in the reflection of the role of the poet as he saw it. From the start, he aspired to be a new-old kind of poet who remains aloof from society in order to critique it, a bard, a figure of the folk, a voice of the people, an advocate of the land itself.

We see MacSweeney playing with these poetic roles very early on in poems such as 'Our Mutual Scarlet Boulevard' where he cites 'the waggy man' and 'the wayfarer'. Clive Bush has described this poem as being about 'placing the poet in the world'.[66] The long poem in which we see MacSweeney most evidently aligning himself with the folk protest tradition is *Ranter*, as Sears notes:

The persona of Ranter links MacSweeney with the English radical tradition, stretching back to the Diggers of St George's Hill, and coinciding, in the year of this poem's publication, with folk-protest movements like those suppressed at the Battle of the Beanfield.[67]

Ranter does indeed lope, wolf-like, between past and present, representing in effect the English revolutionary impulse in its various guises (p.141):

> Ranter: Leveller, Lollard,
> Luddite, Man of Kent, Tyneside
> broadsheet printer,
> whisperer of sedition,
> wrecker of looms

Although oppressed, Ranter remains a hopeful figure 'searching for the good thing / the place with a centre' (p.143), imagining an England full of 'heroes and heroines / reading Shelley / taking up anarchy like a pen' (p.145).

The ancient role of folk poet and rebel is reflected in his tone and style. Peter Manson, always an astute reviewer of the avantgarde, notes that

> MacSweeney is one of those writers whose work becomes richer and more coherent the more of it you read. Tics of phrase, character and landscape recur in poems written years apart, with a cumulative effect like the products of an oral-formulaic bard with the dee tees.[68]

Repetition was of course at the heart of English oral poetry and it occurs on a phonemic, lexical and phrasal basis right across MacSweeney's work both within and between poems and sequences. *Ranter*, 'Liz Hard' and *The Book of Demons* are all suffused with anaphora, which was also one of Anne Sexton's "tics", and Sexton herself makes repeated appearances in MacSweeney's later poems. In a manner reminiscent of the oral bard, MacSweeney's poems and sequences often open flamboyantly, sometimes addressing the reader directly, as in *The Book of Demons*: 'Forgive my almost unforgivable delay – I have been laying the world to waste / beyond any faintest signal of former recognition' (p.218). After a brief, epigraphic poem, the first lines of *Pearl* hark back self-consciously to this ancient tradition, the poet's voice running into Pearl's own words (p.196):

> Listen, hark, attend; wait a moment
> as they used to say
> in the ancient tongue of literacy, before
> language was poisoned to a wreckage...

MacSweeney's description of the voice as a 'very English' idea, 'back to the source...just the voice, what you hear; I think it's stronger'[69] refers us to the oral origins of poetry. Turning to his poetry, we find it to be full of voices: that of the poet, the story-teller, the personae, the hero, the demons, the lover and multiple others, weaving in and out of each other's stories. Story-telling is of course another seminal element of traditional poetry and the narrative impulse is strong in MacSweeney's work. Although fractured and disjunctive, his work is full of tales, the doings of such diverse "characters" as Chatterton, Shelley, Liz Hard, Ranter, Pearl, Tom and Sweeno.

Many of the historical and contemporary figures who appear in MacSweeney's work were extreme young men who burnt-out young: Chatterton, Keats, Shelley, Rimbaud, Robert Johnson and Jim Morrison. These figures have usually been seen as MacSweeney's personal obsessions. Gordon Burn for instance describes him as 'married to the sense of romantic mystery which allied him with the roster of flame-outs and fuck-ups and holy losers he had been fixated on from his youth'.[70] Both Burn and Sears associate them with the 'Romantic myth of genius'.[71] This is undoubtedly the case, but there is more to be said about MacSweeney's engagement with the romantic cult of the individual. It is for him a matter of enquiry, not just adulation. When Mottram tries to persuade him to use the term 'romantic anarchists' about his heroes, he retorts:

> I don't like these bloody names. You see, I've come more and more to the point where I've returned to thinking about people in our society, in their environment, not as individuals.[72]

Once again, MacSweeney uses Chatterton to explore these ideas. In the poems, he is closely allied with Shelley and becomes emblematic of the wider romantic cult of the youthful poet. In *Brother Wolf*, the poet figure becomes a sacrifice for English poetry and is re-absorbed into nature in a manner both comic and dramatic. The mole underground encounters 'the lad's frayed body' and mourns it (p.24):

Shelley's heart which later turned out to be
Liver
& the fish had a whale of a time munching english poetry
It still happens…

Similarly, just as Eric Bloodaxe appeared in Bunting's *Briggflatts*, Harry Hotspur appears in 'Wolf Tongue'. Hotspur, like Chatterton and MacSweeney, was a prodigy, fighting his first battle as a boy and dying before he was forty, his body being subsequently dismembered and displayed around England by Henry IV as a warning to rebels. In the closing lines of the poem the various characters, including the protagonist, are palimpsested into one figure, his blood scattered through the poem, assimilating the essence of the dead as the sky draws Chatterton up at the end of *Brother Wolf*.

Harold Bloom has suggested that Chatterton was, for the Romantics, a muse, appearing as an image of the young poet as god, the glorious, youthful figures who appear in Coleridge's 'Kubla Khan', Shelley's 'Adonais' and Keats's *Endymion*. MacSweeney picks up on this. As Sears notes, his cultural heroes are Dionysic figures and this seems to be borne out in these references to the scattered body, reminiscent of Osiris, Dionysus and Actaeon. These avatars are all identifiable with the archetypal fertility god who dies young and beautiful, and is reborn through the next spring or, perhaps, in MacSweeney's poetic heritage, through the next poet. Some scholars include Jesus Christ in the list. MacSweeney hints at this with his sustained image of the cup. In the odes that, in *Wolf Tongue*, lie between the two long Chatterton poems, Chatterton appears as a Christ-like figure with 'flaming / side' (p.37). He is portrayed in this 'Chatterton Ode' as holding a cup (p.37):

He holds
what blood there is in
side an acorne-coppe.

The acorne-coppe derives from Chatterton's 'AElla: a Tragycal Enterlude' where the 'MYNSTRELLES SONGE' includes the lines:

Comme, wythe acorne-coppe & thorne,
Drayne mie hartys blodde awaie;
Lyfe & all yttes goode I scorne [73]

These lines, also echoed by Keats are, in situ, a lament for a lost love.

In MacSweeney's poetry, the cup invariably contains blood, the blood of the slaughtered, scattered poet. The acorne-coppe returns us to the English oak, suggesting that the poet sacrifices himself for the nation. Like Christ, he is a scapegoat or 'leper', to cite *Ranter*. Shelley saw himself as such a figure in 'Adonais', a lament for the death of Keats. He portrays himself at Adonais' funeral as an unknown figure who reveals himself as both cursed and Christ-like:

> ... sad Urania scanned
> The Stranger's mien, and murmured: 'Who art thou?'
> He answered not, but with a sudden hand
> Made bare his branded and ensanguined brow,
> Which was like Cain's or Christ's – oh! that it should be so! [74]

By the end of the poem, this figure is 'borne darkly, fearfully afar' by his own spirit while 'The soul of Adonais, like a star / Beacons from the abode where the Eternal are'. It is easy to read beckon for beacon in this poem where the dead are portrayed as having 'outsoared the shadow of our night', while the living must linger on in 'Envy and calumny, and hate and pain' exposed to 'the contagion of the world's slow stain'.

However, after all, these god-like young poets are only human and can also be perceived as reckless, suicidal figures. As Bloom notes, at the heart of the Romantic myth, 'the young poet is a god, a rebirth of Apollo, stimulating new life and representing the perpetual freshness of the earth, but only so long as his spirits remain glorious and joyful'.[75] Once fallen or disillusioned, like Shelley in 'Adonais', they see the lure of burning out. It was in this spirit, this awareness that there is a 'fatal cycle' from gladness to despair, that Wordsworth remembers Chatterton:

> I thought of Chatterton, the marvellous Boy,
> The sleepless Soul that perished in his pride;
> Of Him who walked in glory and in joy
> Following his plough, along the mountain-side:
> By our own spirits are we deified:
> We Poets in our youth begin in gladness;
> But thereof come in the end despondency and madness.[76]

Wordsworth, past the first flush of youth in his late thirties, is citing poets (Chatterton and Robert Burns) who did not achieve the eponymous 'resolution and independence' that he seeks in this poem of encounter with the ancient leech-gatherer.

MacSweeney identified strongly with youth. In *Elegy for January* he refers to the older Wordsworth as a 'crabbed bigot'[77] and claims that he wrote these lines about Chatterton 'before bigotry and old old age'[78] set in. Yet the Romantic ambivalence about Chatterton is echoed in MacSweeney. The suicidal urge, born of disillusionment and the fear of growing old, is powerfully articulated in *Elegy for January*:

> Thomas, what is there, after all, after youth. All these poems dedicated to you by poets past their teens. Our resilient animal instinctiveness fails us, with age – we cannot hunt any longer, but lag behind for scraps....
>
> Can we allow ourselves to grow neatly into bigotry? Is that, too, a necessary portion of our making? Then it is better to be unnatural. (I think of the motorcyclist who does not attempt to avoid the head-on crash, but accelerates into his death).[79]

As Wilkinson notes, Chatterton's iconic status with MacSweeney was based on his pride and self-reliance, the independence of spirit that led ultimately to his death.[80] Chatterton chooses suicide over compromise, a sign of strength and integrity. However, there is another way to read MacSweeney's use of the Chatterton legend and that is as a critique of our attitude to poets and poetry. His own essay about Chatterton exposes this, referring to the 'romantic myth' or the 'myth we are fed' throughout.[81] In one stringent passage, he argues, via McClure, that Chatterton's suicide was an act of weakness in which we the consumer can indulge:

> You committed the expected, Thomas...to destroy yourself then was weak and we love you madly and the rosy myth for it. We feed like maggots off your death. Off the spinning insane agony, when head and body do not clinch, but drift apart, and snap.
>
> You were no sheep but momentarily you acted as one![82]

Rowe reads *Brother Wolf* in the same spirit as this quotation. It is for him 'an allegory of the poet as a "rosy myth" to be consumed'[83] who, far from interfering with power simply feeds it with what it demands, his life. Rowe claims that MacSweeney 'rejects this low-cost romanticism'.[84] Ultimately, both Wilkinson's and Rowe's interpretations are convincing. The truth of course lies somewhere in between: Chatterton is both weak and strong in his final act. MacSweeney mourns, valorises, and yet self-consciously mocks, his own devotion to Chatterton, but the devotion is surely there.

We can see it in the lines that immediately follow those cited above: 'You are the elegant, eloquent, poet, my brother! The creator of the most beautiful poetry. You are the wolf.'[85] We can see it in the ending of the book with its reference to Chatterton almost in possession of MacSweeney's body: 'You pace behind my eyes, in a deep room...And we merge'.[86] The pacing of course suggests the wolf of *Brother Wolf* and there we have the nexus of the drawing together of the two poets. For MacSweeney, Chatterton, despite his ultimate failure, is an important English poet, a poet to emulate. He admired and, I would argue, emulated Chatterton's ambition to '*settle the nation before he had done*'.[87]

On the one hand, there is the perhaps inevitable disillusionment of the committed poet living on with 'the contagion of the world's slow stain', the desire to turn to Dis; on the other, there is the counter-balancing desire to pursue the Wordsworthian values of resolution and independence. Early in MacSweeney's career, we find this debate played out in the odes via the Romantic influence (indeed the very use of 'ode' as a collective title reveals that influence). In 'Ode:Resolution', its title recalling Wordsworth's poem, MacSweeney almost translates Keats's 'Ode on Melancholy', the poem in which Keats warns his reader against turning to death- or trance-inducing drugs in the face of the 'melancholy fit':

> No, no, go not to Lethe, neither twist
> Wolf's bane, tight-rooted, for its poisonous wine
> Nor suffer thy pale forehead to be kissed
> By nightshade, ruby grape of Proserpine[88]

With witty contemporary concision, MacSweeney writes (p.56)

> Pass the aconite.
> Wear monk's hood
>   ringed with
>   wolf bane.

This suicidal opening appears to be a negation of Keats's injunction not to partake of the dangerous herb. The three herbs mentioned are in fact all names for aconite; the poison seems unavoidable. MacSweeney would of course wish to include the wolf bane, usually wolfsbane, a name which refers to the drug's use for poisoning wolves or as one used to transform a human into a wolf. Either way, the idea of poisoning the wolf poet is at the back of this. As the poem continues however, MacSweeney draws back from the suicidal into a more warning tone (p.56):

> Chatterton knew
> his way to a
> northern
> Cup. That kind
>
> of final act
> is difficult
> to follow. He lay down
>
> & was Recognised
> in romantic oils.
>
> Watch yr breath.
> It will lie
> to you then lie
> down and stop. Blank
>
> is the colour
> of his separation
> from language & life.
>
> Asbestos.
>
> Cadmium.

At first, Chatterton's suicide is portrayed as an impressive final act. Yet there follows the somewhat sarcastic reference to its appeal to the Romantic poets and, finally, a sense that preoccupation with his last act is dangerous ('Watch yr breath'). Suicide is a separation from poetry as well as life, echoing Chatterton's 'Lyfe & all yttes goode I scorne'. The two chemicals named at the end of the poem, asbestos and cadmium, bring the poem strikingly into the 1970s present, both being forms of industrial toxicity with a deal less romantic appeal than aconite. As a journalist, MacSweeney would have been aware of the asbestos scandal just breaking at this time. There is a sense of the poet putting the lure of aconite into a wholly new context through these uncompromising one-word lines each with its own deathly final full stop.

The figure of the sacrificed dead or dying poet lingers on in MacSweeney, haunting his late work as much as his early poems and is often perceived as an object for consumption: 'Here the poet will die, pickled and puce' he writes in *The Book of Demons*. 'Demons In My Pocket' is his answer to Shelley's 'Adonais', in particular the closing lines of the poem (p.241):

> I am 72-inches tall, yet when I go to meet John
> and Percy and Kazimir and Pearl, stick me in
> an oven and burn me just the same. Then I will
> be a true Jew, a poet through and through.

His list of fellow-victims on first-name terms, Keats, Shelley, Malevich and his own Pearl, is just one of many lists of the dead that recur throughout the sequence. In 'Adonais', the throng of lost poets who receive Keats include Chatterton 'Rose pale, his solemn agony had not / Yet faded from him' and other 'inheritors of unfulfilled renown'. The scene of the lost poets, not appreciated on earth, meeting together after death finds a parallel in Mac-Sweeney's images of the exquisite car in *Brother Wolf* (p.31):

> the exquisite car
> comes holds all
> who go wanting
> to now we may
> not go
> back none now
> wants but
> stay and
> go not
> wanting

In this seemingly simple stanza, words twist around wonderfully to articulate the complexity of the desire to be part of and yet not be part of the culture and society into which one is born. There are several meanings possible in this set of short lines without guiding punctuation. At one level, MacSweeney plays here with the question of Chatterton's much-debated suicide: did he 'go wanting / to'; was the only way to 'not want' to 'go', as in 'go not / wanting'? The line-breaks also allow for the reading that wanting more, to 'go' (as in die or turn aside, to 'dis') still wanting, expecting more is, for MacSweeney the role of the poet.

Much has been made of MacSweeney's identification with the wolf, 'the most noble, handsome, poetic animal there is'.[89] It is relevant however that, beginning with Chatterton, the wolf is related to a succession of writers and thinkers in MacSweeney's work, not just to himself. We might see these as a brotherhood of wolves. Each of these is not only a "lone wolf", but exists in relationship to society, howling on the outskirts of the settlement. Each is a creature who chooses 'to prefer hunger in the woods to slavery in a palace', to cite the Victor Hugo quotation which MacSweeney chose as epigraph to *Brother Wolf*. The wolf is also an archaic figure, a native animal to these isles, extinct since the seventeenth century. So he also represents MacSweeney's quest back into the past for that which is valuable in previous generations of English culture and poetry. Perhaps then the blurb-writer for *The Boy from the Green Cabaret Tells of His Mother* was right about MacSweeney as a new and innovative talent concerned with the 'restatement of old truths that have fallen out of currency'.

WORKS CITED:

Acknowledgement: with many thanks to the staff of Newcastle University and its Robinson Library for help in accessing the MacSweeney Archive held there.

Batchelor, Paul. 'Morphic Cubism: The Strange Case of Gwilliam Mad Mac-Sweeney'. *Modern Poetry in Translation* 3:3 (2005): 131-136.

Barry, Peter. 'Barry MacSweeney *Hellhound Memos*', from 'Writing the Inner City', in *Contemporary British Poetry and the City* (Manchester: Manchester University Press, 2000), pp.67-77.

Bloom, Harold. *The Visionary Company: A Reading of English Romantic Poetry* (Ithaca and London: Cornell University Press, 1971).

Bunyan, John. *The Life and Death of Mr Badman* (1680) http://www.gutenberg.org/dirs/etext99/badmn10.txt

Bush, Clive. *Out of Dissent: A Study of Five Contemporary British Poets* (Talus Editions, 1997).

Burn, Gordon. 'Message in a Bottle'. *The Guardian*, Thursday 1 June 2000, http://www.guardian.co.uk/books/2000/jun/01/poetry.features

Blake, William. *Poems and Prophecies*, ed. Max Plowman. (London and Melbourne: Everyman's Library, J.M. Dent, 1975).

Chatterton, Thomas. *The Poetical Works of Thomas Chatterton* (London and Newcastle-on-Tyne: Walter Scott, 1885).

Crozier, Andrew. 'Barry MacSweeney: Tyneside poet who lived out the myth of exemplary failure'. *The Guardian*, Thursday 18 May 2000, http://www.guardian.co.uk/news/2000/may/18/guardianobituaries

Greaves, Richard L. *Glimpses of Glory: John Bunyan and English Dissent* (Stanford University Press, 2002).

Hampson, Robert and Barry, Peter. *New British Poetries: The Scope of the Possible.* Manchester and New York: Manchester University Press, 1993.

Jarvis, Matthew. 'Barry MacSweeney's Moorland Romance', *Culture, Creativity and Environment: New Environmentalist Criticism*, eds. Fiona Becket and Terry Gifford (Amsterdam and New York: Rodopi, 2007), 181-96.

Johnston, Arthur. *Enchanted Ground: The Study of Medieval Romance in the Eighteenth Century* (London: The Athlone Press, 1964).

Keats, John. *The Complete Poems*, ed. John Barnard (Harmondsworth: Penguin, 1977).

Keith, Jennifer. "'Pre-Romanticism' and the ends of eighteenth-century poetry'. *The Cambridge Companion to Eighteenth-Century Poetry*, ed. John Sitter (Cambridge: Cambridge University Press, 2001).

MacSweeney, Barry. *The Boy from the Green Cabaret Tells of His Mother*. (London: Hutchinson, 1968).

—— *Black Torch* (London: London Pride Editions, 1978).

—— *Flames on the Beach at Viareggio* (Blacksuede Boot Press, 1970).

—— *Elegy for January* (London: Menard Press, 1970).

—— *Our Mutual Scarlet Boulevard* (London: Fulcrum Press, 1971).

—— *Hellhound Memos* (London: The Many Press, 1993).

—— *Wolf Tongue: Selected Poems 1965-2000* (Tarset: Bloodaxe Books, 2003).

—— *Horses in Boiling Blood* (Cambridge: Equipage, 2005).

Manson, Peter. 'Barry MacSweeney *Hellhound Memos*', originally published in *Object Permanence* 1 (January 1994) http://www.petermanson.com/Macsweeney.htm

Morris, Marianne. 'The Abused Become the Abusers: the Poetry of Barry MacSweeney', *Quid* 14 October 2004: 4-21 http://www.barquepress.com/quid14.pdf.

Mottram, Eric. Introduction to 'A Treacherous Assault on British Poetry', *The New British Poetry* (London: Paladin, 1988).

'MACSWEENEY / PICKARD / SMITH: Poets from North-East England interviewed by Eric Mottram, *Poetry Information*, No. 18 (1978): 21-39. The interview was recorded 14.12.74.

Rowe, William Walton. *Three Lyric Poets: Harwood, Torrance, MacSweeney* (Tavistock: Northcote House Publishers, 2009).

Sears, John. 'Out of Control' (review of *Wolf Tongue*). www.popmatters.com/books/reviews/w/wolf-tongue.shtml

Shelley, Percy Bysshe. *The Poetical Works of Percy Bysshe Shelley* (London and New York: Frederick Warne, 1888).

Smith, Rebecca A. 'Barry MacSweeney and the Bunting Influence: A key figure in his literary universe?' *Jacket* 35 (2008) http://jacketmagazine.com/35/smith-macsweeney.shtml

Tarlo, Harriet. 'Radical Landscapes: Contemporary Poetry in the Bunting Tradition', *The Star You Steer By: Basil Bunting and British Modernism* (Amsterdam and Atlanta: Rodopi, 2000), 149-80.

Walker, Carol Kyros. *Walking North With Keat* (New Haven and London: Yale University Press, 1992).

Wilkinson, John. 'A Single Striking Soviet: The Poetry of Barry MacSweeney', *The Lyric Touch: Essays on the Poetry of Excess* (Cambridge: Salt, 2007).

Williams, Jonathan. 'Some Jazz from the Baz: The Bunting-Williams Letters', *The Star You Steer By: Basil Bunting and British Modernism* (Amsterdam and Atlanta, 2000), 253-84.

Wordsworth, William. *The Poems, Volume One*, ed. John O. Hayden (Harmondsworth: Penguin, 1977).

MATTHEW JARVIS

Hard Hats in Heather:
Barry MacSweeney's North-East

In the second section of Barry MacSweeney's early sequence *Brother Wolf* (1972), the poet-speaker declares (p.23):

> There is so much *land* in Northumberland. The sea
> Taught me to sing
>   the river to hold my nose. When
> it rains it rains glue.

In these lines, Northumberland appears most obviously as a physical entity: first, in terms of its sheer expanse and, second, through the olfactory character of an unspecified river (the smell of which teaches the speaker to hold his nose). However, it is important to recognise that Northumberland is also construed culturally here, through the speaker's artistic response to his environment that is figured in those sea-taught songs. This double-barrelled response serves as a useful model for much of MacSweeney's poetic reaction to the North-East of England – the area which forms the primary physical territory of his poetry (particularly the county of Northumberland, although by no means exclusively so). For MacSweeney, in other words, the English North-East is emphatically a landscape of physical experience; but it is also one which is a significantly cultural event. Indeed, in the closing image of the lines quoted above, the human and the non-human are intriguingly mixed, with rain (representative of the non-human elements) manifest as glue (representative of human manufacture). Notwithstanding the fact that, as the *Encyclopædia Britannica* puts it in its entry on Northumberland, 'parts of the moors are still among the most sparsely populated areas of England',[1] for MacSweeney, the poetic construction of this region is emphatically one in which the non-human and the human are inextricably bound together. Such an approach is important because it suggests that what is called human/ nature dualism – the long-standing Western mode of thought which divides humanity from the non-human world – is being, in some way, questioned by MacSweeney. According to environmentalist philosopher Val Plumwood, human/nature dualism 'situates human life outside and above an inferiorised and manipulable nature', thus creating 'ideals of culture and human identity that promote human distance from, control of and ruthlessness towards the sphere of nature as the Other, while minimising non-human claims to the earth and to elements of mind, reason and ethical consideration'.[2] Although my main concern in this essay is to detail MacSweeney's response to his North-East English environment, the question of whether his human/non-human negotiations work to erode the sort of dualistic thinking that Plumwood identifies is also part of what interests me here.

The eighth section of *Brother Wolf* suggests very much the same sort of fusion of physical and cultural responses to place that was apparent in the second section of the poem, although here the art-istic experience of song has been replaced by dance. MacSweeney's particular geographical point of reference in these lines is the Northumberland hamlet of Sparty Lea – to where, according to Nicholas Johnson, MacSweeney would escape in his youth:

> Raised in the poor quarters of Newcastle, the contrast of surrounding moorland hamlets were oxygen to a suppressed wisdom. He would 'plodge' in the river Allen, at the moorland hamlet, Sparty Lea, tick-ling trout and picking rosehips at Allendale for NHS syrup quotas.[3]

In *Brother Wolf*, then, it is the trees at Sparty Lea which are danc-ing (p.25):

> At Sparty Lea the trees don't want Orpheus
> to invoke any magic
> they dance by themselves.
> Up there they
> strap two
> rams together the
> hardest-headed
> wins. Death
> on the horns.
> The trees dance by themselves.

Not needing Orpheus's music to make them move, the trees by the River East Allen seemingly make their own magic and thus 'dance by themselves'. Of course, such dancing could be construed as a simple reference to trees being blown by the wind. However, by invoking the legend of Orpheus – whose music was so powerful that inanimate forms such as rocks and trees literally followed him as he played – it is, I would suggest, far more accurate to see these lines as indicating that the dancing of the Sparty Lea trees parallels the responsive Orphic world, and therefore constitutes an *actual* dance, rather than merely movement in the air.[4] Thus, even though Orpheus is not needed by the trees themselves, it is through his image that MacSweeney approaches the Northumberland landscape – and through his image that we are consequently provided with the frame within which we are to view aspects of the activity in that landscape. In other words, the natural (Sparty Lea's trees) is accessed through the cultural (the Orpheus myth), rendering the non-human forms of landscape a human event.

However, it is important to note that the mystical and magical are not allowed to *overrun* the physical in these lines – the physical being most obviously encapsulated here in the potential for death. Having observed Sparty Lea's dancing trees, MacSweeney describes what seems to be some sort of tough moorland game, in his reference to the rams which are strapped together until 'the / hardestheaded / wins' – the upshot of which is seemingly death for the losing beast ('Death / on the horns'). That such an event is a cultural exercise cannot be denied: it is apparently a game undertaken by an unspecified, but obviously human, 'they'. It is, in this sense, just as much an act of culture as the legend of Orpheus. But it simultaneously places a concrete sense of physicality (bodies strapped together; the clashing of heads; death) alongside the image of the artistic or mystical that is provided by those dancing trees. Yet finding such a combination at Sparty Lea should really be no surprise. As Nicholas Johnson observes, as well as being the locus of splashing in streams and tickling trout for the youthful MacSweeney, Sparty Lea was also a formative *poetic* event:

> MacSweeney opened the doors of his aunts' cottages for ten days [in 1967] to a new generation of English poets who met head on for 'Sparty Lea Poetry Festival'. Sparks flew and Sparty Lea – like The Tower [Tom Pickard's Morden Tower], set the benchmark: for its pollenation [sic] of radical poetics.[5]

Perhaps this is why *Brother Wolf* sees the trees at Sparty Lea as having no need for Orpheus: they dance on their own because the music of poetry is inherently and already part and parcel of this place.

*

Like the sense of exposure to land in section two of *Brother Wolf*, MacSweeney's 1985 sequence *Ranter* begins with a similar and striking sense of being out in open country. Thus, in the first stanza of the long opening poem (also called 'Ranter'), the speaker describes the eponymous character of both poem and sequence as 'sniffing the trail', his 'eyes on any horizon', 'leaping the fence of his enclosure / nose down in open fields' (p.140). The description offered of the Ranter character here renders him as a dog, thus fundamentally aligning him with the green space of the 'open fields' in which he runs. To put it simply, Ranter is, at this point, a non-human form – notwithstanding the significance of his name, which associates him with a radical, anarchic religious movement of the seventeenth century.[6] Thus, rather than merely combining the human and the non-human in the manner of the rain-as-glue which appeared in *Brother Wolf*, the experience of being out in the land at the beginning of *Ranter* reaches the point where the human is apparently subsumed into the non-human – thus going significantly beyond that need to reverse the 'weakened sense of the reality of our embeddedness in nature' which Val Plumwood suggests is integral to humanity's long-term ecological survival.[7] By contrast, what MacSweeney offers here is a profound human re-engagement with what it means to be a creature. As such, at this point, Ranter's name is a near-solitary link between the character himself and human culture, which is otherwise submerged beneath the primal and animalistic experience of a nose full of scent, 'stunned with blood'.

Alongside this striking move towards the non-human, the imagery used in the opening stanza of the sequence is substantially to do with the pursuit of openness – significantly echoing that sense of physical expansiveness which was identifiable in the response of *Brother Wolf* to the landscape of Northumberland. Eyes are fixed on the horizon, an enclosure is escaped from, the fields in which Ranter runs are 'open', and – in the final line of the stanza – he becomes a 'greyhound quick from his trap'. The suggestion is of landscape as the locus for a kind of physical release. However, this stanza does not identify the countryside within which its main character is moving, and it is arguably the case that the territory being engaged with here is more psychological than it is physically actual. The premise of these opening lines is that Ranter is searching for an unnamed 'her' (the lover from whom he has separated, as the sequence goes on to make clear), and the action of 'trailing her scent' is thus as much a metaphor for this quest as it is an indicator of genuine pursuit along the ground. Indeed, in the lines immediately following the stanza's end, the greyhound-formed Ranter is heard 'Moaning: *this must be the last lap* // And it isn't / even the first'. These lines work strikingly against the images of openness offered a few lines earlier (the greyhound is restricted to lapping a track), whilst they also suggest the sense of being caught in an continuing emotional struggle. Ranter is seemingly trapped within a persistent cycle of trauma, whirled round and round, unable to escape.

Having said this, however, it is important to recognise that, even if the poem's opening lines are more to do with psychological than actual territory, the notion of real-world geographical space is, in *Ranter*, never far away. There is, in other words, a persistent urge within the sequence to respond to – to return to – *literal* territory. Thus, the poem's very next lines offer up the description of Ranter as (p.140):

    swooping aloft
    skylark on Skye
    swanning around
    gliding over glades
    snipe drumming
    stealing into empty nests
    shimmering in hillhaze
    Cheviot to Killhope Law

In these lines, then, we begin to see the physical scope of MacSweeney's imaginative north as it is manifest in *Ranter* – here, stretching down from Scotland, from the furthest-north of the Inner Hebrides, through the Cheviot Hills (which mark the border between England and Scotland, with The Cheviot itself being their highest point),[8] before finally ending up at the peak of Killhope Law, which is situated on the border of Northumberland and

County Durham and which rises to 2,208 feet in the area to the west of Allenheads.[9] This arrival at Killhope Law is particularly significant, as it suggests the centrality to *Ranter* of the moorland region in which this particular peak is to be found – although there is a striking breadth of geographical vision in the sequence as a whole, which drifts as far afield as Canterbury, London and Ireland. But the journey down from Skye to Killhope Law in this stanza does seem to imply a kind of coming into focus – the arrival of Ranter at what may be understood as his physical-emotional heartland. Alongside all this, of course, the stanza is another pointer towards expansiveness, in the sheer landscape breadth it captures in the 240-mile sweep of its movement from Skye to Killhope Law via The Cheviot, with the imagery of skylark and snipe similarly indicative of a certain freedom in 'swooping', 'gliding', and being almost lost to sight in the 'shimmering [...] hillhaze'. In other words, in *Ranter*'s opening stanzas, MacSweeney's poetic oscillates sharply between a sense of physical freedom or expansiveness and the notion of being caught within some cycle of psychological or emotional torment. As such, the point of place here seems to be to offer a significantly *physical* release from the traps of the mind.

As my opening analysis suggested, MacSweeney is profoundly bound up with place-as-cultural-event as well as place-as-physical-space. Thus, alongside its physical responses to the English North-East, *Ranter* also defines the region in terms of its socio-cultural life. That MacSweeney's poetic in *Ranter* is intimately concerned with aspects of the history of English culture in general – and not just specifically *northern* English culture – is made abundantly clear in the associations that MacSweeney achieves through the array of names he gives to his central character. Thus, and still in the opening poem of the sequence, he writes of Ranter as (p.141):

> [...] Leveller, Lollard,
> Luddite, Man of Kent, Tyneside
> broadsheet printer,
> whisperer of sedition,
> wrecker of looms

These lines wrap Ranter around with a variety of oppositional labels from English history, from the religious radicalism of the Ranters themselves, through the Levellers (a 'popular democratic movement', again from the seventeenth century, which believed in the abolition of both the monarchy and the House of Lords),[10] the Lollards (late medieval religious radicals, critical of the established church and its practices),[11] and the nineteenth-century Luddites (craftsmen who smashed the machinery which was replacing them),[12] to the 'Kentish rebels' who followed Wat Tyler during the Peasants' Revolt of 1381.[13] Ranter is thus not merely dog, skylark, or snipe: he is also the embodiment of English cultural opposition, the historic propagator of seditious ideas, and one who – in his identity as 'wrecker of looms' – is significantly in sympathy with the threatened and displaced. Such concern with drawing together animal and cultural into one character does suggest that MacSweeney's poetic is, to a certain extent, out of sympathy with human/nature dualism: Ranter is emphatically double, culture *and* creature, rather than merely (or predominantly) one or the other.

Given this, it is hardly surprising to observe a similar sort of physical-cultural doubleness emerging in MacSweeney's sense of place, too. For example, we find Ranter 'Picking up Bede and Cuthbert / on the ham radio / in his birdbrain wolfskull' (p.141) – thus tuning-in to two of the archetypal voices of the North-East's religious history and drawing them into the sphere of Ranter's creaturely brain and skull ('birdbrain wolfskull'). Indeed, in the figure of Cuthbert, MacSweeney accesses at least two of the most significant high-status locations of the area's religious past: the monastery of Lindisfarne (over which Cuthbert became bishop in 685, having been made prior there some years earlier) and Durham Cathedral (the final resting place for Cuthbert's bones).[14] But MacSweeney's cultural vision of the North-East is emphatically not merely religious: he also construes it as a space of political – indeed, of military – conflict, through references to the figures of Halfdan (rendered by MacSweeney as 'Halfden') and Hadrian. Thus, MacSweeney pictures (p.142)

Halfden's longboats
ploughing the shore
Bamburgh at bay

Newcastle gets ready

These lines recall the military incursions of Halfdan into the North-East during the ninth century,[15] and even imagine the great fortress of Bamburgh (iconic symbol of power within historic Northumberland) as cowed by him.[16] However, the sense of threat figured here is not allowed to remain as a distant historical vision. Rather, Ranter himself becomes directly involved in the struggles of the past, as the opening poem of the sequence goes on to depict his own subjugation in the face of military violence (p.142):

> Ranter roped up
> hurt in him
> heel on his neck
> Halfden's heel
> under the Raven banner
>
> Hadrian's leather boot

Admittedly, MacSweeney here conflates two very different historical moments, with Ranter's neck trodden down both by the ninth-century Halfdan and the second-century Roman emperor Hadrian (who came to Britain in 122 AD).[17] But this merely accentuates Ranter as a kind of focal point for cultural experience within the context of the work – as did the numerous names with which MacSweeney invested his central character early in the sequence. However, what is perhaps more important is that these lines simultaneously make such cultural experience immediately physical: the cultural events of North-East history are literally heavy on Ranter, as they find form in the twinned boot-leather of Halfdan and Hadrian. In other words, the cultural and the physical are again bound inextricably together. Thus, recalling 'militiamen / academy-trained' or the 'swinish from pubs', Ranter tells how he is 'hurled off the causeway / asking for Bede' (p.142). The place invoked here is Lindisfarne (Holy Island), which is linked to the mainland by a causeway that can be crossed at low tide. *Ranter* may, it seems, be crucially responsive to the cultural history of the North-East – here figured in Bede, archetype of history-as-such – but his engagement with such culture often seems to be inevitably and concurrently physical: 'asking for Bede' gets him ejected bodily from the route to one of Northumberland's most famous cultural locations. This is, in other words, the body in history. As the next stanza puts it (p.142):

> Salt.
> I got salt.

Asking for Aidan
I was shown the shore.

Here, rather than Bede, and in another of MacSweeney's apparent historical conflations, Ranter recalls seeking the seventh-century founder of Lindisfarne's monastery. But the result is the same: he is 'shown the shore' – which I take to be a euphemistic reference to being thrown into the sea, where he 'gets' the salt of the previous lines. The cultural history of the North-East is thus bound up with taste at this point – specifically the taste of the place when one is thrown face-down onto the ground (or into the sea). Perhaps this is why, in the following stanza, Ranter talks of 'Aching for seawind taste': it is only through an experience of its physical qualities that he can begin to experience a place – including its culture and its history.

In these terms, it is interesting that when the poem's speaker turns his attention to Ranter's own arena of power – in the Northumberland moorland region around the River East Allen, broadly north-east of Killhope Law – he describes it thus (p.146):

Allendale's princedom
running with streams.[18]

In the previous two stanzas, Ranter's personal power has been pictured in terms which strikingly recall the movement of human to animal that I observed at the beginning of the sequence as a whole. Thus, Ranter proclaims that (p.146):

This is my power:
To peck and roar.
To be feathered,
furred and fanged.

To hunt,
sky above him.
Grub-hunting
earth at his feet.

In other words, Ranter's power is a matter of animalistic aggression ('To peck and roar'), but is also to be identified more generally in the displacement of human form by qualities of animal physiology (being 'feathered, / furred and fanged'). Ranter's personal strengths, it seems, are precisely in his movement away from the human. Matching this is the notion of his 'princedom' as being defined in terms of waterways: it is, as the poem puts it, 'running with streams'. Within environmentalist thinking, the concept of bioregionalism approaches place – and the human and non-human communities within it – by thinking in terms of 'territory of limited magnitude whose borders may not be precisely specifiable but are conceived in terms of "natural" rather than jurisdictional units, often in terms of watershed or constellation of watersheds'.[19] In such an approach to place, human administrative units – such as the concept of the county (e.g. Northumberland) – are abandoned for definition by non-human spatial markers (albeit potentially less precise than their human counterparts) such as the drainage basins of rivers. It is this sort of bioregionalist or watershed thinking which seems to appear in the notion of Ranter's 'princedom' as a place of streams. Thus, by contrast with MacSweeney's approach to the landscape of Sparty Lea in *Brother Wolf* through the cultural imagery of Orpheus, the landscape of Ranter's realm (the human concept of the 'princedom') is here approached by means of *non-human* spatial markers (streams). Of course – and as we might expect from the constant shifting between the physical and the cultural which seems to define MacSweeney's approach to place – although Ranter's 'princedom' is here defined in terms of its non-human qualities, in the penultimate poem of the sequence ('Ranter's Reel'), it is a locale that is crucially over-written by acts of culture (p.165):

Broken stiles
littering the princedom
neglected ditches
clogged with clarts

locked-up chapels
where lamenting starts

sheepwire stapling
her fells and fields

wild Northumberland
hemmed in, stitched up

more dismay
for me and my fiefdom

Ranter opens these lines with a lament for a countryside whose rural character has become run-down in the sense that the markers of humanity within it are decaying (broken stiles, ditches neglected and left to fill with sticky mud). By the latter part of this quotation, however, the human itself seems to be understood as an assault on the land, with 'sheepwire' enclosures likened to stapling, hemming in, and stitching up the 'wild' Northumberland environment. Of course, from a bioregionalist point of view, there is something of a problem here, with the notion of the human hemming in something that is a human construct anyway – by which I mean the *county* of Northumberland. But this is less important than the fact that, as the overall movement of these lines suggests, the operations of human culture appear to be significantly equivocal in MacSweeney's North-East. In other words, although the decay of stiles and ditches – markers of human agricultural life – is a cause for lament, the presence of another marker of farming practice ('sheepwire') is seen as a trussing up of the county. Similarly, whilst the Christian heroes of the area's past may be characters to whom Ranter calls out for help, they seem to be significantly out of reach or unavailable (p.147):

Listen Cuthbert.
Come in Bede.

Your time's up
I need help.

Aidan
where are you?

This is Ranter calling
on VHF

Indeed, towards the beginning of the sequence, Ranter explicitly wonders why Bede and Cuthbert 'don't answer back' (p.141). Oppressors, by contrast, are close at hand: Ranter has 'Halfden's heel on his neck' (p.147), whilst in 'Ranter's Reel', an unspecified 'Titled Lord' (p.167) has seemingly usurped Ranter's territory. Thus, Ranter proclaims (pp.166-67):

I'm red grouse,
pride of the moor.
I won't flit
this hole in the heather

because you say so.
[…]

Won't lie in duckdown
when there is bracken & slurry.
Wander the fellsides
rather than be used by you.

You're Boss Lip
brass in his pocket
and a brass neck

Titled Lord
but I'll tell you this:
this is my princedom
you're on the wrong ground

Northumberland's moorland areas become places of guerrilla combat
as Ranter commits himself to ousting the apparent usurper, which
he can achieve – he contends – because 'this is my palace / I know
every bolt-hole / better than the veins / on her [his former lover's]
back' (p.167). In other words, and paralleling lines earlier in the
sequence which describe him as 'conversant with Brock / swooper
with Kes' (p.150), Ranter crucially suggests that he is at one with
the land itself – significantly undivided from the non-human. So
out of this earthy connectedness, he pledges a campaign of usurp-
ation that will continue until 'you're broken / begging for friends',
brought down by the 'Mighty Leveller / one you thought resigned /
to books' (p.167) – the neat ambiguity here suggesting either a
withdrawal into the writing of books (Ranter as MacSweeney the
poet) or the sense of one who has been consigned to history books
(Ranter as the historical figure of the Leveller). Either way, for
MacSweeney, being in the North-East – or more precisely at this
point, being in 'wild Northumberland' – is an acutely human
experience, but one that is at its strongest when it emerges out of
a rooted connectedness with the land itself. Moreover, the human
experience that is involved here is crucially not an easy nostalgia
for the great figures of the region's past. Rather, with such figures
apparently failing to respond to his calls for help, MacSweeney's
representative in *Ranter* – that is, the eponymous Ranter himself –
must set *himself* against the tyrannies of the powerful (pp.167-68):

Shot from a Range Rover
I will rise

Freed from neck-chains
walking in your door
armed with centuries of anger

At this point, the 'centuries of anger' – figured in the list of oppositional movements which Ranter's various names encapsulate – come together in the contest for MacSweeney's heartland, 'Allendale's princedom' (p.146). In this contest, then, Northumberland's open spaces – river-defined, locus of identification with the non-human – become the focal point of a struggle for power over territory, between the status quo (the 'Titled Lord') and the dissident (Ranter, Leveller, Lollard, Luddite, Man of Kent).

*

As a way of moving towards a conclusion, it is useful to compare the construction of the North-East in *Ranter* with MacSweeney's later sequences, *Pearl* (1995) and *Pearl in the Silver Morning* (1999) – both of which also emerge substantially out of the 'princedom' of the moorland areas around the River East Allen. It is, I think, fair to say that MacSweeney's profoundly physical response to the landscape of the North-East is sustained in these later works. Thus, *Pearl* contains a significant amount of what amounts to celebration of the topography and climate of its upland setting (p.207):

> white water,
> foaming tumblestones, wet and grey days, or
> brilliant Aprils and Septembers, shine, shine, shine

The sheer physical ferocity of the poem's environment is something which is also emphasised, in phrases such as 'the rain-soaked law' and 'I stand on the top road and bow / in sleet, knuckle-bunching cold' (p.198), Moreover, the main characters of the sequence – the poet-figure Bar (both young and in later life) and his first love, the eponymous Pearl – are themselves substantially defined by their relationship with the material facts of the land. For example, in 'Cavalry at Calvary' (p.206), the poet-speaker declares that he 'could not stop dreaming of Pearl, / her bare feet driving the brown trout mad', whilst at the start of 'Mony Ryal Ray' (p.200) he proclaims:

> Skybrightness drove me
> to the cool of the lake
> to muscle the wind
> and wrestle the clouds
> and forever dream of Pearl.

In these extracts, Pearl is recalled through her splashing in streams and her interaction with the creatures of the water, whilst the speaker himself becomes a kind of elemental presence, interacting directly with wind and clouds. Moreover, as I have argued elsewhere, in the previous poem of the sequence, 'No Such Thing' (p.199), 'the sense of colour shared by Pearl and the speaker is drawn from non-human sources: feldspar, peat, marigolds, cowslips'.[20] There is, in other words, a persistent suggestion of human embeddedness within the land which makes clear what was also apparent in *Ranter*: that elements of MacSweeney's poetic work against ways of thinking which sunder the human from the non-human, and that his poetry is thus, in part at least, interestingly congruent with environmentalist tendencies – such as Val Plumwood's – to emphasise 'the reality of our embeddedness in nature'.[21] However, this is emphatically not to suggest that MacSweeney's poetic is, in any way, programmatically "green". Indeed, all I have just said must be set against the concluding lines of the 1999 addition to the *Pearl* sequence, *Pearl in the Silver Morning*. In 'We Are Not Stones', looking back to his youth with Pearl in the Northumberland moors, the poet-speaker declares (p.325):

> It was all, all of it, all for us, from the wonders
> of our mysterious heaven
> to the trout's opal seed-sac bubbling with jewels.

On one level, there is a sense of ownership of the non-human in these lines which keys into the conventional dualist sense of humanity being in some way, in Val Plumwood's words, 'outside and above an inferiorised and manipulable nature'.[22] But, nonetheless, the sense of self-identification through association with the non-human is striking. By contrast, in the present, the speaker declares that he is 'miles from our happiness' ('We Are Not Stones', p.325) – that happiness being, very precisely, his time with Pearl in the specific location of upland Northumberland. He is thus sharply cut off from the non-human affiliations which the 'princedom' of Allendale seemed to generate, with the upshot being that – in the words which form the tragic end to both 'We Are Not Stones' and MacSweeney's 2003 volume of selected poems *Wolf Tongue* – 'Everything is lost, and we are dust and done for'. Whatever moves towards some sort of rapprochement with the non-human we might identify in MacSweeney's poetry, for the poet-speaker at least, they appear to come to nothing at the last. This does not, however, overturn the intense physicality of the response to the Northumberland area that is identifiable in *Pearl*. Indeed, as a lament for its loss, the final line of 'We Are Not Stones' rather reinforces its importance.

Just as with *Ranter*, however, such physicality marches side-by-side with a sense of place as cultural event. In the case of *Pearl*, the entire sequence is enveloped by the fourteenth-century alliterative poem of the same name, which provides a kind of literary frame in which MacSweeney's work operates. Thus, for example, although the poet-speaker may be driven to 'the cool of the lake' (p.200), to spar, elemental fashion, with wind and clouds, the poem in which this happens is called 'Mony Ryal Ray' – these words being a quotation from the medieval *Pearl*, with the line from which they are taken referring to the light emanating from a 'crystal clyffe' in heaven.[23] In other words, the 'Skybrightness' of MacSweeney's Northumberland becomes intriguingly mixed with the divine brightness of a medieval literary vision of Christian paradise. Moreover, on a more down-to-earth level, although the landscape of the sequence is recurrently defined as green space (thus non-human), there are persistent indicators of cultural activity within it. The opening of 'No Buses to Damascus' (p.201) declares:

Wonder Pearl distemper pale, queen
of Blanchland who rode mare Bonny
by stooks and stiles in the land
of waving wings and borage blue
and striving storms of stalks and stems.[24]

Although this is a land of birds' wings, 'borage blue', stalks, stems, it is also a place of stooks ('stook' being a dialect word for bundles of straw) and stiles – both of which indicate the human management of land. Moreover, alongside heather and 'heifer-trampled marigold', the poem has Pearl 'on the Leadgate Road', whilst her finger points 'towards the rusty coloured dry stone wall' – both road and wall being prime evidence of human habitation and building. Given such markers of human culture, it also makes considerable sense to find echoes in *Pearl* of that sense of place as the locale of human contest which was so significant in *Ranter*. For example, in 'Pearl Suddenly Awake' (p.202), not only does Pearl consider the 'ghosts of now forsaken four-wheeled bogies' – testimony to the now-abandoned lead mines in the area – but she declares:

> They –
> you call it government – are killing everything
> now. Hard hats abandoned in heather. Locked-up
> company huts
> useless to bird, beast or humankind.

MacSweeney's 'princedom' of blue-flowered borage, streams, cloud, and skybrightness is also a place over which is written both industrial history and what Pearl reads as the destruction wrought on the region by the policies of a literally murderous government (they are, she says, 'killing everything / now'). Certainly, on one level, MacSweeney's poetry may figure a kind of pastoral – or, in the case of *Pearl*, romantic – release within the various physicality (whether beautiful or fierce) of his North-East. But, simultaneously, his work is profoundly caught up with the sense of this land as a place where Halfdan's heel may suddenly be on his neck, where a guerrilla-style campaign may be required to oust a usurping 'Lord', and where both economic failure and subjugation to higher socio-political powers are recorded by hard hats left lying in the heather. Indeed, this latter image of hard hats in heather captures especially neatly the intertwining of human and non-human which is seemingly integral to MacSweeney's poetics of place – thus aligning MacSweeney's topographical vision with Leo Marx's notion of 'complex' pastoral in which, according to Marx, literature 'manage[s] to qualify, or call into question, or bring irony to bear against the illusion of peace and harmony in green pasture'.[25] Whilst MacSweeney's North-East may demand that the human and the non-human be thought of together, it does so in a way which declares that closing the human-nature divide is never a matter of simply retreating into some sort of unproblematic green space. Rather, MacSweeney's North-East binds together release, beauty, and struggle. It is a place where a degree of identification with the non-human may be achieved – but where, at the same time, the diverse marks of humanity and human conflict are absolutely unavoidable.

ANDREW DUNCAN

Revolt in the Backlands: *Black Torch* Book One and the Silenced Voices of History

This wonderful book was announced, in 1977, as follows:

> *Black Torch*, book 1, a first part of a long projected work, drawing on the political/social activity of Northumberland and Durham miners, will be published by London Pride Editions this autumn. Much of it is in Northumbrian dialect. Book 2, half finished, works around John Martin's diaries – he is the Northumbrian painter – tracts by radical Baptist ministers, and the trial of T. Dan Smith. Book 3 is planned to be based on tape recordings with residents of Sparty Lea and the Allen Valley in Northumberland.[1]

This is a note by the poet himself. Book One did come out in 1978, but Books Two and Three were never written. *Blackbird*, an elegy for MacSweeney's grandfather, published in 1979, is Book Two of the work as redesigned. The *Black Torch* is coal itself ('where beds of black torch / reach magnesian limestone / last of the shelves / german ocean'),[2] the heroes of the poem are miners:

> black dusted prometheans
> black fur of moles
> jet phlegm chalked in black dust
> white eye balls teeth groin
> black suede tongue
> ripping fire
> for the national hearth[3]

'Torch' would fit into a Marxist collocation as what a pathfinder carries; it resonates with other charged words like 'vanguard', 'advanced', and 'progress'. It shows us a beacon. We are in darkness, as in a mine, from which we can only exit when led by someone who holds the illuminating torch – of Marxist theory, perhaps.

63

But it also reminds us of the passage in the Book of Revelations where John the Divine talks about touching a burning coal to his lips. Prometheus carried hidden fire and liberated mankind, making him too a popular Marxist symbol.

MacSweeney's works are complex and stand outside genre conventions; the flow of sense is not always easy to follow. *Black Torch* is about seventy-five pages long, and has the following parts: a dedication to Eric Mottram; an account of (probably two) miners' strikes in 1854 occupying the bulk of the book; a poem about a girl, Pearl, set in the 1950s; a legend, 'Melrose to South Shields', slipped in; 'Black Lamp Strike', a poem about many different seditious and protest activities in around 1817; and a final poem, 'Black Torch Sunrise', set in the present day of 1977, with the poet watching television and talking about politics.

The anthropologist Victor Turner has spoken of a 'social drama' studied in depth as providing 'a limited area of transparency on the otherwise opaque surface of regular, uneventful social life. Through it we are enabled to observe the crucial principles of the social structure in their operation'.[4] Every poet is a *soi-disant* poet. They are what they say – and inevitably brush up against the norms of appraising humans. Strikers also want a say in what they're worth – four shillings a day, or however much. A bundle of prices and statuses make up social structure, you could say. Sometimes we notice that the price of goods or labour can vary, and that the status of an individual can also vary. Different people may remember different versions of the rules. We can get a much more accurate view of society by looking for the conflicts and asking who defends the set-up, and how they mend it. Turner was a pupil of Max Gluckman, founder of a school which studied the process of law in African societies. The assumption is that there is competition for key roles, and the goal is to find out how the rivals fight it out, and what the volume of conflict is. After this, one could resolve the structure of a given society including the exceptions.

Evidently, a strike is a classic contest, if only one among many. Evidently, too, *Black Torch* uses conflict to show fundamental aspects of English society. It is what Turner would call a 'social drama'. Its community of the strike may be an example of an anti-structure (to use another of Turner's phrases) where a group develops a strong sense of community along with a set of values which is wholly the opposite of the official set. Such an anti-structure is often associated with fundamentalist religion – as with the Ranters and with the Sicilian slave revolt discussed below – and with genres such as apocalypse and creation myths. It is possible – though there is some debate about this – to regard Northern society as a whole as an anti-structure with regard to the dominant values of politics, law, and history, as upheld in the South.

Shock troops

Throughout the 1960s, English politicians were obsessed with prices and incomes policy. The commodities boom of 1972 encouraged the OPEC oil price rises of 1972-73, which led to high inflation in Western economies. Quarrels attendant on saving wages from rapid deflation then dominated British politics until the early 1980s. People wanted stability and could only obtain it through conflict. Workers in nationalised industries, whose wages were paid by the government, were test cases: the government would either win by holding their wages down, or, in the other case, if the workers refused to be cajoled or coerced, the government would visibly fail, and loud voices would say it was unable to govern. The relationship between the government and the coalminers was thus a charged one. There was a Conservative government from 1970 to 1974. In 1972 the first national miners' strike since 1926 [5] was called, and Prime Minister Edward Heath declared a State of Emergency. In January 1974, another one was called; Heath declared a compulsory three-day working week (power would be shut down on the other days to save fuel), and called a general election on the strength of it, which he lost in February 1974. Many observers stated that the miners had brought the government down. (Conservative strategists had probably thought the issue was a chance to fight an anti-Red ticket and beat Labour that way – the deputy leader of the miners' union, Mick McGahey, was chairman of the Communist Party. If so, they lied and miscalculated.)

In 1995 I conducted an interview with Barry during which he said: 'I read 'Babi Yar' [...] And then I thought, right, this is what poetry's about. It's about fighting, commitment, lyricism. I think even then I was a Communist. I was a member of the Young Communists in Newcastle when I was 17 and I just thought, that's what poetry's all about really'.[6] Barry came from Newcastle, a coal port; there was a whole coalfield around the Tyne. Barry's view of politics was radical but not original – it was plugged into popular narratives; however, we need to reconstruct the shared narratives of the time. Most of *Black Torch* is documentary, like this:

> thats six ton of coal yi knaa
> hoo aboot that then
> we had ti make a stand when we did
> we ownly orn 3 and 6 a day
> for six ton
> aah havent orned more than 3 bob a day
> in twenty yor
> oh wull stay solid till the end like
> till we die [7]

but it also includes argument:

> that the See of Durham
> represented, initiated and actively partook
> in fierce accumulation of common land
> this warlike custom laid the base
> of ecclesiastical capitalism
> in Northumbria
> and the churches' vast collection
> of properties, in other words
> profit
>   without work [8]

Some is written in an elliptical and rhapsodic manner:

> combatants to back fell blue rain
> masons' handshake northern wall to Kielder
> if go south is to soften the weave
> undurable iron such
> electric gardens tended by her when
> her champions all are all in earth
> her champions scarves feet are dead *if*
> *they have gone no course to run or see*
> *that there is any time so they fell and died*
>
> each word a kerbstone [9]

All three modes require interpretation. In order to reconstruct the political thought behind *Black Torch*, we have to uncover the Marxist ideas of the time. I have chosen to do this from the pages of *Past and Present*. This was the central organ of English Marxist historians, where the narrative modules that Barry and the poets of his generation ate up were first tested out. If I understand correctly, these were non-Party historians. The magazine was founded already in 1952, the height of the Cold War, and bore at that time the banner 'magazine of scientific history'. This was explicitly Marxist, as no one else would have used the phrase 'scientific history'. According to Issue Four, 'It was greeted with whispered imputations of sectarianism and of tendencious bias'.

My favourite article appears in Issue Two, where E.A. Thompson re-analyses obscure and passing mentions in late Imperial panegyrics to identify an insurrection of the masses in third, fourth and fifth century Gaul and Spain: the movement of the Bacaudae, a heroic (if true) uprising from below aiming to create a flatter social order. Thompson reports one Eudoxius, a Bacaudae leader and an educated man, as defecting *ad Chunos*, to the Huns. I can't imagine what the Huns would do with a train of intellectuals. But the idea of changing sides to repay ingratitude is always appealing. Thompson says 'When it is dangerously threatened, a propertied class will often conceal (if it can), and even deny, the very existence of those who seek to overthrow it'. This is a magical moment. Has most of history been cut out of the records? But the idea that "I speak for the silent" can so easily soften and rot into "I foist on the Silenced the ideas precious to me". In understanding *Black Torch*, we need to focus on the related processes whereby a few words reveal a whole unsuspected world, and a fat flow of words is capsized and shattered.

Issue Twenty has an article by Peter Green on the First Sicilian Slave War, waged during the second century BC. The slave army reached 70,000 men at one point. Green reports a chronicle by one Caecilius, written from the point of view of the slaves, and says that its loss is irreparable. We have the narratives of the victors. This footnote opens a frustration to which *Black Torch* is the response: this workers' revolt is going to be recorded. Green has interesting details on Eunus, the religious leader of the slaves, breathing flame: 'with a pierced walnut filled with burning sulphur and tinder, and concealed in his mouth'. Green connects this to John the Revelator's report of applying a burning hot coal to his lips, from which his revelation was spoken: '[Eunus's] symbolic fire-breathing trick reminds us of the belief that God spoke through His prophets' lips with tongues of flame'. This is the *Black Torch*, the mineral glow of truth.

The whole endeavour is linked by a shared story about challenging class society and the distribution of property; it is the same story from the third millennium on, with ever-new actors filling the same roles. The two books that are most likely to have influenced Barry are *The Making of the English Working Class* by E.P. Thompson, and *The World Turned Upside Down* by Christopher Hill. (Books by Gerrard Winstanley, Eric Hobsbawm, and George Rudé are also candidates.) However, both of these were part of a stream which begins far, far higher up, and express ideas which are found in hundreds of other writers on history. MacSweeney obviously was not the first socialist poet: we should also consider *The Angry Summer*, Idris Davies's classic account of the 1926 miners' strike; *We the River*, Joseph Macleod's still unpublished documentary-epic on the depression in Huntingdonshire; *Lamentation for the Children*, by Walter Perrie (a miner's son), an account of mining in the Lanarkshire field; and Jeffrey Wainwright's poems on socialist history collected in *Heart's Desire*.

'Black lamp' is certainly a variant of 'dark lantern', a device of the time which lit the way for one person but was invisible (at least from far off) because it did not scatter light. It was used by criminals or conspirators – in this case, obviously, the seditionaries plotting in the terrible trade recession which followed the peace of 1815. '*Black Torch*' is another variant of it:

Masked orator   harangues in midnight shire fields
letters from
distant societies   burn them with candles
Drag the Constitution
from its hidden place   attend Black Lamp's penumbra treason
joined to Black Torch
& Black Torch Strike   chains of seditious affection [10]

We can now return to the political intent of MacSweeney's poem. He is challenging the legitimacy of the legal order by showing significant dissent against it; he is telling us about the shock troops of the working class, whose courage and solidarity makes them able to take on the bosses; they are a torch showing the working class as a whole the way. The decisive conflict will be decided by numbers, and the working class will win.

Pride and Melancholy

The Marxist critic L.C. Knights offers us, in an appendix to his 1937 book on Jonson and early capitalism, *Drama and Society in the Age of Jonson*, a whole essay on melancholy. He locates a rush of interest in the affliction in the early decades of the seventeenth century, and says that 'the root cause of melancholy and discontent is to be found in the social and economic conditions of the time'.[11] He finds this to be an excess number of educated men, equipped with abilities but unable to find fitting office. 'Under Elizabeth, there had been a considerable increase of educational activity, with a consequent heightening of men's expectations'.[12] Richard Mulcaster in 1581 says 'To have so many gaping for preferment, as no gulf hath store enough to suffice, and to let them roam helpless whom nothing else can help [...] For youth being let go forward upon hope, and checked with despair while it roameth without purveyance, makes marvellous ado before it will die'.[13] Lifted up into the air by the Faustian ambition of what seemed to be a world where barriers were breaking, they fell victims to a specific malady in the downstroke. Green says that the First Sicilian Slave War 'was sparked off by the presence in the latifundia of intelligent Syrians and Cilicians'. He speaks of recent mass slave raids by pirates, so that 'this infiltration of educated men [...] into the vast servile plantation which Sicily had become could hardly fail to have disruptive and far-reaching effects'. The loss of their freedom implies a melancholy of unusual proportions. This leads us towards Chatterton, MacSweeney's favourite symbol of upwardly mobile, vaulting, doomed talent. We may think of the flying-suit which lifted Bladud up into the air before his fatal fall over London. He was flying to the Temple of Apollo, associated with lyric poetry and the Nine Muses – like Chatterton in *Brother Wolf* (p.28):

> I will have Fame
> the Nine will be mine

Walpole slew that fact in
vented a smart from the enclosure
Death on a quill
the Nine will be mine
in the arms of Moloch
land of the black goose

The quill was a leak-proof store for arsenic, used for treating syphilis, as well as the writer's fix and what lifts the goose into the air. Chatterton died of arsenic poisoning. It leads us too to MacSweeney's own melancholia. The hangover from individualism may be a political malady: melancholy. There is a mythic arc: pride – flight – revolt – wrath – combat – punishment – wretchedness. Both *Ranter* and *Black Torch* fit this arc, although they cover different segments of it. The "feathered man" imagery occurs frequently in MacSweeney's work. The flight part fits with "high flier", "getting high", and not being "down to earth". We may also think of Iain Sinclair's myth-cycle *Suicide Bridge* (1979), which links three doomed figures who had fallen from the heights: they were Bladud, Harold Godwinsson, and Chatterton. (Chatterton had written a poem about Hastings, including Harold's death; Sinclair added in Bladud.)

The word 'enclosure' in the passage quoted above is without obvious links to the rest of the stanza, but we can guess that it comes trailing associations with the enclosures of the commons in the sixteenth century, identified by Knights and others as the rich abusing the law to steal the rights of the poor. The sense is that Walpole was using his privileges to enclose the sky and arrest Chatterton's flight, bringing his downfall. It may also be helpful to be told that some of MacSweeney's more baffling lines are quotations from Chatterton's fake fifteenth-century English.

One of the key drifts among the authors of *Past and Present* was towards the history of the individual – the over-mighty subjects who broke up collective harmony. That is, you start with a fear of individualism, observe it narrowly, and end up as its biographer. When you see someone like Chatterton who totally breaks out of any nourishing social bonds, who is simply nowhere, who becomes a totally self-conscious individual because he has lost all these relationships and their stabilising customs, you realise that there is a story to be uncovered. He forged mediaeval poetry in an extraordinary loss of self, because he had left his social niche. He sued the literary world to change his status – another social drama, whose course shows the structure of the field.

The breakup of relationships is exactly what most of Barry's poetry is about. This would imply that Barry's trajectory was not willful but predestined, a path he was forced to travel even though he experienced it either as improvisation or disaster. This was a long way from the preplanned battles of Marxist epic. In the 1960s, the Chattertons won the day. Working-class art arrived on the scene in a big way but was neither austere nor collective, had discharged any Marxist residues it might once have harboured. Barry's inability to write books Two and Three of *Black Torch* is not just the redirection of precious resources away from an unprofitable project: more is at stake than that. He could not stably combine a collective and realist approach with his own inclinations.

Crisis and turning-point

There is a whole discussion in Issue Eighteen of *Past and Present* of the general crisis of the seventeenth century, referring to all of Western Europe, and we hear a lot about crisis. This is part of a cherished fantasy: the state reaches a crisis, where small amounts of force can overturn the vehicle, and this is the opportunity for the organised working class to seize power. The more frequent crises in history are, the more rational it is to plot revolutionary politics rather than engage in democratic change. *Past and Present* shows us a kind of park of crashed vehicles, wrecked states; this one has a shell hole in the side, that one has been partly eaten by termites. You can see the whole anatomy of crashed polities. Actually, Marxists are only interested in car wrecks. It's a kind of Ballardian gallery. A specialist collection. In Issue Eighteen, Lawrence Stone writes: 'Psychologically isolated, economically harmful, financially burdensome, numerically small, the central Establishment lacked the resources, numbers and nerve to stand up to the attack when it came. Compared with the court and administrative structures of the Continent, those of England were mean and pitiful things. Hence their collapse in 1640'. Should '1640' read '1974'?

The missing history of the North

Neville Williams' essay on the Tudor Court describes it as travelling between five royal palaces, all of which were in the south-east.[14] Frank Musgrove gives a survey of royal estates and palaces, showing that very few of them were in the North, so the Court almost never went there. Historians who were on hand to record the words and deeds of Parliament and the court would physically never leave the South. High culture, too, was tied to the Court; Elizabethan and Jacobean drama was based in London, but while it did venture out on tour, and for royal visits to the homes of magnates, it left the North untouched.[15] We can say that the Renaissance, which was based in France and North Italy, left most of the British Isles untouched: it was a luxury culture, affordable by the monarchs and by a few noble families, all of whom lived in the South, which was richer and closer to the centre of power.

Historians noticing this at any point (say in 1952, say in 1970) would have realised that most textbooks were really histories of the political elite in the south-east. If they wanted to compensate for this historical deficit, they would have their work cut out to locate good sources. However, major events and processes could have happened in the North (as in Wales, etc., too) and completely escaped the notice of the modern world. *Black Torch* is a voice starting from this silence.

The trial of T. Dan Smith was slated for Book Two. Smith, the son of a communist miner, was on trial three times in 1974-75, and was a brilliant socialist politician who in the 60s seemed to be emerging as leader of the North-East, through interlocking posts. He said he was going to make Newcastle the Brasilia of the North. The agenda was planning for expansion, developing modern industries by directing public money at infrastructure projects. Subsidy and profit were flowing gaily in all directions, or perhaps a little too much in the same direction. Many schemes were facilitated by John Poulson, an architect and head of a firm called Open Systems Building. Ways through bureaucracy were lit, nets were worked, slums were cleared, cogs were oiled, bottlenecks were popped, bungs were trousered, the police popped up, Dan drew a six. Maybe a hundred people were arrested. You may well think that the reading public knew nothing of this story until the bankruptcy officials got at Poulson's accounts. You may also surmise that what came out in the courts and media was not quite the real story, and that Barry was going to tell it. There is one stanza, actually written, about the redevelopment of Newcastle, in *Black Torch*:

city well-gutted   georgian crescents ripped
back alleys gouged   holes in centre cells
spaghetti roadway experimental roundabouts
metro stations into the city crust   breathes
freshness, advancement, progression, okay [16]

John Martin (1789-1854), also set for the proposed Book Two, was a fervent Baptist who painted apocalyptic scenes. These would present the visual imaginary of the radical Methodists, the 'ranters', who crop up in *Black Torch* encouraging the miners. These paintings led to engravings in popular religious works and have a direct link to Cecil B. de Mille's Biblical films, imitating the engravings. Martin also published a number of pamphlets on civic improvements, waterways, shipbuilding, etc, and these included ideas about coalmining.

Any reference to the kings of Northumbria (and its components, Deira and Bernicia) reminds us of the right of the North to have its own government and history, and Ida, first king of Bernicia (including the Tyne valley), from AD 547 to 559, appears several times in our poem. We know that Barry identified him with the flamebearer, *y fflamddwyn*, an Anglian who appears in sixth-century Welsh poetry as attacking King Urien, as in these lines from 'Gweith Argoet Llwyfein' ('The Battle of Argoed Llwyfain', believed to have taken place on the banks of the River Lyne in Cumbria):

Atorelwis flamdwyn vawr trebystawt.
A dodynt yg gwystlon a ynt parawt.
Ys attebwys. Owein dwyrein ffossawt.
nyt dodynt nyt ydynt nyt yn parawt. [17]

(With a great swaggering din, Fflamddwyn shouted,
'Are these the hostages come? Are they ready?'
To him then Owain, scourge of the eastlands,
'They've not come, no! They're not, nor shall they be ready!') [18]

Barry is probably linking this flame with burning coal.

There is a question to answer about how 'Blackbird' fits in with the overall concept of *Black Torch*. To start with, the original design was one of writing about the people of Northumberland. This poem about William Gordon Calvert, Barry's grandfather, is properly part of the project, but seems isolated because the other, connecting works were never written. I think we can add to this, and say that the concept of a formal, exalted elegy to a working-class man is part of a Marxist approach to culture, is a violation of literary gentility, and very well complements a heroic poem about Northumbrian miners.

A burnt-out conflict?

Recalling the initial proposal, that MacSweeney's work is outside genre conventions, we can answer now that *Black Torch* does conform to a genre, that it fits in perfectly with English Marxist historiography of the time, and that it is very carefully designed. The great thing about Marxism was that it swung you out of social reality like a door swinging out into thin air. I always experienced it as a fight which I lost. The Marxist skinned you; stole all your protective ideas; your image of the world was dissolved, left your possession; the outside world vanished, and you were faced with the task of reconstructing it from luminous fragments. This experience may sound familiar to anyone who has tried to read modern poetry. This drags on stage the notion that the wild and difficult element of modern poetry correlates with political radicalism, and that the resistance to it has been social conservatism – whether conscious or not. After a certain point, you could move off to live in the new world you had imagined. The spectral linguistic universe of modernity – half so empty it wasn't there, half so vivid it was hardly bearable – was a revolution at half-turn, halfway between negation and actuality. Barry's poetry comes out of another space. Do we find Barry's style has the sound of a space where the social order has dissolved; as a message coming in from outside, clashing with our accepted norms at every step? Information from outside must be fragmentary, but subject to wonderful transformations.

Having brought this notion on stage, I have to admit that I don't know whether to believe it or not. The brain functions most intensively when its relation with its environment is violently destabilised. It's quite possible that the modernisation process does that to you anyway! It's also credible that writers deliberately induce this as a literary effect.

If we accept that most of the goals the radicals were fighting for were desirable, it follows that we should admire both their revolt against invested values and the quality of their independent thought. It would be perverse, also, to imagine that writers could articulate the issues, denounce the inequalities, and have no influence on the movement of opinion which led to a more egalitarian society. Some gratitude would be in order, I think. I detect some surreptitious rewriting to make out that the radical thinkers, including poets, wanted silly and incondite and incredible things; some commentators would smugly denounce them, while pretending that society has not changed for the better, or that there was no political process.

In the long run of time, poetry has been linked with the celebration of status – the proof that virtue is the companion of wealth and land. In recent times, poetry has tried to prove the opposite. MacSweeney's artistic status oscillated violently during his life. His career went "underground" along with many others; this was part of a larger pattern, a 'social drama' in poetry, where hundreds of poets made their individual suits for status, and the adversarial principle led to counter-suits, slander or simply erasure. An inflationary and wonderful competition in style was part of these suits. A related notion is the one that British poetry was much more exciting in the late 60s and 70s because of the social revolution that hit shore, or at least hung around offshore making storm noises, at that time, and that poetry now is too privatised (and professional?) to achieve greatness. I don't know whether to believe this. The waging of class war was exhausting and capable of blocking anything else from happening (or at least succeeding) in public affairs – it may well be that a similar conflict was taking place within poetry, and that life is more pleasant in an era where character assassination is no longer an act of civic virtue. We should use the leisure to re-evaluate the occulted poetry of the era.

WILLIAM WALTON ROWE

Barry MacSweeney: Pain, Anger, Politics

Spirit attains its truth only by finding itself in absolute dismemberment.

– Hegel, *Phenomenology of Spirit*

To revitalise the language is the high ambition of *Brother Wolf*,
MacSweeney's first important book, which found in Thomas
Chatterton (1752-1770) a figure of the poet unsupported by
society and cynically used by the literary establishment, his work
unscrupulously raided.[1] We readers are held responsible for this
vampirism that turns the poet's life into a 'rosy myth': 'Bee-like
we cluster / and suck' (p.23). What the comforting myth cannot
swallow is the poet's vitality (p.24):

> A young poet's life burns
> Presses
>   (july wind on Hartfell)

Yet just as the poem rises to that highest point the poet's body
breaks and is scattered (pp.24-25):

> taking our hearts (and poetry) higher
> as if to be cleaned
> & not one fish with an answer.   You can't expect advice
> from someone you eat then criticise for having bones
> because he wants to keep his body in shape & not spread it around
> all over the estuary
> (and poetry)

The word 'cleaned' begins to undermine the Romantic sublime
with the possibility of more mundane meanings: cleaning a dead
fish, or cheating someone out of their money (taking them to the
cleaners). After that, the real physical body appears: it is vulnerable
to damage; it needs bones to keep its shape and to maintain its

ability to stand up vertically. The body remembers what the discourse conceals. Who owns the discourse? This is precisely the point at which the poem breaks too: the high-intensity short lines fall into the longer prose sentences of hard fact. The Romantic ideal of transcending the current state of things fails in the face of a ruling class that makes use of the poet; the vertical urge falls into the real body, the material support of poetry trashed by the rulers, which is, as the poem says, what 'still happens'.

The fish stand for the material substrate of life, actual survival, and they undermine the myth of Shelley's heart, the Shelley of 'Mont Blanc' whose heart 'later turned out to be / Liver / & the fish had a whale of a time munching english poetry / It still happens' (p.24). The poem acknowledges this damage and rejects the cowardly stratagem of nostalgia, disenchanted irony and witty metaphor as ways of saving lyrical song from a hostile reality. MacSweeney's pursuit of how to write is far more radical. The image of the poet torn apart sets its seal on his work, but it isn't a myth: 'The mullet used his body for a staircase // They float enviously around the meniscus in the dewy light' (p.23). An uncanny stillness accompanies the scattered image of the poet already dead, offering a glimpse of MacSweeney's self-presentation in *The Book of Demons*.

For Shelley, Mont Blanc embodies the Romantic sublime: 'Far, far above, piercing the infinite sky'. One alternative to this vertical sense of the ideal is Coleridge's conception that reading resembles the movement of a serpent, whose articulations spread along the entire body without there being a centre, whether heart or phallus:

> The reader should be carried forward...by the pleasurable activity of mind excited by the attractions of the journey itself. Like the motion of a serpent...at every step he pauses and half recedes, and from the retrogressive movement collects the force which again carries him onward.[2]

The serpent represents the temporal movement of desire in the act of reading. Yet the shape MacSweeney chooses for the *Odes*, where each line is centred on the page, preserves the upward movement towards a utopian transcendence of society as it is. Damage does not go away, though: it takes on a different manifestation. With their axial organisation around a vertical spine, the poems restore the unity of shape that had begun to disintegrate in *Brother Wolf*, where the poet's body was scattered. Coleridge's idea of the serpent allows multiple connections and disconnections to occur between – but not inside – words. Conversely, to read the *Odes* is to experience the splitting and collision of meanings inside individual words. This is what determines the time of reading, and this time-duration produces displacements of meaning which place the body of the poem at risk. We sense that it could collapse. In other words, the *Odes* keep the upward thrust of the Shelleyan idea but add to it the internal fracture of language.

One of the key characteristics of the *Odes* is compression, the sense that vast tracts have been condensed into few words. Thus 'Wing Ode' begins (p.36):

> The feet are white boats. Hands are
> unlocked keys of colour & shape. Love
>   me.   Feel me beside you
>   and within.

Wide expanses of space and thought are traversed in few words. There's a similarity with Pierre Reverdy's idea of the image: 'it cannot spring from any comparison but from the bringing together of two more or less remote realities. The more distant and legitimate the relation between the two realities brought together, the stronger the image will be'.[3] Here, by way of illustration, are the opening lines of Reverdy's 'Inn':

> An eye closes
>
>   Deep inside and flat against the wall
>   the thought which doesn't go out
>
>   Ideas step by step go their way
> Death could happen
>
> What I hold in my arms could slip away[4]

As with MacSweeney, the gaps or distances draw us into their ambit, and to traverse this space is the strangeness and pleasure of the poetry. But in Reverdy's poem, each line stands alone in a homogeneous space. The effect is dream-like because all the displacements (the possible associative pathways between the separate elements of the image) are in a single instant affirmed and suppressed: there hasn't been time for them to happen. This is dream time: we have crossed a distance but time doesn't seem to have passed. That is its attraction: a waking dream.

The *Odes* do not suppress time in this way. If in Reverdy the intensity produced by compression relates to distance covered, in the *Odes* intensity is felt inside the body ('Feel me beside you / and within') and is bound up with the time of the body. Part of the making of that physical time is the work of the senses as they produce the world ('Hands are / unlocked keys of colour & shape'), an action which takes time. The lines do not, as in Reverdy, stand alone: the breaks between one line and another are cuts but also joinings. The sense of time passing through words is acute in 'New Ode' (p.37):

> Moon goes like
>   a woman
>   through time
>
>   Un-
>   broken

Disarticulated/articulated, the poem's breaks are soldered by desire and myth as we travel through them; the object of love is their broken/unbroken body, as time passes through the word 'un- / broken' when we move through the line-break.

Michael McClure's centred poems are perhaps the closest parallel to the *Odes* in contemporary poetry. Here is part of 'The Column', whose theme and shape spells out vertical energy:

> the flame reflected from all things
> THE BRIGHT COALS OF ALL RAISING SCENT
>
> HEART AND COILED, THE TRACERY GLEAM
> of pink meat
> unfurrowed from blackness.[5]

Here there are no breaks, no division, as the substance of being ('pink meat') is embraced. Burning, it is not consumed. The lines are non-temporal, they are exclamations made by and directed to some kind of pure undivided substance, 'BLOOD AND MUSCLE'.[6] The temporal progression of desire through the material of words is absent; pain is also absent, replaced by a fusing of need with satisfaction, a condition which is beyond desire, as is the region where Blake's sunflower 'wishes to go'. The condition is ecstatic but turns its back on society. Flesh, in McClure, is subtracted from the social.

In the *Odes*, the body which is the subject of desire is riven by excess, dis-joined by the intensity of its states. 'Snake Paint Sky' begins with a reference to J.H. Prynne's *White Stones*, locating itself beyond the boundaries of Prynne's discourse, 'forever in excess' to it (p.45):

> beaming Anaconda of parthian monumentalism your
> votes gloss acidly these white stone derivations
> I'm forever in excess to

While 'acidly' most likely refers to LSD (the poem goes on to speak of 'equally mad / sources'), something else nevertheless breaks in:

> Tenderly those
> crackling head-waters
>   fray
>   to porky
>   mitts
>   in blood

Instead of a drug, chemical or otherwise, that temporarily cancels the work of the senses, the reality that breaks in here is tender and familiar, marked by working-class speech. The final lines unify the body, by means of myth plus sex:

> the sky & I widen, aching
>
>   for the vulva
>   clam.

The body is brought back into relationship with the other, and at that point unified.

However, the *Odes* lack any consistent myth that might hold self and world in reconciled unity. 'Chatterton Ode' returns to the figure of the poet as vitalising maker, but his relationship to his materials is a long way from the terrain of pastoral (p.37):

>   He holds
> what blood there is in
> side an acorne-coppe.
>
>   Spiky yellow buds
>   between
> his making fingers.
>
>   Bread.
>   Cyanide.

Rather than the natural product of spring, 'buds' are what the poet forms with his hands, hands necessary for bringing bread to the mouth, or for taking cyanide to the mouth. Any hope of reconciling the body with nature is riven apart.

The form of many of the *Odes* consists of columns of words kept in shape by desire, whose aim is 'the vulva / clam'. But sometimes their segments are also fused by messages of pain travelling up the spine. 'Real Ode' compresses marriage, separation and divorce, all in a single space: there is no explanation, just the time of pain that leads nowhere except to itself. Section two includes 'Two / of us / in segments', and ends: 'It's in the / human blood / / Now cry' (p.64). Section three begins with 'The struggle / is love', and ends:

> You walked
> up, good
> bye.
>
> Wear your
> seatbelt and
> fix
> that rearlight
>
> soon.

The phrases are like agonisingly painful incisions. There is no relief in telling the story. What holds the words together is an open wound.

In MacSweeney's 1980s poems, pain ceases to be the condition of an isolated self. Instead, it's where community, an 'us', is grasped, albeit at the very moment when it's most at risk of destruction. Anger is what forces this change. These poems are marked by the large scale dislocation caused by Thatcherism. This was the first onslaught of neoliberalism against the structures of post-war social democracy, which had until then tolerated those forms of working class militancy that could be contained by the welfare state. A central aim of Thatcherism was to smash the working class movement, with its base in trade unionism. Its greatest success was the defeat of the miners' strike of 1984 and its long term effect, the defeat of the left. MacSweeney's first response to the intensification of class conflict was *Black Torch*, a poem of sixty eight pages published as a book in 1978, which documents the history of miners' struggles against the pit owners. Its principal modes are factual narrative alongside passages of testimony in North-East dialect. The problems of this method are registered in the final section, 'Black Torch Sunrise', the only part MacSweeney chose to include in his selected poems, *Wolf Tongue*. The problem is that the poet and his language are located outside the life and struggles of the miners: do the new forms of politics of Paris 1968 signify a new political community? The poem leaves the question unresolved.

New content requires new forms. *Black Torch* still uses the old forms. But in the series of political poems he wrote in the 1980s, MacSweeney makes a radical break with the past. Poetry ceases to be shaped by an arc of desire stretched over time ('Bring me my arrows of desire!'). The very function of desire is brought to crisis, and this fissure in the fabric of poetry exposes an antagonistic division in reality itself. 'Jury Vet' (1979-1981) expropriates the instruments of state secrecy fetishism and with them produces a new kind of book. Instead of the production of reality by the media, taking the form of hyper-real events such as a catwalk show, 'Jury Vet' is an anti-production, designed to make the event of Thatcherism impossible, no less. It does this formally by tracing the reduction of the event that could change history, to a fashion show. Let this brief comment suffice: an entire chapter of the present book is dedicated to 'Jury Vet'.

'Wild Knitting' is dated 1983, the year of the Falklands (Malvinas) war, from which one of the British warships returned draped with the banner: 'Now the enemy within'. Instead of individual solitude, the 'I' of the poem has to confront the loss of community. After the utopian social ferment of the 1960s and 1970s, the poem runs into the destruction of hope for a socialist future. With the large-scale scrapping of industrial production, the core historical strength of the working class movement was destroyed, and the dole queue became, for large numbers of people, the seal of their social uselessness. And then there were new types of employment in service industries, signalled in the poem by the worker who gets off the dole by taking a job with Securicor, jobs marked by the kick of becoming a representative of the underlying violence of the system: 'dark / glasses staring / from redundant Albion Mills (Idle)' (p.132). Dubious types of pleasure, such as porn and SM videos, came to occupy the empty time.

At stake here is how proletarian work, once a source of pride and a connection with how society produces itself, has been de-graded. We have moved from the utopian image of self-creation in the *Odes* ('I break my chrysalis / & Rise! // Walk as a golden man' [p.36]) to a state of abjection. Arthur Rimbaud had traced a similar trajectory in his response to the massacre of the Paris Commune: the equivalent, for his time, to the defeat of 1968 in ours. Rimbaud begins by celebrating the abolition of the division of labour, a crucial emancipatory action on the part of the Commune, but then confronts its defeat with a nihilistic gesture, a kind of negative transcendence that abolishes work as such: 'I loathe all trades. All of them, foremen and workmen, are base peasants. A writer's hand is no better than a ploughman's. What a century of hands! I will never possess my hand'.[7] The voided transcendence is the form taken by his anger, verging on despair, at the massacre of the Communards. If the Commune had taken work as the creation of freedom to its highest historical point, that is what Rimbaud is forced to renounce. In response, he defiantly degrades himself. Though his anger does not directly speak from an 'us', Rimbaud's stance remains connected to the masses by refusing to forget what has happened. MacSweeney's 'Wild Knitting' is similar in its refusal to forget, and perhaps anticipates the triumph of Thatcher's politics of social amnesia, well documented by Iain Sinclair. To read Rimbaud or MacSweeney in terms of the myth of the *poète maudit* is to misunderstand their anger.

More than simply registering the conditions that were to permit the defeat of the left, 'Wild Knitting' seeks first to calibrate the subjective marks of submission and then turn them round towards rebellion (p.132):

> all
> the broken dollpeople say: Meat meat, give me
> meat, boss: Boss me
> Up
> or I go Bostick nostril
> & totally Sickrude, need to be
> ordered, regular fishcakes & spam

MacSweeney uses a punk aesthetic (Bostick is a brand of glue) to mirror and express as disgust the process of social submission. As 'boss' becomes 'Bostick', the syllable turns through 180 degrees from the idea of business management to one of disgusting submission.

The rhymes jerk like automata, the syllables have broken loose from syntax. They are driven by something that is repetitive and mechanical, like 'skanking' and pogo (later, moshing), which can be thought of as counter-cultural resistance insofar as they rebelliously mimic the rhythms of social obedience required by the rulers. But it is more accurate to think of them as a form of expression given to the underlying social antagonism of class struggle, which the society itself pretends does not exist. In this sense these rhythms are more like the act of subjecting yourself defiantly to a type of controlled or conscious hysteria, where part of the effect is that it embodies and displays the violence that official representations deny. Margaret Thatcher declared that society didn't exist precisely at the moment when the attack on the organised working class was at its height. But of course there exists the danger that in becoming a subject of hysteria a person might lose the ability to act: though they seek to preserve their anger by displacing it, the very displacement that gives an image to anger and helps it to stay alive, isolates it from its real sources. But direct, realist representation doesn't resolve the problem either, in an epoch when reality is its own ideology. Poetry that is radical has to smash open the regime of appearances.

'The bluebeat skanking jobcentre' (p.132) uses West Indian rhythms to turn round the police signs (blue, beat), emblems of the police society, towards an alternative perception. But the poem overall moves between an anger that breaks apart social space, and anger turned to self-wounding: 'I wreck the cot & cuddle corner in my head, burn the children, / AGAIN' (p.134), 'Hoover / my head for once, clamp it' (p.137). The pain falls into identification with damage and defeat, and the sharp rhythms which break the coherence of the social descend into abject imitation of it (p.133):

all these moody
Italian perfume ads, ponce clusters, tongueclamps,
rant money, bent fivers, all the Christmas crackers &
cubist cripples, spastix in the dollshop,
looking for an Airfix head

'Ponce clusters, tongueclamps' condenses with precision the capture of language by the enemy, and spits it back. But then there's also a strain of machismo (Italians as poncy men) as if, to keep its flame alive, the anger needed to find identification with unthinking resentment. And then the zone of pity ('cripples, spastix') is mobilised and brings with it a state of being unable to move. 'Cubist cripples' declares the defeat of avant-gardism, the cubist experiment that sought to dismantle bourgeois space has been horribly reduced. The poem uses cubist rapid montage and invokes surrealist madness but then states that these have, through market-isation and cynical enjoyment, become blocks to the expression of any alternative: 'totally / cost effective madness, writhing blisses, wordblocks / jamming the entrance' (p.135). The fact that the current state of things is a choice, and that it remains possible to choose an alternative, disappears.[8]

The poem searches the wreckage for something else (p.135):

Albion, you're just a bruise, steamy day wreckage.
     Wound, far penetration, sickness on my gentle sleeve
                     […] all
    the people lurch past my frosted windows,
         creatures
             & clones. I seek yr bones
             & desyre

     whatever touches you
      can lend me
      Now.

The image of the poet seeing 'all / the people' through 'frosted windows' suggests a self cut off and isolated, the opposite of John Lennon's exhortation to 'Imagine all the people'. Does Lennon's 1971 song stand up to MacSweeney's onslaught? MacSweeney takes the measure of what had changed by the 1980s. His poem wants to find in the wound of the nation a means of exit from defeated hope, but the only Real it finds outside that defeat is the fading image of Northumberland, entangled with an unresolved relationship with the poet's wife:

You the wronged woman. You the complexity [. . .]
   You beneath the curlew-whooping sky, sinking
      in my northern arms. Dimming forest of touches
        blest with Real.

Here the figure of the wife, divided and complex, anticipates the simpler figure of Pearl, the girl of MacSweeney's book of that name: 'Wild Knitting was named after me, I know you did, Bar' (p.204) says Pearl, punning on purl knitting. Yet it could be argued that *Pearl*, probably MacSweeney's most admired book, replaces complexity of feeling (and the sense that the Real is found in division) with a more straightforward attachment to a childhood love and a northern landscape. Loss or gain? Certainly, an atmosphere of morning, of first discovery of world and language in childhood, adheres to this book. But perhaps the renewal of love and vision relies too much on turning the fractured reality and fractured language of the poems of the 1980s into a simple evil ('language poisoned to a wreckage', p.196) against which *Pearl* can appear in pristine light.

There exists in some quarters a belief that Barry MacSweeney's political poetry of the 1980s is inferior to the rest of his work. This view sees him as an essentially pastoral poet who, after the aberration of the 80s, returned to form with *Pearl* and *The Book of Demons*. But this image of MacSweeney doesn't fit the evidence. 'Jury Vet' and 'Wild Knitting' not only represent some of MacSweeney's finest writing, they grapple with a crisis that goes to the heart of the survival of poetry itself at a time when its means of expression, language, is under attack. The historical ground of the crisis is the rise of Thatcherism and the subsequent thirty-plus years of neoliberalism in Britain. MacSweeney confronts the attempt to expropriate the commons, our common intellectual inheritance, of which language is the chief part, head on. The terrain that these poems open forms the foundation of *Pearl* and *The Book of Demons*.

JOHN WILKINSON

The Iron Lady and The Pearl: Male Panic in Barry MacSweeney's 'Jury Vet'

Thirty years after they appeared, how peculiarly deranged seem some of the more enduring artistic reactions to Mrs Thatcher. Such an observation takes Thatcher at her own estimate and her contemporaries' in stamping her name on the economic and social changes of the period she dominated in Britain. This essay is concerned with one mode of artistic derangement, a male panic here associated with deregulation. Such panic reaction was not widespread, although it was linked to features of a wider, popular response. Some responses which seemed both more symptomatic and more hopeful, including forms of social resistance exemplified by the women of Greenham Common, came to appear poignant in their anachronism before the camps of the Occupy movement forty years later signalled a resumed contrarian life. In the interim progressives, a baleful term, developed good intentions for "the earth" but made little call on solidarity, a value rooted in a political tradition of much-reduced potency. Under Tony Blair solidarity dissolved into strategic and tactical "partnerships" in politics, in sexual relations and in business. The embodiment of hope in a collectivity, once invested in communities of resistance, seemed to regress into fundamentalist religion. An ironised consumerism infested visual arts and popular music, while British poetry slumped onto the turf of transcendent values stretched across landscape, a milquetoast romanticism.

Retrospection has encouraged some fuller, more humane, and more complex narrative reckonings of the Thatcher period. Most notable are Jonathan Coe's novels, depicting Thatcher's liberation of the ambitious youth of the provinces through the shattering of provincialism (or a disdain for tradition, if you wish), as well as showing the malign effects of commodifying everything including human and animal bodies. The most positive aspect of the post-Thatcher period, an urban life transformed by a far more various population, has been expressed through novels and popular music which negotiate difference with élan, and celebrate small-scale solidarity (local and familial) in hybridity. One effect of this new artistic strain is to make the Thatcher period seem even more grim than it did when mitigated by the exhilarations of resistance; that was the grey time of pain without the payoff, and when population change was framed routinely as a problem always liable to generate crisis.

At this distance and after Thatcherism has been installed as the scarcely-challenged basis of British political and economic life, the poetry of Barry MacSweeney, the novels of Martin Amis and the songs of Elvis Costello, oscillating frantically between enraged resistance and hedonistic capitulation during the mid to late 1970s, look at once impressively premonitory and weirdly pathological. The pathology is obvious enough when it comes to the gynophobia which spills over from the vitriol directed at Mrs Thatcher herself – less so in Costello than in the two writers, for Costello was more self-scrutinising than Amis with his satirical puppetry or MacSweeney with his vaunted aggression and victimhood. Still, Costello's vocal delivery at this period could sound like sexual assault, and the gynophobia of these artists can be understood as expressing male panic, a meltdown occasioned by a historical process of deregulation affecting both financial and sexual domains. This led in these artists to a crisis of subjectivity later marked more publicly in the swaggering vacuity of Brit Art.

From their crisis stemmed a conviction in these different artists that a coherent individual subjectivity must depend upon a stabilising collectivity. The later work of Amis and Costello has entailed a regime of self-rectification, of variable success, assertively promulgating collective and historically-rooted values, whether in Christian civilisation, or in country music and art song. Nonetheless their work of the mid to late 1970s continues to exercise a grip on the collective imagination exceeding their subsequent work, evident in both critical and popular estimates of the two artists. Barry MacSweeney's later work came to be organised around addiction, a perverse return to the maternal origins of solidarity with its dynamics of unassuageable need, aggression and demands for forgiveness; and formally incorporated a return to the blues in *Hellhound Memos* (1993). In confessing the blues he achieved finally a limited celebrity in a culture more interested in a poet's personal suffering than in poetry. The impact of MacSweeney's poetry of the late 1970s and early 1980s has unfortunately been more restricted, which may also be attributable to the lack of a poetic movement comparable to the *Granta* brat-pack which helped to launch Martin Amis, or to Punk Rock which proved fortuitous for Elvis Costello.

The new century has seen an energetic rebirth of narrative history, supplying digests of the twentieth century in the West to a public more or less consciously exercised by a sense of secularism's decline. In Britain an obsession with the century's criminal dictators has been succeeded by a nostalgic fascination with the welfare state, public health, the solidarity of postwar austerity, and civil liberties – among other achievements attributable to secular social democracy. Such popular history registers the erosion of such achievements, contrived to prefigure a staged rescue by the "private sector" of G4S and its like. Through such a lens, Mrs Thatcher continues to polarise views, whether as the bringer of liberty or the personification of selfish greed. For Britain and indeed for Europe, Mrs Thatcher bestrides the second half of the twentieth century, since the economic policies named for her have not only transformed Britain, but have become normative, triumphing across central and Eastern Europe and exported (or enforced) around the globe. In a sense however, her decisions may have been of minor influence in a process she regarded as inevitable but in some respects deprecated, as Andrew Marr points out:

> She wanted to re-moralise society, creating a nation whose Victorian values were expressed through secure marriages, self-reliance and savings, restraint, good neighbourliness and hard work…. Yet Thatcherism heralded an age of unparalleled consumption, credit, show-off wealth, quick bucks and sexual libertinism.[1]

On the other hand, her reckless decisiveness seized responsibility for historical processes, and so far as Britain was concerned, acted as their accelerator, even if not invariably in the direction she might have chosen.

Popular depiction of Thatcher made much of such contradictions. For instance in the political puppet show *Spitting Image* Thatcher was guyed simultaneously as a sadistic disciplinarian presiding over a cabinet of cowed but sexually-aroused males, and as scarcely in control of her own features and speech. To personify in one individual contradictory historical forces which played out over several decades, placed considerable strain on coherent characterisation, but also tended to mislead through attributing structural change to the commands of the Iron Lady – her métier being more a fearless acceptance of changing circumstances than strategic control. This was true even of fundamental economic policy; for instance, the abolition of exchange controls in 1979 was highly risky, responding to an already substantial trade in Eurobonds by a leap into the deregulated unknown. Still, the image of Thatcher as both strict nanny and almost unhinged, powerfully represented a nation in which abjection followed discontent, willing to take the medicine even if the prescriber seemed swivel-eyed. The financial market liberalisation associated with Thatcher and known as the Big Bang, may have had its heyday from the development of the Eurobond market in the mid-1960s until the collapse of Barings Bank in the mid-1990s, but the facade of tradition and "Victorian values" maintained by financial institutions of august name, disguised increasingly buccaneering and deregulated behaviour. So indeed did the brand-name of the Conservative Party.

The Barings collapse showed just how skin-deep the appearance of prudence and unimpeachable reliability had become, reminiscent of the Victorian vicarage of Martin Amis's *Dead Babies* (1975) where frantic drug, alcohol and sexual debauch is pursued by British semi-aristocratic wide boys with their American guests as technical advisors. The unstable language of this novel skitters between upper-class English languor, a gloating nastiness derived from Evelyn Waugh, passages of frenetic scramble half-inched from William Burroughs, and American dude-talk. Licentiousness continues improbably to be associated with hippiedom or privilege, half the characters sounding like offspring of Hunter S. Thompson and the other half like Wodehouse waifs; but both sets have turned sour and selfish, the old retainers in the grounds reduced to butts of abuse. The novel's stock characters are made obnoxious by forces yet to find apt embodiment in chancers, traders and the likes of Jeffrey Archer. This entire farrago is encased in a formal parody of the country-house novel; Jeeves seems to be hovering just off-stage, but sure to have his feet kicked from under him if he ankles forward.

A decade later, in Amis's *Money* (1984), the main character shuttles between Manhattan and London, but this is London/Manhattan as global moneymart, and the language is a panic-driven composite of British and American street-talk, all pornography and money and scrapping, a high-octane macho mix obsessed with gaining and sustaining erections and advantages. Amis's novel is evidently the prime antecedent of the psychopathic object-world of Bret Easton Ellis's *American Psycho* (1991), where deregulation has run its course and money is wholly free – free to tyrannise through a Sadean staging of humiliation and murder, and no longer at risk from uprisings, nationalisations or market failures. Amis's language is still about getting and devouring, with the appetite of the individual entrepreneur propelling history and the novel's narrative; the entrepreneur's world is filled with incalculables, from his own sexual responses to the threats black New Yorkers pose to the whims of movie stars. This does not faze John Self, the novel's main man. His every move challenges defeat and snarls at ruin and sympathy alike. Violence erupts unpredictably. A commitment to first strike is essential to survival. Risk and reward collapse into one so as continuously to feed appetite. But by the 1990s every developing market and every pension fund lay and continues to lie open to the masters of the universe like a crack-dependent prostitute, ready for their investment; and transparent too is the language of Ellis's novel.

This was the end of history, as an influential thesis had it, and Amis saw it coming. John Self, the protagonist of *Money*, encounters the healthy original of *American Psycho*'s Patrick Bateman in Fielding Goodney, a man made of money and money's enraptured partisan:

> And he was away, his voice full of passionate connoisseurship, with many parallels and precedents, Italian banking, liquidity preference, composition fallacy, hyperinflation, business confidence syndrome, booms and panics, US corporations, the sobriety of financial architecture, the Bust of '29, the suicides on La Salle and Wall Street...[2]

Self knows that the age of street-fighting and pickups, of the individual operator surviving on sleeping tablets and adrenaline is nearing its close. And he was right; after the Falklands War and during the second Thatcher government (1983-87) with Nigel Lawson as Chancellor, Thatcher's economic policies became more radical, again in response to changes already reshaping financial markets. Banks were consolidating internationally, and the traditional firewalls between speculators and bankers had begun to crumble. A neoliberal vision of governments as little more than market facilitators gripped both American and British legislators, with privatisation believed inevitable for efficiency in core utilities and in the technology sector (with some reason in the latter case and very little in the former). The more chaotic and uncertain the world, the more inevitability would be invoked. The resistance of British Trades Unions to market dictates was broken by the failure of the Miners' Strike, and remains broken; with the outlawing of secondary picketing, the rhetoric of solidarity has been succeeded by a rhetoric of representing members' interests, indistinguishable from shareholder meetings.

The period 1983-85 was marked by the three shocks of the Falklands War, with its resurgence of a jingoism thought long-dead by the left; the defeat of the Miners; and financial deregulation. This last designated the liberation of capitalism from the "shackles", the "controls" and the redistributive corrections of state policy – profit was to be "no longer a dirty word", as the cant of the time announced. "Control" was now to be applied mainly to money supply and public sector pay. Small wonder that the left, once its fury was spent in defence of the miners, suffered a severe disorientation. Accustomed to confronting a rather timorous social democracy, it found itself helpless in the face of more radical and eventually more disciplined forces (the market needed some help from police batons, as it turned out). In the arts, well-tried radical idioms had looked weary and pointless for some time. Consider for instance Barry MacSweeney's 'Black Torch Sunrise' (1977-78), from his Socialist Realist book *Black Torch*, written in a reportage idiom which should have been more convincing since, as it acknowledges (p.77)

> I deal in secret financial reports
>> confidential manpower utilisation documents
>>> council Deep-Throats with secrets to tell

This refers to the trial for corruption in 1974 of the powerful regional politician T. Dan Smith, Leader of Newcastle upon Tyne

City Council and a partner in crime of the architect John Poulson, together shamelessly exploiting contracts for redeveloping slum housing. Had MacSweeney drilled into this world poetically as well as journalistically, for he was a news reporter by profession, he might have developed a vital style of investigative poetry, but this poem (as its epigraph warns) adopts Allen Ginsberg's middle-style of poetic witness without the verve, conviction and egotism which drove Ginsberg's tireless reportage. MacSweeney's denunc-iation of university-tenured and Sunday newspaper-approved poets sounds peevish, and his recourse to a disingenuous insistence on the 'real' lacks power: 'Breasts are for kissing / & for bairns' milk' and 'Real miners / ripped that coal'. Such decently banal sentiment was soon to be swept aside, historically and poetically, or in any event to require more conviction and more art to assert. Real miners were to become vanishingly rare in the United Kingdom, while real breasts would be used for competitive advantage in bairns' admission to top nurseries. Working class infants faced forward in their buggies, confronting the bleak street with the inferior goods of formula and bottle.

MacSweeney approached the language of 'Liz Hard' and 'Jury Vet' by steps traceable from the *Odes* (with the related long poem 'Far Cliff Babylon') through 'Colonel B', as though succumbing by stages to total freak-out. By the end of 'Wild Knitting' he was seeking a more stable mode of resistance to Thatcher, to shut her out by demarcating an enclave of love in the heartless world she presided over. Chronology is not straightforward, and the *Selected Poems*, *Wolf Tongue*, prints 'Liz Hard' before 'Jury Vet' while ascribing a later date to the former text without explanation. How-ever, the period of maximum panic in MacSweeney's poetry can be dated as 1979-1983. His subsequent writing until his death in 2000 might plausibly be framed as a series of defences against the panic which overwhelmed him, involving a capitulation to neediness eventually fixed as addiction. What occasions panic historically is not always visible in 'Liz Hard' and 'Jury Vet', two works appearing at first sight to be driven by unbridled sexual appetite rather than defence mechanisms; rather, the two 'state of the nation bulletins' 'Colonel B' and 'Wild Knitting' which immediately precede and follow them, are symptomatically more fluent and historically specific.

Fluency in MacSweeney's writing is categorically female. Its origins lie in amniotic fluid and breast milk; more problematic is menstrual flow, and 'Colonel B' is unusual for addressing 'the bloody mistress of his pleasant ayre. / Blood whose with [sic] my waters fat flow thick' (p.89). It is such a 'dark stream', such 'red snow' that herald the entrance of 'THE MAGGIE BOEAST [*sic*]' (p.93). Fluency would become the prime attribute of Pearl, the girl with a cleft palate MacSweeney taught to read during his own adolescence, but an attribute surrounding her rather than embodied in her, for she is virginally intact; flow also signifies a shared belonging to the Northumbrian landscape – a watery place of becks and falls, watercress, borage and watermint. The wateriness of the later Pearl poems might therefore be read as a turning away from mature female sexuality. 'Colonel B''s rapid glissando from menstrual blood to the Maggie Beast by way of a scrambled regurgitation of MacSweeney's earlier poetry mixed with 'rubber policies' and 'pulsing / velour cravats' (p.91), foreshadows the male panic immediately ahead.

The *Pearl* poems, always threatened by sentimentality, are redeemed in some measure through their watery landscape. It helps that, as with Basil Bunting's poem *Briggflatts* (1966) and Ken Loach's film *Kes* (1969), MacSweeney's work reflects a Northern working-class topography where industrial town and the wildness of heath and moor closely interpenetrate; indeed, the location of industrial towns was determined by geology and water-force. Experientially, country and city are still less separate (as in a distinct urban or rural "upbringing") than in the South of the country; hence water does not set up an uncomplicated opposition between spirituality and materialism, or between authenticity and sophistication. Rather, in MacSweeney's poetry after 'Colonel B' the salient opposition plays out between two economies, each psychic and political. One of these is the water world, interlacing, associating, shape-shifting, touching but not grasping or possessing. The other is a world of shards – part-objects rent from larger entities, hard and shiny, biting and aggressive. The water world is not characterised by amniotic oceanic feelings, although some of its affective force may derive from them, especially through sound; rather, it is a world in which fully-formed entities communicate through watery and linguistic flow. Because its entities are complete (and in the case of *Pearl*, inviolably so), they can associate sexually, familially, communally, intellectually; and because they are set in a landscape, their associations are not arbitrary and fleeting but continuous even if ever-mutative.

By contrast the world of shards is governed by panic-driven substitutions, permitting no object to achieve integrity or to detain desire. The *Pearl* poems, succeeding these poems invaded by panic, can be quite explicit about the difference: for instance, the *Pearl* poem 'No Such Thing' opposes lipstick and colour charts, whose colours are no attributes but are presented as applicable, made hard in sticks and glossy on sample cards, to colour inherent in 'feldspar heaved from the streambed; / cusloppe, burnt peat in summer / and wild trampled marigolds' (p.199). While attributes inhere in their proper subjects and the *Pearl* poems accept no substitute or overlay, it should be noticed that for Pearl herself no change or development can be contemplated, she must remain immature and speechless as the figure of pure need; already the structure of addiction is installed in this insatiable lack.

A most vivid distinction between the worlds of water and of shards can be drawn through what happens to human feet. In the *Pearl* poems, feet are either bare or protected in hiking boots of defensively-asserted practicality. The prevalence of feet becomes intrusive once noticed. A few instances include 'without / Dunlop lace-up boots, one bare foot / should do it' (p.196), 'my heather-crashing feet, splash happy / kneefalls' (p.197), 'Pearl walked barefoot down the rain-soaked flags' (p.204), 'waterproof / lace-up Dunlop boots' (p.210) and 'toes wetted in the berylmintbed' (p.210), 'toes in the watermint' (p.212), and 'Wet-footed / I tread home alone' (p.216) – to say nothing of the plethora of splashings implying bare feet, or the compulsive play of bare hands in water.

Compare this with the substitution of shoes for feet in 'Jury Vet' (p.103):

We'll gleam like thongs
    & dovegrey
      straps
   on high-heeled
    Bordeaux
     shoes!

and 'cream sandal shoes' (p.106) and '((INK LEATHER COURT

SHOES ON VERY HIGH HEELS))' (p.106) and 'Brown heels on JOSE. / Blue heels on JANE' (p.107) and 'Cup Court Shoes' (p.108). These examples are pulled from the earliest 'Jury Vet' poems and are characteristic in their proximity to shiny accessories such as buckles, while throughout the sequence skin vulcanises into leather.

MacSweeney's fetishism has been discussed by Marianne Morris in her pioneering account of these poems, 'The Abused Become The Abusers', with particular emphasis on substitution and inter-changeability:

> His reaction against social systems and political grievances, particularly in the Deneuve-inspired 'Jury Vet', gives special attention to the com-modity of sexuality in particular over other commodities, fetishising the female body and its commercial paraphernalia of shoes and make-up, but the obsessive structures of fetishes are interchangeable.[3]

Morris refers here to 'the female body' attended by 'paraphernalia' because she is following the Freudian account of fetishism as substitute for the mother's penis, which the infant boy once believed in and does not wish to give up. The fetish is highly specific and to that extent stable as a substitution; it must lead back to the maternal phallus. However, the female body in MacSweeney's poems is broken up into a heap of paraphernalia or junk, with the clit or the quim or the tit of a bint as disjunct as a thong or a heel; female fluency is frozen then smashed into a scree of weapon-like monosyllables, axe-heads, little phalloi – not so much a fetish as a fusillade of fetishes. Such multiplication and panic substitution signify the revenge of the castrated woman on the man who would subjugate her, turning the appurtenances of her seductiveness into weapons. The fetish that would defend against female phallicism, returns as a flight of arrows. The mechanism is comparable to the Kleinian paranoid-schizoid position, but what is important for this discussion is that the part-objects, these fetishes, are *hard*.

Morris discusses Barry MacSweeney's 'Liz Hard' in detail, adducing helpful information about its origins in his encounter with an immigration official, but neglects to gloss the eponymous heroine's name. The name is more than a little significant – for hardness points to the maternal phallicism which is a defining attribute of male heterosexual fetishism. The very name 'Liz Hard' is phallic, for 'Hard' is a surname that is no name, since a name must be arbitrary – rather, 'hard' is a hardened attribute. Liz Hard belongs to the shock troops of the Iron Lady, with her phallicism linked directly to homosexual rape: 'Luggage will be collected and searched. Strip down. // BEND OVER NOW' (p.97). The men of the British left felt shafted by Liz Hard and her ilk in an uncanny remobilisation of the German extreme right's castration myths of harridan Red Army and Sparticist women in the early 1920s, as recounted by Klaus Theweleit:

> The fact that the rifle-woman, the woman with the castrating penis, is expressly named suggests that the name itself has a sexual and an agg-ressive quality; that it functions, then, as a penis-attribute. Just like waitresses, barmaids, cleaning women, prostitutes, dancers, and circus performers, the rifle-women are given only first names. Women who have only first names are somehow on offer to the public [...]
> All of that makes them, on the one hand, objects at the disposal of men; whereas on the other, they are footloose, powerful, dangerous – especially in time of disintegrating political "order".[4]

Several ironies are at play here, notably the disintegration of the public order on which the right always believes it has a monopoly. For the *Freikorps* activists whom Theweleit examines, the asserted goal of re-imposing public order was approached practically through rape, murder, pillage and beatings, reacting (as he demonstrates) to a perceived feminising of German manhood effected through the wiles of women, Jews, leftist intellectuals etc. Such viciousness suggests strongly the dynamic of "homosexual panic" proposed by defence lawyers to excuse murderously homophobic actions. While the exculpatory proposition that an individual might become help-lessly bestial when propositioned homosexually is patently oppor-tunistic, the male panic induced by "hard" women is related strongly to unconscious fear of homosexual desire and submission. The 'rifle-women', the hard women who so terrified the *Freikorps*, were felt to be in some sense invited by the feminised body politic. The reactionary defence, self-proclaimed to be harder than hard but actually in a state of paranoid derangement, is consistent with the modernist association of hardness with a manly resistance to flux (as in Wyndham Lewis's deranged attacks on Bergsonian flux in the name of hard-edged reason and precision).[5]

Feminised decadence is transmuted into a feminised commodity world in MacSweeney's poems of panic, and the cosmetic goes ballistic. Both the society which *asks for it*, that is, which invites sexual aggression, and the avenger who deals it out in response, alike turn phallic-female, one the marauding female band, the other the forces of order mesmerised by consumer goods. Threatening to become one and the same, a truly intolerable prospect, they disintegrate into a whirl of commodified body-parts not to be distinguished from clothing and makeup. When a feminised patriarchal order looked at the Iron Lady, its ministers and grandees saw a clit which was a cock, and recognised also the allure of hard and polished parts – hard as the "hard bodies" of pornography. In their collectivity they turned out to be dead soft, or as Mrs Thatcher would taunt, no more than a group of *wets* squalling for their mother's milk; but individually they loved the 'little triggers' hymned by Elvis Costello in *This Year's Model* (1978). For every kind of wet, the Iron Lady stood for the end of wholeness; the end of "organic communities" and of solidarity. She was the entity which broke the wholes, which buggered everything taken for granted and everything socially-owned, despising and dismissing all motivations other than the financial (when it came down to brass tacks and hard bargaining).

What is wholeness? Wholeness had been maternal, the state looking after you 'from cradle to grave', the matron, the woman given to reproduction. That was then, and this is the world regulated by money supply, requiring both a disciplined economy and an economy fuelled by credit and desire. Money and wants always agitate to break free. Discipline versus unbridled, deregulated consumerism: that was a conflict endemic to the Thatcher period and to the image of Mrs Thatcher. Where was wholeness? Wholeness is always phallic, the object of desire is whole in itself, whole in being wanted, whole embodied in another through the satisfactions and reintegration another makes possible. But the condition of consumerism and of pornography is that nothing fixes or detains desire; fashion and pornography were waiting for internet search engines, sorting and naming scarcely differentiable attributes to fill the eye, displaced immediately by another cut, another tint, all definite, all defined. The female world in 'Jury Vet' is a phallic plurality. Consider the following (p.108):

> woman car. female lorry of all delights. Her mudguard thighs.
> bonnet indicators blinking. fine

98

suede trousers grey gabardine (cloudy) thick-lined
AVEC BILBERRY SATIN: green wool
stockings (If you are
deceptive fragility – YOU ARE!), brass eardrops, red
suede cuffed
winter boots. Add silver, lampblack leather
court shoes

((mix duck egg & moss)) – *Rain trench*
Rainjacket. warm
lined lichen green
zipped &
buckled.   GOLD dropping
chunky, clip-ons. Easy satchel. YOUR NATURAL

SLENDER WAIST.

This section, defined by a line across the page, from '1980 Colour Grid: Cinnebar Jury Stitch: Up / 1983 Colour Grid: Cinnebar Perfume Worn by Sue', forms a section of a sub-section of a poem within the series 'Jury Vet'; sectional break-up is the principle of 'Jury Vet''s larger-scale construction, as much as of local prosody. By contrast both 'Colonel B' and 'Wild Knitting' are fluent poems submitting to breakup, set as continuous but with their continuity interrupted by sectional numbers. Here the disposition of verse draws attention to the materiality of its words, through the use of capital letters, italics, double bracketing, leading lower case, and the almost scopophiliac isolation of some phrases, especially 'zipped & / buckled'. This kind of materiality has become a tic of post-modern poetry, but the verse's lasciviousness is MacSweeney's own, emerging from the oral retrieval of these linguistic shards, their mouthing, spitting, pouting and shouting. The objectification and fragmentation of the female body makes every fragment suck-able, a nipple or a penis, and each fragment stands for a potential entity, one which might fill the mouth: 'lampblack leather' obviously enough, but even '*Rainjacket*'. They insist on this sucking, smacking, licking orality, tasting everything in the make-up bag and jewellery box. In Kleinian terms, this could be likened to the infant's desire to evacuate the mother's body of good things ('part objects'), and terror of the retribution they will exact.

The dismemberment of Catherine Deneuve in these poems probably responds to the ice-cool and sexually voracious screen persona developed in *Repulsion*, *Belle de Jour*, and *Tristana*; preternatural self-possession in the midst of the disorder she provokes was also the key to Mrs Thatcher's compelling presence. Thatcher's representation as a dominatrix was commonplace, but the complexity of her relationship to order unfolds through further contradictions in the "discipline" she represented. While proclaiming the virtues of fiscal discipline, both at the macro-level of money supply and in the family budget, at the same time Thatcher was arraigned for the collapse of discipline and "traditional British values" associated with financial deregulation and the liberalisation of professions, a charge not confined to moderate conservatives but often heard from Trade Union leaders. Barry MacSweeney's pornographic assaults on Catherine Deneuve are proxy assaults on the Iron Lady, who sexually disconcerted even Alan Clark, the shameless Lothario of her cabinet, as his diaries attest. The 'woman car' and 'female lorry' of the 'Colour Grid' passage, are stripped down to 'mudguard thighs' and 'bonnet indicators' in the breakers' yard of MacSweeney's verse, then translated into dress accessories via the British term 'bonnet' for a car hood. This is power dressing, a weapon of the Iron Lady (here called 'steely') described by a schoolfriend who observed the Margaret Roberts/Mrs Thatcher phallic rigour, from schoolbench to standing erect at the House of Commons dispatch box:

> Her appearance continued to be immaculate. She always knew that important messages were sent out by dress. I doubt if she ever had any leisure wear, but the uniform of power, the suit, was usually chosen. A Labour MP who was also careful about her dress, Barbara Castle remarked that on Mrs Thatcher's first day in the Commons she found Margaret pressing a blouse in some nook of the building, with a selection of suits on hangers. Many politicians were appreciative of her looks and she used her femininity to good effect – Alan Clark pays his leader many compliments in his Diaries, calling her 'The Lady' – it was a political weapon. The combination of womanly good looks and stylishness, together with a steely personality made her a powerful force.[6]

The transformation of emblem of femininity into phallic weapon was shown vividly in the swiftly-adopted tabloid coinage of the verb 'to handbag' for Mrs Thatcher's confounding of male politicians, through her implacable negativity. (The use of refusal as a weapon is of course another dreaded female phallicism.) In the MacSweeney passage, a handbag appears in a phrase at once lip-smackingly delicious – 'chunky, clip-ons' preparing the mouth for 'easy satchel'; sexually promiscuous – a woman is 'easy' if sexually available, and 'easy satchel' then suggests female genitalia; and also aggressively expectorant ('satchel'). Words here are not only sticks and stones, but are gendered projectiles. From the handbagging victim they demand his abasement so as to avoid the sight of what they substitute for incessantly. The victim is then made speechless when the fetish bites. Words do not run communicatively as in the water-world, but are the snapped-off attributes of what they signify, flying, spearing, stamping: 'Feet religious. / SHOES, I AM ABASED' (p.106). This flipflop, this oscillation makes 'Jury Vet' an unsettling experience. The disgraceful comedy of Martin Amis, the sadistic froideur of Bret Easton Ellis, Elvis Costello's yelps of pain, at once adopt and direct positions by their address; all exact from the presumed-male recipient a gratifying exercise in self-control where arousal and its disavowal are simultaneously at work. In 'Jury Vet' the deictics point to a subject shattered into multiplicity, simultaneously seductive and punitive, seduced and punished, and integrated only through an insistence that an addressee exists; the addressee forms through the subject's exercise of will. But the subject's explosive finger-pointing, his effort to reassert his own phallic dominance, collapses because the addressee is in truth an empty term – what the subject seeks to penetrate has no inside, and its inner life has been evacuated in a whirl of concretised, superficial attributes. Shoes substitute for feet. Belts substitute for waists. Clit, quim and 'silk manholes' (p.128) lead nowhere in a hiding to nothing.

Thus the attempt to impose discipline is doomed, and deregulation offers its ceaseless pornographic substitutions. Pornography and consumerism are treated as the same phenomenon, holding out the promise of desire fulfilled only to withdraw it and flaunt another. The real thing is no more whole and no more capable of holding the desirer together through his desire, than 'YOUR NATURAL // SLENDER WAIST'. Next year's natural is this year's artifice. Returning to the passage, it is striking how attributes of MacSweeney's water-world and of Northumbrian landscape are transformed into the part-objects of consumer and sexual desire; they become especially sharp darts, *poignant* indeed. 'BILBERRY', 'duck egg', 'moss' and 'lichen' alike draw on the vocabulary of the water world, but reified in the 'colour chart' of the poem's title, while 'cloudy', 'rain' and 'winter' become fashion items (p.108). Such a conversion is effected most brutally near the beginning of the Jury Vet series in 'Jury Vet Failure/Woman's Piece' (p.105), where the water-world receives its earliest full treatment, a trailer despoiling what later will be celebrated in the main feature of the *Pearl* poems. This treatment inverts the systematic ironies of Martin Amis, dependent on outraging a nostalgia for the forms and discourses his novels distort; the water-world may precede the world of shards autobiographically, while it succeeds it poetically, and will offer redemption rather than tending to bemoan (or besmirch) a lost paradise. And redemption will surely be required, since 'Jury Vet Failure/Woman's Piece' performs violence beyond anything Catherine Deneuve endures. This is significant: repeatedly the adolescent and specifically virgin Pearl is raped by 'sex weaponry / in her go root', whereupon the abject rapist seeks to restore her, once again by addressing her as whole, in the language of the medieval poem which names Pearl – 'YOU THE SHIMMERTEXING PEARL / WITHOUTEN SPOT OR BODY BRUISE'.

The summons to Pearl is a verbal offence as brutal as the verbal record of rape, from the first words of this poem 'BE LOGGED) LOVED', where 'logged' brilliantly and appallingly compresses definition, cataloguing and rape, and then proceeding to attempt Pearl's restoration and to expunge her bruises. Then is followed immediately by 'take the mould, pube lichen pistol come, quim / trigger fanny juice [...]', and then the further restorative command 'Be / SIGNIFICANT'. Significance requires Pearl's 'tent fold nighties' to be 'PULLED DOWN' – to display her displaced cleft. Restoration is enforced so she can 'ask for' a further assault. Why is this dynamic necessary for MacSweeney's substitutive fetishism? Because the only tolerable whole body is the spotless body, without organs (particularly the intolerable phallus) and without menstrual flow. Washing Pearl in the beck here promotes her restoration to pre-sexuality, when she invites again being raped and restored: she is not broken, she cannot be allowed to disintegrate into vengeful bits. Only insistent and violent invocation can restore Pearl, but is ineffectual on a sexualised and powerful woman; the attempt in the 'Colour Grid' passage to summon Deneuve in 'deceptive fragility' with the childish pronouncement 'YOU ARE!', is a parenthesised failure amidst a biting swarm of accessories.

For Pearl to be washed clean and restored is insufficient in itself; for her to be closed up as a body without organs is still insufficient to protect MacSweeney from the maternal phallus. Pearl's cleft palate blazons her castration, a castration which silences her physically. Pearl is simply a gap. Her insubstantiality will later compromise the *Pearl* poems, which would have benefited from a reflexive understanding of the roots of MacSweeney's utterance in Pearl's silence rather than the awkward and ill-deserved identification claimed in 'Pearl's Final Say-So' (p.216).

While invocation is deployed often in the internal drama of 'Jury Vet', the definitive agent of invocation in lyric poetry must be prosody. 'Invocation' here designates an imaginative restoration through verbal fiat of destroyed or damaged and persecutory part-objects, in an integrated body. In the instance of Pearl, invocation fails because it instals a symbol – a "virgin" whose intact status cannot contain conflict but can only be smashed or restored. Even restored she is a cleft, a gap. The invocation of Catherine Deneuve fails because every shard aspires to a hard completeness in itself, and because what is being avoided is exactly the complete and sexually active female body. Although these dramas of invocation are bound to fail, the invocative dynamic of the poems is satisfying, because through the act of reading, of following the poems, the reader becomes a Prospero-like summoner.

Taking "invocation" in this sense of managing impossible conflict through incorporating a mélange instead of reaching a rational resolution, 'Jury Vet' provides an exemplary instance. This is how lyric poetry should work. Returning once more to the 'Colour Grid' passage, no reading aloud could fail to discover the licking sounds necessary to negotiate its trail of 'l's and short 'i's; the very act of reading becomes restorative and developmental, like an animal licking her young. From 'lorry' to 'slender', sheer relish draws out from this poetry an unlikely tenderness. Here is the answer to the question which has shadowed the discussion so far and is unavoidable: what does such poetry offer beyond the patho-logically symptomatic? How can poetry of this sexual violence and terror, a madly animated fetishism which harries the fetishist, interest anyone other than a connoisseur of perversion or a cultural historian? The satisfactions it offers are categorically poetic, operative not through metaphor but through sound and lexicon. Persecutory part-objects combine in vocal performance to sound out a complete and generous world which the reader both creates and consorts with. Such an activity always risks poeticism, and MacSweeney faces down that risk boldly with avidly poetic language calling attention to itself, forever breaking up and being restored by its reader. In 'Jury Vet' the activity is extreme, both in destruction/persecution, and in restoration.

This is why the poetry of 'Jury Vet' and 'Liz Hard' yields rewards as least as generous as the more widely-admired poetry which followed. The *Pearl* poems (1995-99) and *The Book of Demons* (1997) muster around neediness and addiction, and pleas for forgiveness. Their rewards are inevitably of a more passive and compassionate order – identification, pity, self-pity and gratitude. Such poems are more appealing in both senses, and their invocations of the Pearl-cipher as well as the cries of betrayal and damage, resolve into a manner. Pearl no longer needs summoning because she is invariably present as an empty wholeness. The whole of need along with her wretched addict, associate in the fluent linguistic landscape. For Pearl's increasingly relied-upon presence anticipates the self-glorifying and self-abasing poems of alcoholism. With MacSweeney's later writing the reader is engaged or repelled by the poet's personal drama, and largely excused from the poetic work – being "swept along" or withdrawing. Fluency too can be coercive, after all; *The Book of Demons* becomes torrential, and if you are not with Barry MacSweeney you (in common with most of the world) are against him. The later work also seems anachronistic. Self-exposure and self-abasement not only recall the 1960s poetics of confessionalism, but the strip joints which preceded mass consumer pornography: what would be revealed would be *everything*. Everything comes before *things*; the organic world of MacSweeney's youth was to be shattered into the inorganic shards of consumerism. Though never forget that the everything the addict tells may well be a self-serving lie.

Because a particular dispensation has been superseded does not mean its life is at an end, and because its recollection is self-serving does not discredit its values. That said, it is disappointing that the post-Thatcher variety of the British population and its cultures which 'Far Cliff Babylon' (1978) and the later *Odes* adumbrated, sank from MacSweeney's view as he became preoccupied with his Irish and Northern origins, the myth of Pearl, apostrophising his poetic forebears, and addiction to alcohol. The discursive hybridity of his poems of the late 1970s to the early 1980s is already yielding in 'Wild Knitting' (1983) to an expressive voice demanding identification, or even empathy. The *Odes* had seemed about to instigate a summons at the social level, calling into being a collectedness out of improbable variety. Such a possibility was certainly beyond the imagination of Martin Amis, who as late as *London Fields* (1989) introduced a set of *Sun* newspaper racial stereotypes into a London staged as a tabloid delirium. But satire is a weapon dangerous to the soul of its wielder, and Amis now fulminates against alien threats to civilisation and advocates ethnic screening. It is argued here that the power of Barry MacSweeney's best poems lies in their creative and integrative summons to their reader, surprised into poetic activity which has not been advertised according to post-authorial dogma; MacSweeney's prosody shapes the reader into a shaper. Could such an activity be imagined, through its incorporation of the indigestibly hard and hostile and the fetishistically alluring, as itself a premonition of participation in emerging collectivities of variety? In these poems the reader is inveigled prosodically into care.

The violence of 'Liz Hard' and 'Jury Vet' curdled as personal resentment, but for a brief period the Iron Lady helped to re-inscribe MacSweeney's personal demons in an idiom tellingly connected with social damage, just as Elvis Costello connected to his largest audience. What could be harder than the 'greed and avarice' meeting a child's lips in Costello's post-Falklands song 'Tramp the Dirt Down' (1986), a hardness transmogrifying womanly spillage?

> I saw a newspaper picture from the political campaign
> A woman was kissing a child, who was obviously in pain
> She spills with compassion, as that young child's
> face in her hands she grips
> Can you imagine all that greed and avarice
> coming down on that child's lips

Sexually predatory and hard: in the next verse Costello finds a way to pull together discipline, sexuality and commerce in the figure of the brothel madam:

> When England was the whore of the world
> Margeret [sic] was her madam
> And the future looked as bright and as clear as
> the black tarmacadam [7]

The world of light too is transmogrified, into hard road metal. Costello's delivery of this song is among the most ferocious in his recorded catalogue, but also strikingly plaintive and abandoned. After verses in this idiom (an earlier version of the song, 'Betrayal', keeps to a stricter ballad versification, and the title is telling), the song unhinges into a berating of the public's 'pitiful discontent' as they 'line up for punishment'. Part of that punishment is to be reduced to a 'head like a tin can', the Iron Lady's attribute transposed into a sorry redundancy. What Costello wants is revenge, to 'tramp the dirt down' on Margaret Thatcher's grave. But this parting shot betrayed an unacceptable wish to emulate the despised Thatcher. Costello does not shy away from the rifle-woman, from the maternal phallus; he looks her in the eye and declares he would be as hard. As his contemporary song 'Tokyo Storm Warning' pithily puts it, 'He always had a dream of that revolver in her purse'. The revolver points both ways; he can take it like a man and give it with the best.

But without Thatcher, Elvis Costello lost definition, turning his hand to any genre and disastrously in love with his own voice. Martin Amis now pronounces on any and everything, his panic legitimated by the Rushdie fatwa and congealed into a set of positions. The most potent work of these three male artists turns out to have been driven by the different ways in which their panic at the deregulated world of Thatcherism overtook their work:

> Even now public opinion spurns [Thatcher], and shows a confused and wistful sympathy for all those 'wet' notions – consensus, compassion, collectivism – that she so stoutly opposed. Who is this 'dry' mother, whom people can't love, and what kind of children is she rearing? [8]

After their panicky first responses, Costello briefly went hard-boiled, recognised the condition and sought to recover his humanity; Amis would surpass Thatcherism and end up in the same corner as George W. Bush; and Barry MacSweeney would be overwhelmed by loss, yearning for the water-world he blamed himself for polluting, and by his terrible 'neediness visceral, cultural, and political'. [9]

PAUL BATCHELOR

False Fathers, Desperate Readers, and the Prince of Sparty Lea[1]

When Barry Patrick McSweeney published his first poems in *Stand*[2] at the age of seventeen, he did so under his birth name. Every subsequent publication appeared under the variant spelling 'MacSweeney'. Mc/Mac is from the Gaelic for 'son of', and this qualification (not quite a repudiation) of the name of the father was re-enacted compulsively by MacSweeney in his poetry, which is full of part-identifications, appropriated identities, surrogate selves and self-applied names and titles. In MacSweeney's first book, *The Boy from the Green Cabaret Tells of His Mother* (hereafter, *Cabaret*), which appeared when he was nineteen years old, this uncertainty over the identity of the father manifested itself as a marked openness to influence, and an eagerness to establish literary allegiances. MacSweeney himself subsequently dismissed the book as derivative: 'My early poems are just complete and bad imitations of an echo I'd caught from Carlos Williams; they really are bad little lyrical-erotic stuff'.[3] *Cabaret* also contains imitations of Frank O'Hara, E.E. Cummings, Ed Dorn, Allen Ginsberg, the Liverpool Poets, J.H. Prynne and Basil Bunting. As John Wilkinson has remarked, *Cabaret* 'amounts to an anthology of the poetic fashions of its time'.[4]

Cabaret was published by a large press, Hutchinson, and was a considerable commercial success, selling thousands of copies, largely because of a publicity stunt involving someone from Hutchinson bribing two Oxford dons to nominate MacSweeney for the Oxford Chair of Poetry. This generated a great deal of interest: most newspapers ran features on the story, and MacSweeney was interviewed by magazines such as *Queens*, *Honey* and *Penthouse*.[5] In the event, Roy Fuller got the post with 350 votes, and the favourite,

Enid Starkie, came second. MacSweeney received three votes. He was derided as a figure of fun, and Hutchinson dropped him from their list. This public humiliation permanently soured MacSweeney's opinion of official verse culture, and exacerbated his anxieties over his readership and reception. These anxieties would exert a powerful, lifelong influence over the way MacSweeney read other poets, and the way he tried to write himself into, and out of, various poetic traditions and schools.

Many of MacSweeney's poems were written with particular readers in mind, and these primary readers were often father figures. In this essay, I will focus on MacSweeney's habit of presenting two father figures in his key poems, paying particular attention to the importance of Basil Bunting. The first appearance of the two-fathers motif occurs in 'The Last Bud', which is partly addressed to Jeremy Prynne, an appreciative father who can recognise MacSweeney's talents, but also partly aimed at Bunting, an antagonistic father whose territory MacSweeney would like to usurp. I will then consider *Brother Wolf* (1972), in which MacSweeney is putatively concerned with Thomas Chatterton but in fact continues to wrestle with Bunting and Prynne; and *Ranter* (1984), which constitutes MacSweeney's most thoroughgoing attempt to present himself as Bunting's heir, but is ultimately overwhelmed by the influence of Ken Smith. *Brother Wolf* and *Ranter* are only partially successful poems, but they are significant for the role they play in preparing the ground for later, more achieved work such as *Pearl* (1995). Bunting's influence on *Pearl* has been noted by many critics, so I will not linger on it here, but focus instead on the process by which MacSweeney came to harness that influence.

The claim, or assumption, that Bunting was a formative influence on MacSweeney is one many critics and commentators have made, but few examine the nature of the influence in detail. Keith Tuma's verdict, offered in a review of Clive Bush's study *Out of Dissent*, is typical: 'MacSweeney is very much the pupil of Basil Bunting, his *condensare* alternating between bile and sentiment and having also benefitted from study of Rimbaud and French symbolism'.[6] Tuma does not appear to be very familiar with MacSweeney's work,[7] but even a cursory glance would have told him that here was a poet who rarely if ever condensed his work in the stringent manner Bunting advocated; perhaps this is why Tuma pairs '*condensare*' with the antithetical 'bile' and 'sentiment', before adding Rimbaud and French symbolism for good measure.

In 'Barry MacSweeney and the Bunting Influence: "A key figure in his literary universe"?',[8] Rebecca A. Smith surveys many instances of the widespread assumption that some sort of regional-poetical mantle was handed down, in a more or less untroubled fashion, from the elder poet to the younger. Smith has fun interrogating the flimsy evidence for such an assumption. For example, the fact that Bunting was MacSweeney's boss for a short time when they both worked at the *Evening Chronicle* has been eagerly repeated, and MacSweeney's decidedly prosaic recollections of their relationship ('Basil used to have to tell me off every time I made the tidetables incorrect [...] he used to come up and scold me and say you've added this up all wrong') have been embellished. MacSweeney also stated that Bunting offered him feedback on an early poem, editing it down to only four lines, and this incident has been taken to imply a more regular exchange of poems.[9]

That they happened to share an office at the *Evening Chronicle* is not in itself evidence of a 'key' relationship between the poets, but Smith is too quick to conclude that the opposite must be true. It is hard to imagine that MacSweeney, a poet prone to self-mythologising, would have failed to draw a symbolic meaning from Bunting's supervision. Furthermore, MacSweeney was proud and easily wounded, and his embarrassment at having been scolded by Bunting clearly made an impression, for he recalled it at intervals throughout his life, even in his last poems.[10] And, at the risk of taking this too far, it is entirely possible that the notoriously fastidious Bunting, who insisted that a writer should know 'bloody well'[11] what he was writing about, might have drawn conclusions about the likely worth of MacSweeney's poetry from his tidetable complacency. Smith dismisses the incident as one of 'several coincidental biographical similarities' between the poets, along with their difficult relationships with their respective fathers, and their bruising experiences of metropolitan literary society: such commonalities, she claims, are of significance only to the poets' critics, and she does not entertain the possibility that, coincidental or not, they led MacSweeney to view Bunting as a role-model.

When Smith concludes that 'Bunting's presence in MacSweeney's verse and its critical appreciation is both consistent and restricted to several precise themes', she blurs an important distinction between the work and its critical reception. The critics may consistently repeat the same assumptions, but I will argue that Bunting's antagonistic presence in MacSweeney's work manifested itself in a variety of ways: his was an influence that MacSweeney felt compelled to qualify, outflank and reject, before overtly declaring and eventually absorbing it. Furthermore, where Smith sees MacSweeney struggling 'with a legacy provoked by numerous early comparisons', I see MacSweeney instigating and directing those comparisons throughout his career.

'The Last Bud' (1968)

Unlike the other products of MacSweeney's influence-flooded apprenticeship, 'The Last Bud' takes inauthenticity and the threat of being overpowered by one's forebears as its theme, and knowingly invites literary antecedents into its arena. 'The Last Bud' is a sublimation of MacSweeney's feelings about his traumatic literary début, a prophecy of exile from a mainstream audience (an exile that would be partly self-imposed and partly supervised by mentor-figures such as Prynne), and a rehearsal of the end of a relationship. Each of these factors was closely connected to the idea of fatherhood in MacSweeney's mind. MacSweeney's preoccupation with fatherhood, and his tendency to collect father figures, stemmed from the difficult relationship he had with his own father, who displayed a marked favouritism for MacSweeney's younger brother, Paul. The poem 'Daddy Wants To Murder Me', from *The Book of Demons*, also describes regular beatings. In 'The Last Bud', Mac-Sweeney writes (p.16):

> I have only one half of my parenthood.
>   The other isn't dead, but he lingers on
> this side of breath with the tenacity
>   of a rat. That breakdown in relations
> doesn't even bother me now.

Having disowned his birth father, MacSweeney sets about establishing relations with literary fathers. Bunting's significance in this pantheon is not because he represented a literary inheritance, but because he had inadvertently activated MacSweeney's sense of having been *dis*inherited. When he named Tom Pickard as his protégé, and wrote an effusive preface for his first collection ('I find here…a sound that suggests some of the earliest writers in the Greek Anthology'),[12] Bunting made the dynamics of the Newcastle literary scene's family romance painfully clear: once again, Mac-Sweeney was the less favoured son.

By teasing out the tangle of allusions, we can see that 'The Last Bud' is, among other things, a subtle but outrageous attempt by a young poet to present himself as Bunting's equal. For example, there is an allusion to *Briggflatts* in the reference to Israfel, the archangel who sounds the Resurrection Trump, once to destroy the world, once to begin the Resurrection. At the climax of *Briggflatts* we see Alexander the Great climb a mountain until he sees 'the limbs of Israfel, / trumpet in hand'.[13] Confronted with the archangel, Alexander sees the transience of earthly achievements, and understands that permanence is only to be found in the spiritual world. While Bunting only implies a connection between himself and Alexander, MacSweeney makes his identification explicit: 'And her [sic] who is Israfel takes me to / pity through pain…'.[14] Engaged in a creative misreading of Bunting, MacSweeney reads an entirely negative futility into the image of Israfel. Bloom calls this process Daemonisation, 'a movement towards a personalised Counter-Sublime, in reaction to the precursor's Sublime'.[15] Mac-Sweeney eccentrically depicts Israfel as female and describes her as overseeing an apocalyptic abortion (p.18):

> That dark
> continent of man has lived very well
> since this ball of dust aborted itself
> from the sun's legs.

Apart from invoking Alexander and Israfel, MacSweeney does not allude to Bunting directly, but instead to Bunting's own primary antecedents: Dante, Wordsworth and Whitman.[16] W. Jackson Bate calls this technique 'the "leapfrog" use of the past for authority or psychological comfort: the leap over the parental – the principal immediate predecessors – to what Northrop Frye calls the "modal grandfather"'.[17] 'The Last Bud' includes a translation of lines 13-15 from Canto 34 of Dante's *Inferno*, in which we see figures locked in the ice of Cocytus, the frozen river at the lowest point in Hell (p.17):

111

Some lie at length and others stand
      in it. This one upon his head, and
that one upright. Another like a bow
      bent face to feet...

Here, MacSweeney has managed to smuggle in a glancing allusion to Wordsworth's lines from Book VII of *The Prelude*, in which the poet describes his residence in London:

A travelling cripple, by the trunk cut short,
And stumping with his arms. In sailor's garb
Another lies at length, beside a range
Of written characters...[18]

As a northern poet living in London, MacSweeney identifies himself with Wordsworth, simultaneously casting the metropolis as a modern-day Inferno. MacSweeney's allusion to Wordsworth's unremarkable phrase 'another lies at length' is subtly, lovingly done: without announcing itself to a general reader, it is a barb designed for Bunting.

Dante takes centre stage once more in the closing lines of the first section of 'The Last Bud' (p.17):

...In the whirlpool, sleep takes over, the
      boat bobs like a ball: this is the
lullaby of death. Friends and skeletons
      hold hands in the marriage of evil.
There is no evidence.
      Sterility asks how, and I answer from
the Gates of Dis...

These lines refer to various events in Cantos 7-9 of *Inferno*, in which Dante compares the dance-like movement of the Avaricious to Charybdis's whirlpool, crosses the Styx in Phlegyas' boat, sees bodies beneath the muddy water, and finally reaches the Gates of Dis. These Cantos were crucial to Bunting: in *The Well of Lycopolis*, he blends Dante's image of souls under the mud of the Styx with imagery of trench warfare in the First World War, translating lines 117-126 of Canto 7. Bunting later confirmed that 'the whole passage of the *Inferno* is indelibly in my mind'.[19]

The final section of 'The Last Bud' alludes to Whitman's 'Out of the Cradle Endlessly Rocking', the poem Bunting invariably cited when he praised Whitman.[20] In these lines, Whitman speaks in the persona of a shore bird to his mate:

Shine! shine! shine!
Pour down your warmth, great sun!
While we bask, we two together.

Two together!
Winds blow south, or winds blow north,
Day come white, or night come black...[21]

Where Whitman's lines express a joyous love, MacSweeney expresses a stern resolution to turn his back on this world (p.19):

> Enjoy the warmth, soak in
>   the lukewarm sea, wave your naked bodies
> about like freedom flags. Ahead of me
>   is brilliant darkness, and the king
> of night. This is a signed resignation;
>   I am finished with your kingdom of light.

To Whitman, the sea symbolises an ecstatic union of the natural world and human society; but to MacSweeney it is merely 'lukewarm'. Here as elsewhere, 'The Last Bud' differs from *Cabaret* not in the density of allusion but in the allusions' function.

'The Last Bud' not only attempts to supersede Bunting, it also appeals directly to Jeremy Prynne as its preferred father figure and primary reader (p.15):[22]

> He is my friend, so
>   how will he take this, this testament,
> established as he is, as I wanted to be,
>   to be sufficient in all ways, in that
> durable fyre I was after too.

The Chattertonesque 'durable fyre' is a reference to Prynne having introduced MacSweeney to Chatterton's work, and an allusion to Prynne's poem 'Love in the Air', which refers to 'the durable fire'.[23] 'The Last Bud' and 'Love in the Air' share a similar tone, and both are wry reflections on disloyalty. MacSweeney's other borrowings from this poem include the pun on sentiment/sediment and the reference to the 'old owl' that flies from the oak after 'little, little mice', which derives from Prynne's lines 'the owl of / my right hand is ready for flight'.

MacSweeney imagines an ideal relationship with Prynne: 'I have a friend who shelters me, and tho' / beyond me in years, he is brother, / father, teacher, child to me...' (p.15). He sees Prynne not only as a father but as a brother (ie. an equal), and even a 'child to me': a fantasy of non–competitive, non–Bloomian poetic self-begetting based on a reciprocally nurturing relation with the literary antecedent. But while the resounding rhetoric of the closing lines of 'The Last Bud' suggest that MacSweeney has chosen his path, his next important poem, *Brother Wolf*, will more strongly advertise Prynne's influence but will remain indebted to Bunting.

Brother Wolf (1972)

Bunting's 'Villon' and MacSweeney's *Brother Wolf* have much in common. Both are ambitious but derivative apprentice works by writers who would take a long time to come into their own, and both establish a poetic persona by means of identification and opposition: where Bunting identifies with a French poet as a means of attacking parochial English literary culture, MacSweeney sees Southern England as a foreign country because of French influence, and he identifies with Chatterton as a way of asserting a dissenting northern identity. Both poems assert a false father (François Villon and Thomas Chatterton) in order to obscure a genuine literary father (Ezra Pound and Bunting/Prynne).

In 1925, while living in Paris, Bunting was detained by French police for assaulting a police officer and carrying a concealed weapon, and was held for a short time in the same building in which Villon had languished five centuries before. Bunting claims to have always kept a copy of Villon's poetry in his pocket at this time, and the coincidence prompted his first successful poem, 'Villon'. Although its immediate inspiration was a brief spell in a French gaol, 'Villon' draws on Bunting's two-year incarceration in England for his conscientious objection to World War One. Unsupported by his family, and frequently held in solitary confinement, Bunting experienced a profound isolation, to which 'Villon' belatedly responds by asserting its author's literary connectedness. Bunting translates and ventriloquises Villon until his identity merges with that of his antecedent; more importantly, and more covertly, he asserts his relationship to Ezra Pound.

1925 was the year Bunting's father died, and also the year he found his literary father: Pound's 'Homage to Sextus Propertius' (a poem Bunting rated as 'the foundation document' for modern poetry)[24] provided the formal model for 'Villon', and Pound also edited 'Villon', reducing it to half its original length, and saw that it was published in *Poetry* (Chicago), where it won the annual Lyric prize of fifty dollars, launching Bunting's literary career. Pound had used troubadour poetry to critique English literary culture, and Bunting's choice of Villon in a similar role was judicious: close enough to Pound, but respectful of the mentor's turf.

In *Brother Wolf*, the role of false father is played by Thomas Chatterton. Like Bunting, MacSweeney selects his antecedent for reasons of personal identification rather than literary influence. Chatterton's curse is that his life (age, class, sociological significance, reception) is more interesting than his poetry, and it is this curse that interests MacSweeney. This much is clear from his lecture on Chatterton, which was delivered at Newcastle University in January 1970, and subsequently published as *Elegy for January*. The lecture focuses on scandalous biographical information, on the poetry Chatterton inspired, and on how Chatterton was received by the poetry establishment of his day, especially his fraught relationship with Horace Walpole. Aggrieved at the negative reception afforded his own first book, MacSweeney obsesses about the way Chatterton's authority and authenticity were determined by his reception, and in *Brother Wolf* he reads and reconstructs Chatterton afresh.

Following Keats's example, MacSweeney claimed Chatterton as a 'northern' poet. In a letter to Hamilton Reynolds, 19 September 1819, Keats wrote '[Chatterton] is the purest writer in the English Language. He has no French idioms or particles like Chaucer – 'tis genuine English idiom in English words'.[25] Keats added, in a letter to George and Georgiana Keats 17 – 27 September 1819: 'The purest English I think – or what ought to be the purest – is Chatterton's. The language had existed long enough to be entirely uncorrupted of Chaucer's Gallicisms and still the old words are used – Chatterton's language is entirely northern – I prefer the native music of it to Milton's cut by feet'.[26] In an interview with Eric Mottram in 1974, MacSweeney describes Chatterton's work as 'very English, back to the source', before paraphrasing Keats's words and producing a bizarre image: '[Chatterton] was the first English poet with a really northern tongue to escape the Gallic feet of Chaucer…'.[27] Evidently, Keats's pronouncements on Chatterton appealed to MacSweeney, who, in memorising the quotes, interpreted 'northern' in his own fashion.

As for the supposedly pure, genuine, uncorrupted quality of Chatterton's language, it would be truer to say that MacSweeney was attracted to its fraudulence, and its ability to embody contradictions. For example, having been denied a classical education, Chatterton complains '…whoever spekethe Englysch ys despysed, / The Englysch hym to please moste fyrst be latynized'.[28] The content of these lines is intriguingly at odds with the strong iambic rhythm (originally carried over from Latinate languages by translators such as Chaucer), and we remember that Chatterton's fraudulent medieval works were exposed because of their close adherence to the neoclassical standards of his day. Far from avoiding French influence, the lines are alexandrines, a form Chatterton frequently used, and one that appears in *Brother Wolf*: 'It is a leaf which falls in autumn like a poem. / Chatterton looked at Mole and did not hear it fall' (p.29).

MacSweeney's interest in Chatterton's Rowley poems stemmed from the way they had triggered a debate over the ways in which authenticity might be sought out and fought for, rather than conferred by tradition and patronage. Ironically, MacSweeney identified with Chatterton's socio-literary significance before he read any of the poetry. Mottram asks him about this: 'So your interest in Chatterton came about as… an interest in this *kind* of person. But what about his work?'.[29] MacSweeney replies 'Well, I hadn't read any. I'd heard about the guy through Coleridge, Shelley, Wordsworth. So I went and bought the books, what I could find, and I remember I borrowed or was given one by Jeremy Prynne, and started reading his work'.[30] Despite MacSweeney's complaints about critics who focus on 'this fucking social shit',[31] this was the source of his interest in Chatterton, and in *Brother Wolf* he wants to draw attention to similarities between Chatterton's cultural moment and his own.

Brother Wolf begins with some impressionistic lines that contain three images traditionally associated with artistic creation – fire, water and bees (p.23):

the fire-crowned terrain
                    as the sea burns
        wind

116

You can't burn your boats when you live inland
Chatterton
     Knowing this
Died
Rosy myth
     bee-like
          we cluster & suck.

The most important of these images, it transpires, is the bee. In Plato's *Ion*, Socrates claims that the poet gathers poetry from 'honey-springs' because he is 'a light thing, and winged and holy, and cannot compose before he gets inspiration and loses control of his senses and his reason has deserted him. No man, so long as he keeps that, can prophesy or compose'.[32] Where Socrates uses the bee to symbolise the muse-possessed poet, MacSweeney sees the reader, rather than the writer, as the locus of creative energy. The source-rose is a 'myth'. In section eighteen, the more sinister implications of 'cluster & suck' become apparent, as the bees are linked to Chatterton's demise: 'Bee-like. The randomness of (his) death' and we are told that there is 'No rose. No honey / suckle on the vine' (p.28). In other words, there is no reason for the bees to be there: they symbolise uniformity and rigid hierarchy rather than creativity. The readers have triumphed over the writer, just as MacSweeney's readers triumphed over him, and just as he now hopes to triumph over Chatterton.

MacSweeney sees prejudicial reception as a greater threat to a poet than death itself; indeed, Chatterton only appears fully integrated, fully *realised* in death, in Henry Wallis's iconic portrait, *The Death of Chatterton*. Section 23 consists of a quotation from an early reaction to Chatterton (p.30):

'The whole of Chatterton's life presents
a fund of useful instruction to young per-
sons of brilliant and lively talents, and
affords a strong dissuasive against that im-
petuosity of expectation, and those delu-
sive hopes of success, founded upon the
consciousness of genius and merit, which
lead them to neglect the ordinary means of
acquiring competence and independence.'

The system of control and reward that this unnamed critic recom-
mends is precisely the one Chatterton tried to subvert, and the

117

conventional language seems to underline the inadequacy of the response, as the grammatical control of the long sentence with its many sub-clauses contrasts markedly with Chatterton's – and Mac-Sweeney's – impetuosity. Since conventional, official language has been the scene of betrayal and loss of authenticity, it is rejected in *Brother Wolf*: words and images are fragmented and repeated in various tenses and as various parts of speech, destabilising the idea of an author dispensing meaning to a reader, and stressing instead the social expectations that determine reception, and the literary traditions that determine our judgement.

The ideal reader might consider the title of *Brother Wolf* to be a poem in itself, proposing a sympathetic identification with Chatterton while acknowledging the problematic nature of such an enterprise: how exactly does one declare solidarity with a lone wolf? But there is a discrepancy between the title, which suggests a unified, clear and direct utterance, and the poem, which is characterised by fragmentation, quotation, obsessive repetition and collage. The reason for this discrepancy may lie in the dedication to Prynne, which indicates a dialogic exchange from which the general reader is excluded. The complexity MacSweeney has imposed on the poem signals his rejection of the large, general readership that *Cabaret* had reached, in favour of a small, hardcore audience of dedicated readers, almost all of whom were fellow poets. First and foremost, MacSweeney is writing for Prynne, who once said 'It has mostly been my own aspiration, for example, to establish relations not personally with the reader, but with the world and its layers of shifted but recognisable usage; and thereby with the reader's own position within this world'.[33] In *Brother Wolf*, MacSweeney tries to graft such priorities onto his own, quite different agenda, for at this stage (barely four years after his short-lived fame) he still has a subject, a point of view and an argument; and he is still evidently concerned to project a self-image that will be received by a particular readership.

Brother Wolf declares its allegiance to Prynne, but the false father motif, borrowed from 'Villon', shows Bunting's influence remains strong. These father figures were incompatible, not least because they fostered such different relationships with their disciples: Bunting had edited MacSweeney's work, just as Pound had edited his, whereas Prynne encouraged excess. MacSweeney's attempt to

purge Bunting's influence continued with his next collection, *Odes*.
If the title recalls Bunting's two books of odes, the poems them-
selves bear no trace of him. Instead, MacSweeney pairs Prynne
with a range of ancillary father figures, from Mike McClure to
Jim Morrison. *Brother Wolf* is a significant poem in MacSweeney's
oeuvre not because of its own merits, but because the allegiance it
declares to a poetry of Prynne-sanctioned excess would culminate,
ten years later, in some of MacSweeney's finest work: 'Jury Vet'
and 'Wild Knitting'. 'Jury Vet' is a delirious mix of political anger,
sexual fantasy, punk rock and consumerism, while the angry, con-
fessional poem 'Wild Knitting' went too far even for Prynne (the
poem quotes the farewell note MacSweeney's second wife left for
him, and, according to S.J. Litherland, this violation of privacy
offended Prynne).[34] These two works represent the first peak of
MacSweeney's poetic career, and Prynne's influence upon them is
clear in the way they attack the grand narratives, poetic tropes
and linguistic sleights of hand with which a poet might appeal for
sympathy or reassure the reader of a stable self-hood and the con-
tinuity of identity over time. What is remarkable is the way they
somehow manage to square this with MacSweeney's confessional
impulse to replicate his inner turmoil and make it the keynote of
the reading experience.[35]

Ranter (1984)

Ranter was written in Bradford between February and September
1984. An important context in which the poem needs to be read is
that of the aftermath of the poetry wars.[36] By 1984 the wars were a
distant memory. In 1982 the editors of *The Penguin Book of Con-
temporary British Poetry* had air-brushed the period out of the
picture: their introduction refers to 'a stretch, occupying much of
the 1960s and 70s, when very little – in England at any rate –
seemed to be happening. [...] Now, after a spell of lethargy, British
poetry is once again undergoing a transition...'.[37] This is not so
much a case of history being written by the victors, as by those
with no interest in the war. Ken Edwards summarises the new
conditions in his introduction to the anthology *The New British
Poetry*:

119

> Where once, in the 1960s and 1970s, British poets creating the new...
> forced the literary establishment to sit up and take notice, now the
> silence is eerie and almost total. No longer does the establishment
> revile modernism in poetry; it simply ignores it.[38]

The avant-garde scene was changing too: without the focal point
provided by the Poetry Society, the scene fragmented – there had
always been tensions and divisions, especially between Cambridge/
Prynne and London/Mottram – and by the mid 80s there was an
emergent generation of innovative poets who did not wish to
define themselves according to the Revival's terms. MacSweeney
was uncertain of his place in this new landscape. He had been in
close contact with both Prynne and Mottram, but had not allied
himself exclusively with either; nor had he been geographically
tied to London or Cambridge since the early 70s. MacSweeney
sent the finished manuscript to Bloodaxe, Faber and even his old
enemy Hutchinson. His failure to secure a larger publisher and a
new readership precipitated a breakdown and a six-year period of
depression, showing MacSweeney's huge emotional investment in
the project. There were more than commercial considerations at
stake: by 1984, after a disastrous, short-lived second marriage,
MacSweeney not only wanted to become another kind of poet, he
wanted to become another kind of man.

Like many of MacSweeney's key poems, *Ranter* is a quest. The
speaker is searching for his lost love, the Bride; but the poem
itself is a quest for a readership. The sequence consists of four
poems, each containing several sections. The first poem, 'Ranter',
is the longest, and introduces the two principle characters: Ranter
and his Bride. The primary location is Northumberland and the
poem has an extraordinary historical scope, from the first century
to the present day. The second poem, 'Snipe Drumming', is much
shorter, and as most of it is spoken by the Bride. The third poem is
the angriest: 'Ranter's Reel' is the closest Ranter comes to actual
rant, though the target is ambiguous, as I will show. The final
part, 'Flamebearer', is a tender duet between Ranter and his Bride.

In *Ranter*, MacSweeney focuses on how he will be read, and how
he reads others (p.150):

loper, glider,
dashing for game,
loading his gun,

cleaning his blade,
trap setter, marriage-breaker,
reader, desperate for attention,
bruised and mighty,
strangler of cries,
particularly his own
driver and driven

The most unusual epithet here is 'reader'; the others suggest an
animal or a hunter. Few would cite reading as a characteristic of
the hunter-gatherer, but MacSweeney clearly did. 'Reader' is
followed by the equally surprising 'desperate for attention'. While
it might be considered self-aggrandising to call yourself a 'trap
setter, marriage breaker', to say that you are 'desperate for attention'
sounds like a candid admission of a smaller failing.
Ranter distinguishes between the time for fighting and the time
for reading (p.162):

Time for books after the scourge

Sit in my cell with a quiver
of pens, gold-leaf for the page.

Drawing maps, borders
wanting more than I had.

For wisdom return to myself
wearing pelt because I am wolf.
Wolfric my brother a hearty man.

Killed with my axe
and now he is in me.

This is a coded reference to MacSweeney's position after the poetry
wars ('the scourge'), when he withdrew and tried to redraw the
map of British poetry to establish his place on it. 'Wolfric my
brother' recalls *Brother Wolf*: he must not forget the example of
Chatterton's reception. The motif of killing someone and absorbing
their identity as a metaphor for reading will return in 'Finnbar's
Lament' ('I dragged him from a monastery / and made his spirit
mine'), another poem spoken by a warlord who has belatedly dis-
covered the joys of 'the slow business of books' (p.182).
    Evidently, MacSweeney saw issues of readership and reception as
being closely related to issues of territory and invasion. In *Brother
Wolf*, MacSweeney had taken up Keats's association of Chaucer

with the invasion of effete French idioms into English in order to distinguish between the authentic northern English tradition of Chatterton and the Frenchified, Southern-England tradition of his persecutors. This motif reappears when Ranter complains that 'pink fleur de lys / invaded the psalter', and claims to hate 'the French words / invading my books'; by contrast, there is 'blood on the words / which are Northern' (p.156). The fact that Chaucer is bedtime reading for Ranter's southern Bride proves her unsuitability as a mate: 'singing for the sleepless // Chaucer in her lap' (p.157).

Bunting had also taken up Keats's complaint about the Frenchified Chaucer, claiming that Chaucer's verse forms and 'conventions of thought' were French, as were the line, texture, architecture and shape of his poems. French characteristics, as defined by Bunting, include 'the form is a very loose fit for the matter', the poetry is 'slower and much wordier' with many 'elaborations and interruptions and moralisings' that deprive a poem of 'tension'. Instead there tends to be a 'rather misty, garrulous prettiness'.[39] These characteristics are the antithesis of the (presumably northern) qualities Bunting prized in his own writing: concision, shape, and an exact fit between form and content.

Ranter's territorial demarcations show the influence of Bunting's *Briggflatts*. Both poets construct a kingdom of Northumbria, and offer an alternative history of England centred on the north. Bunting peppered *Briggflatts* with hints and buried allusions that he would happily gloss in interviews, lectures and in the footnotes to the poem. Here he is engaging in some distinctly Modernist oppositional mapping:

> There are perhaps half-a-dozen books in the world comparable to the *Codex Lindisfarnensis*. They were all produced by Northumbrians, or by people under the immediate influence of Northumbrians. The Book of Durrow, which is in Ireland, is believed to have been made in Northumberland. The Echternach Book, which is, I forget whether it's [in] Germany or Luxembourg, was made there by Northumbrian missionaries. The Book of Kells, which is about a century younger than these, was made in Ireland, at a time when Ireland was chock full of Northumbrian scholars and monks.[40]

> The image of history is that of continually changing racial identity but continually recurring and lasting cultural identities, and the flowering of art and literature and history in ancient Northumbria has been a lasting thing. You can see quite clearly the same kind of considerations

occurring to Swinburne as those that you will find in the pages of the *Codex Lindisfarniensis* [sic], or in *Beowulf*.[41]

Bunting is using the Lindisfarne illuminations to establish the terms of a native Northumbrian art, one that reflects his own practice of combining complex patterning with a clear overall structure. Bunting made many statements of this kind. It is difficult to engage with them closely: the terms have been left deliberately sketchy in order to tempt a disciple to colour them in. Like Hugh MacDiarmid and David Jones, Bunting was an autodidact who argued for a mythic, ahistoric Britain that draws on an unquantifiable Celtic heritage. These poets valued oral culture above canonical tradition, ephemeral pre-linguistic art forms such as song and dance above the stable text, and myth above history. All defined themselves in opposition to parochial, anti-Modernist English literary culture.[42]

With the Lindisfarne Gospels in place, Bunting's next step was to identify some Northumbrian literary antecedents, but this proved difficult. William the Conqueror's savage response to the Northern uprising against Norman rule in 1069 is often referred to as the 'harrowing of the North'.[43] Within a few months, 150,000 people were slaughtered and a huge amount of the land from the Humber to the Tweed was laid to waste. The cultural damage lasted much longer: Anglo-Danish lords were replaced by Normans, and the native culture was forced underground, where it went largely unrecorded. Northumberland lagged behind the rest of England in terms of education and industrial development for centuries, and continual territorial disputes with Scotland meant that the region was synonymous with lawlessness (the border reivers). These conditions nurtured a thriving oral culture (the border ballads) but precluded a continuous literary culture.

Bunting utilised these extensible borders and unwritten histories in order to contrive Northumbrian roots for poets he admired, such as Edmund Spenser, Wordsworth, the author of *Beowulf*, and Thomas Wyatt. The fact that Wyatt's father came from Yorkshire allowed Bunting to place Wyatt at the head of the English Renaissance and find a northern influence over all that followed. MacSweeney's equally dubious concept of northern-ness takes its bearings from Chatterton (Bristol), John Clare (Nottinghamshire) and the Perle poet (Midlands). Both poets are engaged in a kind of confabulation: constructing a cultural memory to fill the gap left by historical repression. *Briggflatts* sets up a Northumbrian kingdom that extends to Orkney, York and Dublin. In Bunting's view, Northumbrian identity had always been synthetic. The Lindisfarne illuminations were the product of Celtic, Germanic and Mediterranean cultures, hence his belief in 'continually changing racial identity but continually recurring and lasting cultural identities'.

Just as they cite dubious Northumbrian antecedents, Bunting and MacSweeney claim a Northumbrian heritage for their language. Bunting argued that 'southrons' could not understand Wordsworth because they couldn't pronounce his northern sounds,[42] and his introduction to the notes to *Briggflatts* leads the reader to expect a glossary of Northumbrian dialect words:

> The Northumbrian tongue travel has not taken from me sometimes sounds strange to men used to the *koine* or to Americans who may not know how much Northumberland differs from the Saxon south of England. Southrons would maul the music of many lines in *Briggflatts*.[45]

In fact, there are relatively few dialect words in the notes ('oxter' and 'hoy' are the exceptions). Tony Lopez observes:

> It seems to me that the notes themselves reconstruct an ancient Northumbria by harnessing old north-south divisions and prejudices, mixing up some northern words with others not so restricted, and presenting a quick checklist of names and texts to establish the basis for a cultural identity for anyone willing to take up the bait.[46]

MacSweeney took up the bait in *Ranter*, in which one recurrent Bunting-signifier is the word 'fipple', which appears in a key passage of *Briggflatts*. In his notes, Bunting defines the grand Old Norse word as 'the soft wood stop forming with part of the hard wood tube the wind passage of a recorder'.[47] MacSweeney appears to think a fipple is a musical instrument, and uses it several times in *Ranter*, reclaiming the word, by a process of misappropriation, as a signifier of northern-ness.

Such allusive signposting was part of MacSweeney's attempt to present himself as Bunting's heir. We see a similar process at work in MacSweeney's historicising. *Briggflatts*'s greatest confabulation is its revisionist history of Northumberland, structured around the contrasting figures of Eric Bloodaxe and St Cuthbert. Bunting's choice of founding fathers about whom nothing certain is known is reminiscent of MacSweeney's earlier choice of Chatterton as his literary antecedent: these figures do not "mean"; rather, they are a mechanism by which others have construed meaning. Peter Makin has argued convincingly for the significance of Bloodaxe and Cuthbert to *Briggflatts*, and explained the surprising absence of Bede, whom Bunting disdained for (as he saw it) denigrating the Celtic strand of Christianity that Aidan had imported from Ireland.[48] This debate, which goes back to the Synod of Whitby in 664, was alive for Bunting, and it comes as something of a relief that MacSweeney had no such compunction, referring to Bede alongside Cuthbert, Aidan and Eric Bloodaxe as equally-weighted signifiers of northernness, and calling out to Bede and Aidan for help.

Lopez argues that there was a socio-political dimension to Bunting's northern empire-building, and says that Bunting wanted 'to construct Northumbria as a proud and hard kingdom... in a time when the old industrial basis of the North-East's economy has been undermined'.[49] In 1984, when MacSweeney was writing *Ranter*, North-East industries were under a far more sustained attack; but he draws remarkably few parallels between the history of popular dissent and the political landscape of the 1980s. For example, a comparison could easily be made between the Peasants' Revolt in the fourteenth century and the industrial disputes of the 1970s and 80s: in both cases, labourers protested legislation that kept their wages low. But *Ranter* cannot make this argument. Instead, it implies that the progress won through the historical struggles of oppressed communities was due not to collective endeavour but to the self-assertion of heroic individuals: 'Call him Leveller, Lollard, / his various modes' (p.140).

The more closely we examine it, the more suspect MacSweeney's historicising appears. He uses the term Ranter loosely to signify resistance to the established order, as though it were interchangeable with other underground movements such as Levellers and Diggers. He does not refer to the Ranters' radical atheist/pantheist element because that would contradict the speaker's sense of impending retribution; nor does he refer to their levelling social aims, such as the abolition of property, because this would contradict the proud warlord element and the stress on fetishised prestige-objects such as cloakclasps. In fact, the individualist ethos of *Ranter* has more in common with the Puritanism of the Revolution. Social upheaval appears to have reduced the speaker to a state of permanent panic and uncertainty, like Hobbes's man in the state of nature.[50]

In 'Ranter's Reel', political references are gradually superseded by more personal demons. Here, Ranter addresses his enemy with mock-familiarity (p.169):

Listen Pal
Compadre
Colleague
Friend
Listen Dad

The historical/political dimension disappears altogether in the final section, 'Flamebearer', which is spoken in turn by Ranter and his Bride, and the poem turns out to be about personal failings, alcoholism, and the end of a relationship. Much of the poem's anger stems from alcoholic self-disgust. Here Ranter describes an alcoholic black out, followed by waking covered in vomit and blood and trying to piece together what has happened (p.154):

Ranter upright
on the sofa

Bloodcake shirt
vomitbib drying [...]

waking: This is not possible

Later, the speaker tells us he has been 'winedrunk from day one' (p.156), that his resentment is 'rising like liquor' (p.159), and that he has lived for five years 'drink to drink' (p.171). In 'Snipe Drumming', Ranter's Bride pointedly ignores the political dimension and states the case simply: 'You were drunk. // I didn't like / it much' (p.160). The confessional element suggests that *Ranter* is a staging post on the way to *The Book of Demons*: this is the point at which MacSweeney begins to project himself as the hero of his poetry much more directly.

Ironically, given how thoroughly MacSweeney wrote himself into Bunting's territory, *Ranter* was rejected because it sounded too much like Ken Smith. It is not surprising that MacSweeney's poetry should bear the influence of Smith at this point. MacSweeney wanted what Smith had achieved: soon after the Poetry Society walkout in 1977, Smith was picked up by Bloodaxe Books. *Tristan Crazy* was Bloodaxe's first publication [51] and was followed in 1982 by Smith's selected poems, *The Poet Reclining*. Having weathered the poetry wars in the 70s, Smith was billed in the mid-80s as 'Godfather to the New Poetry'.[52] MacSweeney's attempt to assimilate Smith's style proved too successful. Neil Astley, editor of Bloodaxe Books, praised *Ranter* on a technical level, but rejected it on the grounds that

> it is a direct copy of Ken Smith's *Fox*. Not only are the identities identical – or rather your way of exploiting the identity in the poem – but there are numerous similarities in phrasing, rhythm and even in your use of the same words.[53]

There are clear similarities between *Ranter* and *Fox Running*. Both poems are spoken by men on the run from their obligations or the consequences of their actions. Both poems capture a figure on the move by continually shifting the frame of reference, so that images, points of view, situations and settings are taken up and discarded rapidly, reflecting the speakers' restlessness and mistrust of larger organising structures, whether linguistic, social or political. Both Fox and Ranter are self-consciously displaced from language: Ranter says 'word for running / word for betrayal / word for bond [...] rocking down the Dartford Loop Line' (p.145). Fox makes a similar demand:

> I want a word
> a beginning word forming in its water bead
>
> I want a word forming fingers of itself
> in the belly of all language [54]

Smith's disproportionate influence on *Ranter* shows the extent to which the poem represented a break with MacSweeney's previous methods and readership. He was flying blind and, eager to be accepted by his new target audience, reverted to the clumsy, too-obvious imitation that had marred his earliest work.

Ranter invokes a history of political defeats in order to dramatise personal failure; but more than that, it constituted an artistic failure. Only after it had been rejected by Bloodaxe – forcing MacSweeney back into the small press world he had been trying to escape – could MacSweeney complete the poem by writing 'Finnbar's Lament'. Although it changes the name of the speaker, and relocates the story to Ireland, 'Finnbar's Lament' completes *Ranter*'s narrative and emotional arc by having Finnbar speak to us from a position of defeat, as will all of MacSweeney's subsequent personae (p.179):

God forgive me
least of souls

forgive my face
its crookedness

Finnbar has lost his wife, his home, his title, his land, his enthusiasm for battle and his pride: he invites his punishment. The irony is that in being disinherited, Finnbar/MacSweeney comes into his own: as Nicholas Johnson has observed, the lament is MacSweeney's 'natural mode'.[55] When MacSweeney declared his solidarity with dissenters and rebels in *Ranter*, and pledged his allegiance to the radical energies that drive his own best creations, he did not convince because his manner of doing so was derivative. By contrast, 'Finnbar's Lament' is characterised by tremendous beauty and fluency.

Ranter's signposts of kinship with Bunting and Smith have been removed, and 'Finnbar's Lament' emerges as a version of the fall from power endured by King Suibne in *Suibne Geilt*. Ireland is presented as an Edenic Albion: a rural, structured, stable kingdom whose poets know their place, whose men are war chiefs and whose women are grateful. MacSweeney had altered his birth name, but he could not dispense with it altogether because Suibne was an important early model for the poet driven to madness and solitude because of his uncompromising speech and conduct. Ireland held conflicting paternal associations, standing for the poetic vocation, but also for negative masculinity, violence and retribution. (Admittedly, this is also a case of English stereotyping: passionate, violent Ireland is the corollary of effeminate, affected France.) 'Finnbar's Lament' is a return to the father, but since *Ranter* had been so disastrously overpowered by its poetic father figures Bunting and Smith, it is a return in shame and defeat. There is a queasily paternal aspect to Finnbar's unnamed captor; an intimate, humiliating dimension to the punishment (pp.179-80):

Hammer home my rudeness
    strike my head
confirming my badness

making most
    of my humiliation. [...]

Break my blade. I will dance on its fragments

in any public place
you care to name. [...]

Take this small but neatly-written

list of friends.

MacSweeney could find nowhere to go after withdrawing to his imaginary Ireland, and 'Finnbar's Lament' was followed by six years of depression, alcoholism and writer's block. The *Ranter* project had failed, but it was an important failure: like *Brother Wolf*, the poem is a declaration of intent, and one that would bear fruit years later. In 1993 MacSweeney broke his silence with the tentative *Hellhound Memos*, which sketches out the urban landscape of *The Book of Demons* and introduces the figure of a silent young girl. After that, he produced some of his finest work in *Pearl*, the collection in which he declares himself prince of Sparty Lea (p.201), and that once again bore the crucial influence of Bunting.

A detailed study of the similarities between *Pearl* and the opening section of *Briggflatts* is beyond the scope of this essay. (Harriet Tarlo gives a thorough account of the parallels in 'Radical Landscapes: Contemporary British Poetry in the Bunting Tradition'.)[56] In conclusion, I will say that both poems are about childhood, and are set in isolated rural locations (Brigflatts and Allendale) that were not the poets' places of birth, but places where they had enjoyed holidays as children. Both poets seek redemption by belatedly returning to the first loves they had abandoned, and the poems form part of a larger project of self-assessment, following a period of artistic silence. For the most part, Bunting's presence in *Pearl* is felt in terms of an affinity, rather than by means of textual allusion, but we may note that Peggy's 'striped flannel drawers' match Pearl's 'Co-op coat' and 'red mittens' (p.209; p.210); that we see Peggy on the mason's cart, and 'Pearl on Noble's trailer' (p.206); that Bunting contrasts the mason's marble and sandstone with the 'trembling' and 'truculent' river Rawthey, while MacSweeney repeatedly invokes the 'white water, / foaming tumblestones' of Allendale (p.207); that Bunting and Peggy take shelter from the rain while MacSweeney and Pearl delight in it; that all four listen to the singing of peewits; and the way MacSweeney describes food – 'crisps / and ox-cheek for tea' and 'spam on Sundays / and chips if there is coal' (p.214; p.205) – has a pre-echo in *Briggflatts*, in which the children also enjoy simple rustic fare:

> Sour rye porridge from the hob
> with cream and black tea,
> meat, crust and crumb.[57]

In depicting such scenes, both poets favour, to a greater extent than is typical of their work, a Wordsworthian simplicity of diction,[58] a wish to honour 'things'[59] as they are. We are a long way from the Bloomian duel of 'The Last Bud', in which MacSweeney had deployed an allusion to Wordsworth as a barb aimed at Bunting: Wordsworth's influence now appears mediated by Bunting.

MacSweeney's relationship with Bunting was never straight-forward, and was certainly not that of apprentice and master. How-ever, it is equally misleading to claim that there is little or no evidence of Bunting's influence in his poetry. If the competitive edge to MacSweeney's relationship with Bunting has not altogether disappeared in *Pearl*, it has been transcended. Bunting's influence is neither avoided nor denied, but absorbed; his techniques are not imitated but developed; and his northern antecedents are matched with equivalents that have more resonance to MacSweeney. The cloakclasp that Ranter wore so proudly has been traded in for Pearl's 'Woolworth butterfly blue plastic clip, still made in Britain / then' (p.203). The northern territory that MacSweeney had so long staked out is suddenly augmented by passionately felt experience, as he transforms a synthetic heritage into poetry of great authority.

PETER RILEY

Thoughts on Barry MacSweeney

1 *Pearl* and *The Book of Demons*[1]

The whole discipline of *Pearl* is objective and self-purifying. Take any few lines (p.199):

> Grassblade glintstreak in one of the last mornings
> before I come to meet you, Pearl,
> as the rain shies.

The phonetics here effect that tense unison of sight and sound which so intrigued Pound before he capitulated to anger and importance. The shining of water on the earth's surface and the shining spittle in the mouth as it tangles in that initial cluster of palatals, are what make speech possible; the glinting and the saying enforce each other. Pearl's very disability is re-enacted as a vehicle of song. Right through the book the word 'spittle' occurs again and again as a sign of the purity and wisdom of desire. 'Grassblade glintstreak': there is a liquid compaction, a birth channel (a new word echoed out of an old word) and then the sentence walks away in search of belonging and reciprocity. From the first word of the sentence to the last the phonetics phase from one zone to another and the voice walks out into tradition and plainness, knowing exactly where it is (the octosyllabic line, the lyric) towards an objectivity, the rain which is the earth's echo of our vocal fluidity.

'Pearl' is a shifted term of 'earth', the adored but unattainable (because it is always too late) perfect condition of being, the 'lost mournings' lurking behind 'last mornings'. The break into plain language at 'before I come to meet you' is surely the most heartening, even redemptive, sign in these opening lines, a linguistic act

131

which quite transcends the forlorn messages of the poem and restores the earth-light to us beyond the author's condition. It is so exact, the way the rhythm bears the syntax down into the prime focus (Pearl), the way it runs to her. After that, the aftermath, a little ending on two stopped syllables that echo each other: 'rain shies' – new sounds, entering experience, taking the forked passage of ambiguity in the uncertain force of 'as' (at the same time as / in the manner of) and the unanswered question as to how exactly the rain 'shies' (rears up, throws itself at, recoils from). Reluctance is the word for this whole process, re-shining, the shy rain that deflects before a queen.

So the passionate extravagance of the poetical writing (here calm and obvious, elsewhere wild and defeating) is not just effect, it locks into the entire purpose of the poetry. It is the major instrument in moving the poetry out of confessional and into artefact.

Pearl is pastoral poetry in the most serious sense, which takes our experience out of society to a constructed elsewhere, a bright theatre of earth where the ills are real but morally clear and all lessons are fulfilled, then dances with it and returns it. *The Book of Demons* is of course the contrary, where the self is trapped in its own alienation and hatred, its nose stuck in the dereliction of politics, vomit instead of spittle, hallucinated pavements instead of real cold fields. The self cries out for comfort and drowns in it. It can't succeed, as the reader can't be any more than second cousin to the self-murdering self that parades up and down the text. But the two works are not entirely distinct, for *Demons* shares a longing for resolution which intermittently relaxes the diatribe, and is like a *Pearl* that has lost its anchorage. Towards the end, where the redemptive figure of 'Tom' appears and Pearl is referred to again, this longing is the central issue, but refuses to resolve into anything but solid contradiction: 'God Save the Queen' in enormous majuscules and we don't know which queen and so whether to laugh or cry. Published together, the two texts echo and rebound off each other in illuminating ways, and even when *Demons* wallows deepest in rage and splashes its acids wherever they can reach, the calm praises of *Pearl* remain in the back of the reader's trust, and flashes of innocence glint here and there in the devastated townships like sprigs of honeysuckle on a prison wall.

2 Thoughts on Barry MacSweeney

In the last decade of his life, Barry MacSweeney no longer cared: who he was pleasing, what cultural agenda he might attach to, what figure of a poet he struck, what he *should* be writing... He was poisoning himself to death with alcohol and he knew it. From then on he wrote what he knew, and very little else. It was not always accomplished, it was not free of his excesses and imbalances, and there were terrible lapses, but it was what he was sent here to do.

Barry was a traditional lyrical poet, and the whole mode of his writing manifests an essentially familiar and even popular understanding of what a poet is and does. Basically he writes love songs. He "addresses the beloved", he pleads with her for reciprocity, wooing her with all the echoic lures of musical language. This condition survives, I think, through all the vast ranges of his writing, turning increasingly towards lament, and rage, for the loss of love, and all other matter is achieved through that lens. All the socio-political diatribes, 'state of the nation bulletins', laments for dissolving landscapes, etc., are processed through that essentially personal condition. The first person singular presides over everything. She, whether acceding or denying, is the reflective confirmation of his desire; thus it is in the entire tradition. But she is also, traditionally, the desired figure of the earth at its fairest, the figure of redemption.

Barry was not interested in, for instance, language change. If the language got radicalised, disrupted, damaged or destroyed, as it sometimes did, that was not the result of a working agenda; it derived from an inner soul condition, compounded of his nature and his circumstances, pushed to an extreme. The creation and maintenance of this inner poet of the self was his constant task and his claim to both tradition and innovation.

So biography doesn't get you very far in understanding the necessities of the poetry. The alcoholism explains nothing of the quality and force of the writing; it supplied the materials and tone of the central depiction, the contradicted self, because it was both release and imprisonment. It became so much part of him that it is impossible to see the writing without it, but it is not what the poetry is about. It is about an inner creative self-hood the cleft nature of which was understood as a condition of the world. It could be that the more obviously a poet's biography intrudes into the text as a major determinant, as with Paul Celan, the more it is a distraction from what is actually going on in the poetry.

Barry acted out the role of poet possessed, heroic victim, shaman, *poète maudit*...but it was basically a pop version centred on the self, indulging all the swagger and aggression of rock 'n' roll. There was nothing Arctic about it, no slow patience. The poetry began in a pop context and never entirely left it. People like Jim Morrison, Bob Dylan, and Robert Johnson, were chosen as life-long heroes: showmen, all of them, pin-ups of protracted adolescence. At the time such allegiances were valuable for positing adulthood and virility against the nursery mentality of The Beatles, but our resources were limited by our bilateralism: we didn't know about reggae or 'sweet protest'! In selecting Robert Johnson for instance for solitary lionisation out of all those southern songsters Barry made it clear that there was no room for the steady lamentational persistence of blues players like Skip James or Son House. There was only stress, musical muscle. And some of the poet-heroes too: Rimbaud of course, but also Anne Sexton, Sylvia Plath, Thomas Chatterton, Michael McClure... – not all that much to do with poetry really, more with a particularly ambitious casting of the self into the heroic role as worldly victim and artistic victor, the suicide for which the world itself is to blame. All the heroes whether musical, literary or just stars of the circuits, were figures of the MacSweeney poet-self, they spoke the same language of the self struggling against destruction of and by the world, and were claimed as intimates by exclusive affinity.

In the earliest poetry you can see a tension between the search for a poetical discourse of some figurative weight and the intrusion of distracting ostentatious verbal gestures. Many times a promising move is sidetracked into a trick of pop surrealism, or a poem contains little else. A nascent sense of the reach of a fully poetical discourse clashes with career moves. But he did get there sometimes in his way, for example in *The Boy from the Green Cabaret Tells of His Mother*: 'On the burning down...', 'The Margin', 'Death go get yr shoes repaired...'; and in the more seriously inclined *Our Mutual Scarlet Boulevard*: 'Saffron Walden Blues', 'The new light, when it comes...', the coda to the title poem, 'Poem' ('to belong outside of this catastrophe...') and 'Losing at Cards'. A more generous selection from the first two books and the many uncollected poems of that period would have made a better beginning for *Wolf Tongue*. For he also had a skill as an entertainer which didn't require flashy tropes; it is evident at times in the early work in slightly outrageous but telling figurations, playfully tense rhythms and suspended endings, and was revived in 'Letters to Dewey',[2] a splendidly coherent and relaxed work which consummates much that he failed to do between 1965 and 1970, and also shows how openly unpretentious and playful his version of the self could be.

When Barry started, the so-called "youth revolution" of the 1960s was at its end, and faced with the reactionary clampdown youth was passing into a more severe engagement through political action, which in other countries became murderous. Barry was of that fighting spirit and had he been German or Italian his career might have been very different, and his life perhaps even shorter. But our revolution was catchy tunes and smart shoes, and although we had The Angry Brigade there was nothing here like the 1970s terrorist crises in the former Axis countries. Had there been, Barry would have been there in the thick of it; but as it was, the revolt went into poetry. I don't just mean the intermittent shouts of 'fascist!' to cover just about anything he didn't like the looks of, I mean the whole force of his move into an alien poetical language, a language that violates normality by displacements of image, sense, and scene, bearing with it a mounting sense that the society and civilisation he lives in, and ultimately the entire present world socially, politically and biologically, is a site of despoliation for which human evil is responsible, and his business is to hound it down by accusing it and mimicking it and provoking it. His essay on Chatterton is pure youth-cult, accusing age of wrecking the world, a simplification of Blake's lyrical dichotomy (exciting to read at the time but when you're 70 rather depressing). His climactic work of the early 1980s amounts to a kind of poetical terrorism, bombs thrown at any reader's peace of mind or "bourgeois" sense of decency. And the sphere of blame grew and grew until the crisis was permanent, and all that was left was a band of heroes, mostly poets and musicians, who bore messages of defiance and mostly themselves fell victim to the world's enemies. His world virtually rested on these figures as projections of himself. But not much sight of philosophers, political thinkers, historians... not even Marx. Not much accuracy about what was happening and why, and what the alternatives were. It was a world-encompassing rage centred on the immediate mental spaces of the self.

About 1970 then, a plunge into wild figuration, rather like the plunge Dylan Thomas took in about 1934, but without the loco-motive power; rather accumulations of verbal gestures, in a language that was stripped of rationalism but held onto a sense of the real by allowing recognisable forms of usage to emerge piecemeal: periods of passionate address, account, description, letter, ultimatum, in a scenario of dynamic displacement. This magnificently bold and resourceful flawed flight into a new poetry was surely the establish-ment of the real MacSweeney poet, and continued for two more decades to thrust itself forward into violence and fall back into the singing of wish and despair. It was always precarious – always, even here, courting the edge of verbal incompetence. And weaker, I thought, in *Odes* than in *Brother Wolf* because of the reduction of the syntax to broken yelps, pellets of disdain strung on the monolithic central pivot, redeemed only by such tenderness and humour as was allowed in. But by the time he had *Blackbird* under his belt he had clearly got there, and the possibilities were more than merely dynamic or strong. If I choose to demur about the Poundian effort of *Black Torch* because I don't think his powers of understanding could actually reach the substances involved, that is not to deny him a remarkable ascension during the 1970s.

The working of a public language was always a problem. Who is 'Aidan'? Where is 'Sparty Lea'? I know exactly where Sparty Lea is because I was there and I know what it meant to Barry; and I wrote a blurb for Aidan Semmens's latest book. But I am made almost ashamed of this knowledge by the way Barry throws the name around. I don't want to be one of what he called the 'Men in the know / chewing ends off cigars' (p.141) and it is ironic that he created one exclusivity while decrying another. In poems like *Brother Wolf* and *Blackbird* he solved his earlier struggle with accidence, the struggle to make the particulars he encountered inhabit the poetical discourse as necessities, largely by applying intense emotional pressure to them so that they are borne up into the rhythm and power of it all. But for the reader who wants to pause at details and hope for recognition, there is largely contempt.

There are ways of saying local and personal names into a poem which don't cause problems, which establish a sense of narrative and thus a more laid-back discourse. O'Hara had it, and perhaps learned it from Nicholas Moore. MacSweeney approached it only in his late poems.

The violent and obscene poems of the early 1980s are for me the central disaster in Barry's career. His growing confidence crashed into its own absurdity. Somehow he determined, or was persuaded, that things like erotomania or faeces were powerful meanings in the cultural and political order of the world. The possibility of this diatribe had always lurked on the edge of his poetry (see 'poem' 'Still the blue stone lodged asleep...' in *Our Mutual Scarlet Boulevard*); moved to centre stage in total shrillness it emerged as a brutal and simplistic equation of political and sexual failure, with resulting hysteria. His poetry was not politicised in 'Liz Hard' and 'Jury Vet'. It had always been political as he knew and understood politics: on the ground, in the workplace (he had been a union official) and the infantile sexual temper-tantrum reduced politics to crude categories of the person, the Nazi officer in the brothel. And anyway, using poetry as a vehicle of shock is doomed – it only ever reaches the pre-confirmed and they just laugh and yell for more.

Ranter, which rants far less than the texts that precede it, represents the recovery from this. It is a tremendous relief and a brilliant performance: he *runs* out of all that sordidness, into the open air and across the land in a continuously active metric of mostly two or three beat lines, bouncing over rocks and grass and into boudoirs and political meetings... It is the first of his works of real extended telling, and seems to offer hope of healing by a self-sustaining, self-mocking perseverance, with glimpses too of a different author, lower in assertion and deeper into helplessness. The ever-hovering danger of solipsism might have been averted.

I think Barry was easily swayed as a poet, by individuals, by his reading, or by a climate. I think he sometimes took up certain zones into his poetry because he thought he had to in order to be a real contemporary poet, whatever his actual interest or knowledge. Gestures are made throughout his career, for instance, in the direction of economics, finance, money, pressed into the whole structure of the dissolution of hope, but the message rarely goes far beyond: filthy money, stinking rich. Terms of economics and finance are chucked into the discourse on an assumption that they will merge with figures of harm quite automatically. 'Totem Banking', the last of these, is an important poem, but for all its sustained eloquence, indeed its intellectual striving, it is basically a claim for an artistic elitist deliverance from the enemies of the spirit who control the world: fat cats, arts councils, tame poets, 'those who have never heard of Bartok [sic]' (p.315), including, explicitly, all the ordinary stupid people who fall for the bait. It doesn't touch on the actualities or categories of banking, and the tone and manner of it – the heaped disdain, the linguistic pressure and blockage – is not Barry's authentic voice.

His condition forced crudity, banality, even stupidity, into his writing, which were either transcended or not. The poems tend to collapse when "the real MacSweeney" emerges through cracks in them, with its constant liability to crude attitudes, false history, sexual bravado... This self was no more real than any of the other self-personae, or the late-night phone-calling MacSweeney recounting convincingly all sorts of fantasies about himself. Barry's knowledge should not be underestimated, it was wide and purposeful and can emerge when least expected. But extreme emotions, especially anger, distorted both it and its language. Anger, like anxiety, when deeply embodied in the psyche, makes intelligent people stupid and that is the level of fault Barry's poetry falls into when his grip on it slips. But it would be wrong to accuse him of self-pity. All kinds of bravado, misjudgements of the world, destructive urges, whole sequences made up of nothing but vaunted attitudes, many of them second-hand (*Hellhound Memos*). But the self-pity was something he had a right to, it was real and precious, and saved his poetry. It created Pearl out of his warring body fluids.

The poetry needed Pearl. Through her it became possible to bestow unmitigated praise on someone who was not a sexual object and not a model hero or suicidal alter-ego. A lot of the attitudes are dropped; what remain of the diatribes are sad traces of new dereliction on the moors, and images not of upsurgence but of loneliness and resignation, though the force of complaint flows as strongly as ever, and can swell into Shakespearean monologues. But the questions asked are now part of something else, both larger and more particular. 'What does a government do?' — Barry himself would have asked this in spiteful anger, but now it is Pearl's question, 'Can it make you speak?' (p.204) and all the complaint and negation is refocused. Pearl speaks who cannot speak, and the act of writing comes to her aid. This invented voice is not made as the author's mouthpiece, but as a voice offered to the voiceless. And with this voice she tells him what he cannot tell himself; the donated voice becomes the only one he needs to listen to, the voice of what he knows when all the showmanship is stripped away.

The only other figure like Pearl that I can think of in recent poetry is Tom, the Downs Syndrome infant, in Douglas Oliver's *The Diagram Poems* (1974), who is also given a voice to calm down and broaden the author's ambitions. The wisdom that resides in the sheer humanity of the completely inarticulate child.

The lost condition of the *Pearl* poems is not social. The lament is not for a Jerusalem, but neither is it for the survival of mutual aid structures in the North-East villages. It is for a pre-adolescent condition of the self free from booze and failure. A bubble in the mind really. Babes in the wood. Factual or not, that hardly matters. It is the promise that the world broke. But the story of Pearl is not an idyll. It is not the picture of innocence he thought it was. It has its own enemies and dangers and its own termination built into it, from cruel teachers to the weather and Pearl's affliction itself. It does not beg a contrary. He thought it did. He had this rigid binary structure in his mind of innocence and experience, good and evil, which he thought told him that after Pearl's persuasive mellifluous speech it was his duty to ventriloquise Nazi dictators and child murderers, neither of which he was qualified to do, the former because of his simplistic version of historical causality, the latter because the exercise dropped him back into unmitigated hatred of the physical world and the human frame (though if there are in fact, as he claimed, 200 Mary Bell sonnets the story might turn out to be longer and more complicated).

The Book of Demons is not the answering contrary to *Pearl*, rather both of them participate in different ways in a newly fluent mode of passionate writing, a rule-breaking, expansive mode, which was still going strong in 1997. This includes *Horses in Boiling Blood* and maybe about 100 unpublished poems. It particularly broke the "poetry as sculpture" rule which he had struggled with throughout his career, the demand for the discretion of items within the discourse; now it all rolled on impelled by internal need on the edge of the abyss. The productivity became profligate and often careless, substantial poems turned out one after the other in something like desperation, but all of them offering something to an actual reader which had in many respects been denied previously. The fulcrum wavered between love (*Pearl*) and hatred (*Demons*) and it was the former which achieved a liberated mode of writing for him, carried on from there into what he may have thought of as more serious matter. But, as he himself proclaimed at the reading referred to below, the contrary to the 'innocence' of Pearl was not reached until the final evil sonnets, and was not a contrary but a negation.

The final episode, the last two or three years, might be a separate matter. I can only guess what his condition had become at that time from various hints I have picked up. But in April 2000, two weeks before he died, he gave a reading at Dulwich College which was recorded. Listening to it now, there are things which are clearly shocking. He was always a most persuasive reader; his rendering of the *Pearl* poems was remarkably powerful and tender, but now his voice has lost its music. His speech is very slow and full of bitterness, never far from sarcasm. The beautiful Geordie accent is betrayed by vehemence into coarse sliding diphthongs. He reads 'Pearl Alone' (p.205) which is, like most of the best Pearl poems, spoken by Pearl, and every faintly negative value in the poem is triple stressed. Every complaint she makes, which in the written metrics bear the calm and balance of measured speech, becomes a caustic, sneering accusation, a jibe thrown at the world. The 'heifer muck' (line 21) is disgusting. Pearl's only vowel (line 10) becomes McClure's wild-beast roar. And twice (lines 8 and 30) he breaks the poem completely by screaming and banging. This is not Pearl's voice at all; you would cower from this voice before you'd respond to it. And of course by contorting the poem like this he completely violates Pearl's plea to him in the next poem he reads, 'Pearl in the Silver Morning': 'Anger is hot, and Bar you have too much of it' ... 'We were hot, but never blasted' ... 'your raining rage must cease' ... '*Please do it* – cool your raging fire lovelorn heart – for me' (pp.323-24). It seemed that this plea for peace was the only voice from his poetry, now, to offer anything but horror.

140

W.N. HERBERT

Barry MacSweeney and the Demons of Influence: *Pearl* and *The Book of Demons*

When I began my research for this essay, I visited the Robinson Library to pick up a copy of Barry MacSweeney's first book, *The Boy from the Green Cabaret Tells of His Mother*, basically because, much like its successor, *Our Mutual Scarlet Boulevard*, the bare minimum of work from it was chosen by MacSweeney for his selected poems, *Wolf Tongue*. As I was at the counter getting the book stamped, the librarian picked it up and remarked with genuine affection, 'That takes me back!' We then had a short chat about the merits and availability of the volume, and about Barry, as we both referred to him, as a poet.

There was in this something more than anecdotal about Barry MacSweeney's relationship both to place and to the academy within that place. He, like a few other Newcastle and Northumbrian writers, including Basil Bunting, Sid Chaplin, Tom Haddaway and, latterly, David Almond, Julia Darling and Lee Hall, has become talismanic as a literary exemplar that is at once regional and national, indeed international in status. An ironic position, considering the peripherality, half-willed, half-involuntary, of the role he played for most of his writing life.

Indeed to consider the anecdote as an excluded mode within criticism does not seem irrelevant when discussing a poet who both revelled in and despaired of his outsider status. There is a sense in which the position of Barry MacSweeney in relation to the usual dichotomy of mainstream and experimental poetry is illuminated by analogy with the anecdote, invented as an historical genre by Procopius in order to reveal what he could not say in his official work ('an ecdota': not published).

That is the thesis of this essay: that MacSweeney was neither/
both mainstream nor/and experimental, a writer who had to find
his own position almost in despite of these categories. Almost from
the outset, MacSweeney's work displayed an instinct for antithesis,
always swerving away from what he perceived was expected of him,
or of the contemporary poet in the turbulent four decades across
which he wrote. In the two books published toward the end of his
life, *Pearl* and *The Book of Demons*, he finds a way of incorporating
this swerve into the dynamic relationship between the two works.

Peter Barry's opposition, in *Contemporary British Poetry and the
City*, of the poetics of the pastoral to the various urban modes
which critique or envelop it, is highly illuminating, but his analysis
needs a certain repositioning when we look at MacSweeney. For
Peter Barry, the MacSweeney of *Hellhound Memos* is primarily a
poet of Newcastle's inner city:

> The speaker in the sequence materialises ...as a kind of transgenera-
> tional urban Lord of Misrule...an embodiment of the anarchic gang
> spirit of the overspill estates...He is scandalising, reckless and electri-
> fying, like Robert Johnson, claiming a privilege for his destructive/
> deconstructive art....[1]

I'd like to counter that with a short overview of MacSweeney's
career in order to suggest that MacSweeney is best understood as
a poet who sets up a distinctive dynamic between the urban and
the pastoral, locating his poetry in both the towns and cities of the
North-East, Newcastle and Durham, and the surrounding country-
side of Northumberland. Moreover, it is by associating, assigning
and re-assigning the distinctive aspects of his imagination and his
influences with both rural and urban, that he achieves his best work.

In the preface to *The Boy from the Green Cabaret Tells of His
Mother*, 'The autobiography of Barry MacSweeney', this is made
explicit. Beginning '"Born in "The Village", Benwell, Newcastle
upon Tyne..."' MacSweeney enfolds village within suburb within
urban. The first key element for him in Newcastle's topography is
this enfoldedness, that it contains or admits access to both urban
and rural:

> You can walk out of Newcastle for half an hour and be in greenery.
> The city gave words a harshness, like the steel or coal. Then I wd
> [sic] flit off to [sic] little stone cottage on the fells and fish for trout...
> Began to translate Laforgue, Cros, Corbiere.[2]

The 'autobiography' itself is enfolded in a further layer of quote marks, indicating its interview-like, verbatim nature. It therefore has at once a journalistic immediacy and a sense of removal, as though it represents a report on something – it is, appropriately for MacSweeney, trained as a journalist, a mediated encounter. Its use of contractions and pronoun-less sentences is oddly reminiscent of Browning's gestures of garrulous intimacy, for instance in 'Caliban on Setebos', where they signify the primitive 'salvage' [3] man of Shakespeare's Dramatis Personae.

That gesture of cutting as if to essentials is enacted in the key encounter, recounted here, with his most difficult influence, Basil Bunting: "'Showed Bunting Walk poem, it came back sliced down to about 4 lines and a note: Start again from there."' (Note Bunting's instruction is, by contrast to this whole statement, not contained in quotes, but represented as though already absorbed into MacSweeney's own utterance – a tendency which will recur.)

He contrasts this binary interrelation of town and countryside, this eclogue between the aesthetics of the urban and the pastoral, with his journalistic apprenticeship in the south: "'Synthetic new town, a dormitory to London...And the land was flat, that was a shock. An utter antithesis to Newcastle...the people, they didn't *belong*."' Of course the parallels between Harlow and Benwell, their relationship with both a city and a countryside, might have been just as evident, but MacSweeney's resistance to the 'synthetic' is already searching out a further guarantee of authenticity that he locates, ironically, in a duck pond later discovered to be "'one of the town planner's landscaping tricks.'"

One further significant detail is relevant in this little introduction: towards the end, when describing his present situation back in Newcastle, the pronoun-less present tense shifts from first person to third: "'helps run Morden Tower poetry readings... Wants to see poets get away from revisionism.'" Here we see played out for the first time in his prose one of the paradoxes that haunt MacSweeney's poetry: at the moment of supposedly greatest authenticity and intimacy, he is always already distancing himself into persona. 'MacSweeney' is, effectively, to be found neither here nor there, not in the Toon or the country, not the 'he' or the 'I', but in the oscillation between them.

The events following publication of this first volume not only reinforced this oscillatory tendency, but turned it into a mode of response and indeed resistance to the poet's role in the fraught aesthetic politics of the late 60s and 70s. Put forward by his publisher, Hutchinson, via a pair of compliant dons, for the Oxford Professorship of Poetry in 1968, MacSweeney's youth and origins were seized upon by the media as symbolic weapons in opposition to the mainstream. (The poet who won the election, Roy Fuller, was associated with the Movement, a poetic grouping identified with both traditional metrics and Oxbridge.)

The poems of *The Boy from the Green Cabaret Tells of His Mother* were written in the same milieu as those of Morden Tower organiser Tom Pickard (which we might characterise as one aware of modern European writing from an Americanised post-Beat perspective), and under the late Modernist tutelage of Basil Bunting. They were seen as, approximately, cognate with the pop sensibilities of the Liverpool Poets: wasn't one northernness much like another when set against the staid, the middleclass and the Oxonian?

As a journalist, MacSweeney may have understood the simplifications of the 'story' he had become part of, but as a poet he found the attention intolerable. No wonder he increasingly cast Chatterton as his hero (thereby casting himself as Chatterton), the obscure Romantic youth ridiculed and destroyed by a world insensitive to his attempts to recreate and reinvigorate the authentic roots of English poetry. His main reaction was to consolidate his engagement with the experimental agendas of the Cambridge school, simultaneously turning his back on the wider public – or at least that aspect of the public which might be influenced by reading newspapers – and on an Oxford which placed the poet in such a conspicuously public professorial role.

It also seems significant here that, as a teenager back in 1967, when inviting Prynne and other practitioners of the Cambridge School north, he had focused the trip on his rural retreat: the Poetry Festival was located in Sparty Lea, rather than Pickard's (and Bunting's) Morden Tower. In the 70s he would confirm this secondary opposition, rejecting both the wider audience and, perhaps, the aesthetic that had led to the débâcle of the Professorship.

His consistent areas of concern are present from his earliest work: love as the most extreme emotion; the North of England as a territory opening out to earlier poetries; rock music as the alternative to conventional literary influences; and Thomas Chatterton, the Romantics' favourite suicidal teenager, as a personal icon. The poem 'Brother Wolf' announces many of these obsessions (p.23):

> There is so much *land* in Northumberland. The sea
> Taught me to sing
>   the river to hold my nose. When
> it rains it rains glue.
>   Chatterton's eyes were stuck to mountains.
> He saw fires where other men saw firewood.
> One step ahead in recognising signals.
> And leapt into the flames.

MacSweeney's 70s work, exclusively gathered (or, with reference to the anecdote, concealed) in small presses, displayed his interest in both the politically and poetically radical, and his interest in collecting (and speaking through) personae was extended to include that of the experimentalist and the associated technique of manipulated collage (writing that incorporates collage, rather than being solely constituted of collaged materials). It is notable, however, that he seems more comfortable with the expressionistic howling capitals and centre margins of Michael McClure than with the cooler deconstruction of personal and public discourse favoured by Ashbery and Prynne himself.

Avatars from the blues and rock and roll, and lyric stances adopted from punk and reggae, allowed him continued access to direct utterance – all the more necessary as his alcoholism led to personal and professional crises that seemed to parallel the social and political crises of the era. What emerges in these poems is a verse infused with resonant colloquial energy, lines which feel intuitive yet unpredictable, absurd but stingingly apt, as at the close of 'Ode Long Kesh': 'Nouveau Flapless in the garments of rich / hunger, living on potatoes & nitro-glycerine' (p.41).

There was a second retreat from poetic office when, in 1977, caught up in the conflict Peter Barry chronicles in his *Poetry Wars*, MacSweeney resigned as chair of the Poetry Society's committee, writing earlier to Eric Mottram, head of the radical faction which had seized control in the 70s (what Peter Barry categorises as the British Poetry Revival): 'I've done too much compromising and my skull won't take any more'.[4] Certainly he went on to write some of his most aggressive political collage pieces, such as 'Wild Knitting', described in its dedication as 'this State of the Nation bulletin' (p.138). Equally, however, this not very tactical retreat could be seen as demarcating the limits of this group of writers' capacity to engage with any audience broader than its own adherents. Though it should be noted, as Robert Sheppard points out, that this was no simplistic grouping of the avant-garde: 'Jeff Nuttall [was] the only representative of the "Cambridge" grouping of poets to be caught up in the events.'

Certainly by the mid-80s he had swung back to a more recognisably Buntingesque mode, offering the new press in the Toon, Bloodaxe Books, *Ranter*, a poem which cannily combined aspects of two of Bloodaxe's key early poets, the outsider persona presented by Ken Smith in Fox Running, and the pre-Chaucerian frame of reference of the author of *Briggflatts* himself. Its rejection was followed by another oscillation, the partial reversion to the outsider voice of *Hellhound Memos*, which, as Peter Barry notes, 'manifests a constant verbal exuberance and conspicuous, register-blending, excess'. These two books between them marked out the territory of his late style, forged equally from a ruralising Northern Modernism and what Peter Barry goes on to call his 'homodiegetic' urban variation on Cambridge Hermeticism. (Barry, p.76)

The two volumes of *Pearl* and *The Book of Demons* seem to exist for many readers in a Blakean pairing of early Innocence set against late and terrible Experience. Certainly, Pearl is portrayed as an innocent figure in an idealised pastoral setting, in which the flawed orality of that past becomes a kind of ur-poetry – she is a *genius loci* in a Romanticised context, at once Wordsworth's Lucy and MacSweeney's Idiot Girl (p.198):

>   ...I am Pearl.
> So low a nobody I am beneath the cowslip's
> shadow, next to the heifers' hooves.
> I have a roof over my head, but none
> in my mouth. All my words are homeless.

Both Bunting's Peggy Greenbank ('She has been with me fifty years') and the beatified child of the medieval alliterative poem *Pearl* (cited in 'Mony Ryal Ray') are behind this portrait, while the mention of John Clare's Helpston ('I know your heart's in Helpston today'), reminds us of that poet's walk home from the asylum ('John eating grass'), convinced he was going to meet his childhood sweetheart, Mary Joyce (p.204).

Pearl's influences, then, appear mostly ruralised, pre-industrial – its chronotope, to refer to Peter Barry's use of Bakhtinian terminology, is long ago, and, if not so far away from Newcastle, precisely positioned in relation to a further point significant for a writer of Irish descent: 'Donegal sleet spoke to our faces uniquely' (p.210). But unlike the Northumbrian landscapes of Bunting, which appear to disdain any awareness that there is such a city as Newcastle, *Pearl* is also positioned as at an oscillatory extreme, a reaction to the riotous urban setting of its predecessor, *Hellhound Memos* (p.199):

Deep despair destroys and dents delight
now that I have pledged my future to you, Pearl,
from the edge of the broken bypass, from
the home of the broken bottle and fiery
battleground of the sieged estate.

So *Pearl* is in this sense a book which utilises its pastoral material to state a case: those poems in which Pearl describes 'Bar' are not merely persona poems, but a means of depicting its author in a period before poetry, or at least before the wars and wanderings of his poetic career. This image is heroic: Pearl casts him as 'Bar, my trout-catching / hero'; by teaching her to write, he becomes 'my language Lancelot', and her depiction of his fidelity allows glimpses of self-interpretative commentary on previous works: 'I'm still plain Pearl. / Wild Knitting was named after me, I know you did, Bar' (p.198; p.216; p.204).

This mode reflects the strategy of Hardy in a poem like 'The Haunter', where he speaks in the voice of his dead first wife, expiating guilt by depicting her unswerving faithfulness, but ironising the gesture by putting words in the ghost's mouth which, it claims, he cannot hear: 'What a good haunter I am, O tell him! / Quickly make him know...'.[5] In both cases the reader is drawn in and made complicit in an exchange invented by the poet, the true purpose of which is to confide in us.

This subtle directing of the reader's attention is also present in the form of apparently unconscious allusion on Pearl's part, such as the gathering of vowels in 'Lost Pearl', where the couplet 'looking up at the mesmeric flicker of adult mouths / as they said A and E and I and U and O...' (p.213) performs two acts beyond its literal meaning. The first concerns its rearrangement of the usual order of the vowels to suggest a subliminal message: 'A&E' as Accident and Emergency looks forward to the tragedies of *Demons*, while 'I and you' symbolises the couple; 'O' in this context is both lamentation and evocation. Who is being evoked brings in the second layer of reference, as it is another of MacSweeney's avatars, the Rimbaud of 'Voyelles', whose almost-presence is confirmed by the drunken fairground swingboat at the opening of a subsequent lyric, 'Pearl at 4 a.m.' (p.215):

> Moon afloat, drunken opal shuggy boat
> in an ocean of planets and stars.
> Fierce clouds gather over me
> like a plaid shawl –

While the Celticised shawl only takes us back to the third poem in the book ('Argent moon with bruised shawl'), these two references to Rimbaud take us right back to the title of his first book – as a footnote there makes clear: 'The Boy is Rimbaud, and the *Cabaret Vert* is a pub in Central France where he wrote a letter to his mother, and a poem'. And as the last poem in that collection ('To Me Mam, Somewhere To The North Of This Shit') confirms, all identifications in MacSweeney are self-identifications, and Pearl is as much the poet as she is the actual person: that is the underlying implication of the reiterated declaration, 'I am Pearl'. It is in this sense that her education becomes an allegory of his own increasing literary independence: 'I have, I learned later, the emotions / of literate people…' (p.210).

The Book of Demons would appear to contrast with Pearl in several key ways – it refers to a different cast of influences or rather totemic figures including Anne Sexton, Kasimir Malevich and Johnny Rotten. It appears to be more usually urban in its settings and topographic references. Its voices expand to admit significant others to the cast – principally the poet Jackie Litherland. Its lyric voice seems more distended both in line length and in length of poem – although numerically there are not many more poems (26 to 22), it is more than three times longer. Excess is both its subject and its manner (p.253):

> I am gnawing jawface, furman, odd cove
> alone in the tree-line, pawpoison back
> of the track pack, blood beneath the rolling

148

> mills of sense, MC for this mad filthy earth
> whose prancing demon gaffers have me
> straight between the shoulder blades
> and down the garglevomit hole they call
> a throat. I am the bloatstoat, floating
> volevoter at the collapse pollstation.

Except, as we see here, at the same time as he cites the urban, urbane role of the rap MC, he is placing himself in an isolated internal landscape other poems identify as, in emotional terms, utterly remote from any conurbation or indeed anything human: 'You cannot // be wolf or stag alone in taiga treeline forever' – once we understand this internalised wilderness is enfolded within the urban, just as he positions 'The Village' within Benwell, we see that the territories of *The Book of Demons* shift back and forth or rather oscillate wildly between town and countryside, between real, remembered, imaginary and hallucinated landscapes (p.269).

The appearance of the polling station as part of the urban landscape, alongside the medical bureaucracy of 'the Durham Family Practitioner Committee' and the horrors of the locked ward, points to MacSweeney's positioning of his alcoholism within a dysfunctional society, the 'Great United Quelldom' in which self and country are one: 'that's the nation of me too: each of us / in very separate parts brought to our knees' (p.246). We hear the echo of Thatcher's denial of community here, 'There's no such thing as society', as well as noting it is a central trope of *The Book of Demons* that MacSweeney's illness has both symbolic and polemic meaning, in that it links him to a pantheon of suffering poet-heroes (p.241):

> I am 72-inches tall, yet when I go to meet John
> and Percy and Kazimir and Pearl, stick me in
> the oven and burn me just the same. Then I will
> be a true Jew, a poet through and through.

Pearl makes a key reappearance two thirds of the way through the book in 'Pearl Against The Barbed Wire', to reinforce this analogy between poet and Jew, borrowed from either from Plath in 'Daddy Wants To Murder Me', or from Marina Tsvetaeva in 'Poem of the End', or indeed from both. Her stumbling speech recalls the ''Ban 'Ban ca-Caliban' of the drunken and rebellious Caliban's song: 'Bar, Bar, barbed wire. Bar, the barbs / and staples and hooks and eyes. Did / you see the photographs?' (p.250). Here the punning on 'Bar' recalls the 'Dunbar' (Done Bar) of the last poem in *Pearl* and elsewhere, and indeed the 'Barred windows, bedlam' of the locked ward.

Pearl's reappearance not only reminds us that several significant settings in *Demons* are rural, enacting the oscillation between town and country within the frame of the book, but also that her cleft palate has already prefigured the central demonic figure, introduced in the opening poem as 'the Demon with the Mouth of Rustling Knives'. This Demon appears to symbolise the insatiable thirst of the alcoholic (most graphically illustrated in 'Nil By Mouth: The Tongue Poem'), and Pearl's thirst is conceived in similar terms in 'Fever' from the earlier collection (p.203):

> She opens her swan mouth and rain pour in from north
> and south and west, Atlantic squalls from Donegal.
> They cannot lubricate her speech.
> A baked canyon there, my Pearl.

Just as *Pearl* supports the identification of MacSweeney with earlier suffering writers, so too the demons are associated with repressive social forces, becoming KGB and 'Stasi demons' in 'gin-soaked bat-packed overcoats', and 'beating demon daddies'. The familial context is explored most thoroughly in 'Daddy Wants To Murder Me', a poem which, although it cites Plath, would seem to owe as much to the influence of Paul Durcan's *Daddy, Daddy*, particularly the agonised but surreal narrations of 'Ulysses', 'Geronimo' or 'Glocca Morra':

> The sun was going down in the west over the Phoenix Park
> Where Daddy and me
> ('Daddy and I' – he corrects me –
> He was a stickler for grammar)
> Played all sorts of games for years...
> Before he got into his Abraham-and-Isaac phase
> And I got the boat to England...[6]

Not only do father and son play similar language games ('Daddy you personally put the sin in syntax'), but MacSweeney reverses Durcan's flight, returning in his imagination to the source of the Irish rain that falls on Pearl ('the rains of Sparty flower all the way from the ferry landings of / Ireland'), and finding it a cold sectarian space (pp.228-9):

> ...the stricken wastes
> of Crossmaglen and ugly Strabane, in the permanent borders
> of crossfire, bull-horn warnings, rain-dulled crackle of
> walkie-talkies barely heard from soaking ditches, and the cross-hairs
> of my heart...

The father, explicitly identified earlier with the main demon ('you Demon With Knives In The Mouth, / daddy'), is here associated with paramilitaries, completing a nexus of oppressive forces which are associated equally with MacSweeney's alcoholism and his creativity: 'What goes through my cross-hairs heart at this time, in the final trudge, / Are the beatings and berations, the betrayals of one who expected to / be loved'. As he says in 'Himself Bright Starre Northern Within' (dedicated to a sort of substitute father figure, J.H. Prynne), 'Stop beating me over the head. All I wanted was to write a poem, I / really don't know why' (p.259).

While Pearl and the Demon/Daddy balance and negate each other, MacSweeney is unable to escape the self-destructive cycle. The intercessionary figures of his earlier work either fail him ('all the saints – Bede, Bob, Sexton, Messrs Rotten, Johnson, / Presley and Cash – abandoned me...'), or when, as in 'Anne Sexton Blues', they do make an appearance, it is to provide the poetic equivalent of the Last Rites: 'She put her gluey lips to mine, absolutely / lipstick and vine, / someone grieving kissing a person / about to be dead in Tumble Down Town' (p.221; p.263).

The resulting stasis means the book deliberately engages in a lot of repetition, managed formally by two oscillatory devices: parataxis of imagery, and a constant renaming of the drunken self which amounts to a series of virtuoso variations on the theme of self-castigation. Thus, in 'Nil By Mouth' we have a set of painfully graphic images for thirst focused on the vulnerability of the tongue (p.237):

> bladderwrack tongue late of the ebbingtide pools, salt on the rocks,
> tongue of the deep sea trawler lick hull clean department,
> tongue out on rent as a dog's public park hard-on, for
> artists to paint in glory of its pinky stiffness and quality
> as blotting paper for anything as long as it's a double on the rocks.

The litanies of names demonstrate MacSweeney's genius for combining compressed cultural allusion with an abusive, incantatory colloquiality: 'Swanne, Ludlunatic, Moonyswooney, Madstag, Lenin

Wolfboy...' 'Pookah Swanne MacSweeney...' 'Nightjar Sweeno'
'Anti-Lazarus Ludlunatic lolltongue Lollard...' 'Sweeney Furioso...'
(p.238; p.266; p.269; p.273; p.277).

This stasis is broken by the appearance of Jackie Litherland, the
book's dedicatee and the addressee of the prefatory 'Ode', which
tells us that the demonic nightmare does indeed end and that the
book will therefore achieve a (temporary) narrative resolution.
That poem concludes with a vibrant image which links Litherland
both to the city and to Chatterton (note the spelling of 'starre')
(p.219):

> ...a dearest darling spring when we will start again and the curtains
>   will not be drawn at dawn beneath the monumental viaduct of the
> great engineer. The truly great span of the legs above the city, spread
>   and wide, rodded north and south and electrified by power passing
> through beneath the novas and planets and starres. Magnetised!

Here the emotional register depicts the Durham viaduct in un-
ambiguously sexualised terms at a redemptive point of renewal:
both dawn and spring are cited (albeit in a precautionary future
tense), suggesting that the ordeal about to be recounted, together
with the demons to be encountered, can be conceived of as a sort
of *Saison en Enfer*. Rimbaud ends his poem on a similar auroral
and urban note: 'Recevons tous les influx de vigueur et de tendresse
réelle. Et à l'aurore, armés d'une ardente patience, nous entrerons
aux splendides villes.' [7] And in the crux poem in *Demons*, 'Up A
Height And Raining', MacSweeney uses pathetic fallacy to extend
his inebriation not just to society, but to the season (p.276):

> O look at the golden leaves retrieved from the pink-sleeved trees
> by the very act of the earth and its seasons.
> They are bronze and gold, how very precious and horizontal
> they are this regal collapsed November.
> Look how they fall from the trees, quite drunk
> with an unknown dream of renewal.

Litherland's voice resonates through *The Book of Demons*, chal-
lenging the despairing poet to acts of resistance and their equivalent,
acts of love. These are often framed in relation to the most idealised
of MacSweeney's self-images: 'I&I // myself am in a poisoned /
corner, Chatterton-style' (p.247). Famously, Chatterton poisoned
himself at seventeen, just as Rimbaud renounced poetry before the
age of twenty, and Litherland rebukes the poet, poisoning himself

with alcohol while lingering in a state of arrested development: 'And she said: that's the story / of your life. Almost man'.

Her presence is often heralded by Chattertonian constructions ('swannes mate for life'), and a principal event from her life, the burning of Coventry Cathedral in the Second World War, is absorbed into MacSweeney's mythos of hellfire and damnation in 'The Horror' where, as in the *Pearl* poems, he absorbs her voice: 'Nazi airmen torched my childhood / cathedral; me in a shelter, afraid / of flames and fire, as you are now...' (p.255; p.242). We are shown that she alone sees the poet as an unheroicised figure, not collecting awful images and epithets to characterise (and partly valorise) his addiction, but simply suffering (p.243):

> For many days, my man, you were
> a man with a many-layered mask.
> You did not want to know me and
> again as I arrived and arrived you
> bent your head and heart away...

This resistance to Litherland 'seeing everything so damned War-wickshire clearly' gives way in 'Himself Bright Starre Northern Within' and 'Sweeno Sweeno' to moments of unmasking, of attempting to get beyond the chains of both addictive behaviour and identity that have led to the crisis in which he finds himself: 'There was a six-feet man delete with a single silver argent starre. / He cast a long black shadow, high-heeled, & unfortunately, it was me' (p.256; p.261). MacSweeney's use of the totemic terms 'argent' and 'starre' – together with 'sunne' 'moone' 'bloode' and 'buttercoppes' always indicates points of Chattertonian intensity, and therefore points at which he is confronting the pantheon of personae he has built up for himself since adolescence – here the tall rock-star sheriff is seen to cast a destructive shadow in a sort of reversal of Jungian psychology: the persona projects the self.

In 'Sweeno, Sweeno' this self-image vacillates between the literally catastrophic drinker and the youthful innocence of the lover (p.269):

> Sweeno the Olympian champ diver down 20 stairs half an inch
> from a broken neck. Seaweed Sweeno the man on the rocks a wreck.

> Yet there's another side to Sweeno, the man with eyes of borage blue,
> the man high up in the heather hills with his Grace Darling...

And in 'Up A Height And Raining' the same turning and returning is enacted from the drunkenness of the November leaves to the apotheistic self-titling as 'Sweeney Furioso', the epic hero driven mad by unfulfilled love, to the return to Sparty Lea and Pearl: 'Here at the west window is the speaking for Pearl / ...She sails / in galleons of light all the way to Dunbar'. At this point there is a reprise of the ecstatic redemptive love-making with which *The Book of Demons* opens, in which, again, meteorological and railway imagery serve to unite both urban and rural landscapes ('electric discharge between clouds, / fecund trenches and moss cracks. / Zig-zag bones and branch-lines fully displayed...'). Malevich and the Russian Revolution also make an allusive return in the line 'Our passion, darling, is pure 1917...' and the poem ends with a return to Chattertonian erratography: 'our souls brilliant kisses and everlasting starres' (pp.275-9).

It is very interesting that *The Book of Demons* does not end on this note, but requires further poems to be complete. The first of these, 'Tom in the Market Square Outside Boots' is, on first reading, a compassionate, empathic study of a fellow alcoholic which appears to relate him to the figure of Poor Tom in *King Lear* (p.280):

> Tom I saw you in the Heart Foundation shop
> buying a cardigan five sizes too big.
> Tom you're more bent over than when
> we sat together in the locked ward.
> Tom your coat is frayed like the edges of your mind.
> Tom they let you out to the chippy but you're not free.

As with the identification of *Pearl* with the medieval poem, this gestures toward placing *The Book of Demons* within the English canon, and indeed it is illuminating to compare MacSweeney's ranting persona with Lear raving on the heath, but it also hints at further readings. Poor Tom of course is another persona, adopted by Edgar as a way of approaching and protecting his father Gloucester and the father figure of Lear. As Edgar says

> My face I'll grime with filth,
> Blanket my loins, elf all my hair in knots
> And with presented nakedness outface
> The winds and persecutions of the sky.
> The country gives me proof and precedent
> Of Bedlam beggars...[8]

Here both nature and nation give Edgar inspiration for his role, and it would make seem to make sense to cast MacSweeney as Lear in such a scenario. Except he actually alludes more strongly to Hamlet in a passage densely packed with allusions to separate parts of that play: 'Tom are you mad by north-north-west / or do you know a hawk from a handsaw? / ...all the peeping spirits / have ascended to your brain / like region kites...' (p.282). Here is a second allusion to feigned madness, or rather to the relationship between it and actual madness, and it cautions us from making easy identifications. There is another reading, as the final poem makes clear.

'John Bunyan to Johnny Rotten' is more a type of psychic journey from the state of mind of the Pilgrim to that of John Lydon than, as its title might suggest, an epistolary poem. But it is still addressed to someone, and that someone is still called Tom. The season of the poem is still the late autumn of both 'Up a Height And Raining' and Rimbaud's 'Adieu', and the poet declares himself to be 'not a poker-hearted Pooka. In sober raindawn reality I'm a cress-hearted man'. In Seamus Heaney's translation of *Buile Suibhne*, *Sweeney Astray*, the mad king lives on watercress, traditionally a cure for madness.[9]

Rendered sane, then, through the intercession of a determined woman, MacSweeney declares the terms of his sanity: 'I walk alive alone in Alston and lean against the menu of the Bluebell Inn / because it *is* mine'. A few lines later he repeats this unusual act of emphasis: 'This place, Tom, *was* a nation, making trains and ships and cranes...' (p.284). This place, *contra* Peter Barry, is a region: a territory including both cities and Pearl's countryside, Newcastle, Durham, Sparty Lea, and Alston – the latter of which just happens to be where, by this period, the poet Tom Pickard had settled. Pickard is referred to as 'Tom' by both Bunting in 'What the Chairman Told Tom' and by MacSweeney himself in 'On The Apology Owed Tom Pickard' from *Our Mutual Scarlet Boulevard*.

It would seem that a more complex interpretation of the interrelation between Lear and Poor Tom is being referred to here. Especially as Bunting then makes only his second overt appearance in *The Book of Demons*: 'I want to swing on my starres by Bunting...' (p.286). The earlier reference, in 'Nothing Are These Times', prefigures this starry imagery with a reference to section V of Bunting's *Briggflatts* ('Betelgeuse, / calling behind him to Rigel'):

'Each bouncer's waistcoat gemstarred / with fragments of Bunting Betelgeuse' (p.253).

When MacSweeney refers to Betelgeuse in the coda to 'Colonel B' he terms it his 'central star', continuing 'Justice as geography of the soul' (p.93). It would seem that what we are witnessing here is the completion of a larger cycle than that enacted by the rest of *The Book of Demons*, one in which MacSweeney's legitimacy as an heir of Bunting is being insisted upon. As Rebecca A. Smith points out in her study of MacSweeney's relationship with Bunting (and Pickard):

> it is clear from the marked disparity between MacSweeney's ambiguous allusions to his fellow poets and their vociferous celebrations of each other that he undoubtedly – and most likely deliberately – occupied the position of marginalised 'other' in this equation.[10]

Recovery from addiction for MacSweeney seems also to mean recovery of a status lost almost at the outset of his writing career – not just the innocence of Pearl, but the restoration of his original inheritance. Edgar adopts the persona of Poor Tom because he has been driven out by his father Gloucester through the machinations of his illegitimate brother Edmund. Whether MacSweeney is systematically assigning roles or, as so often, adopting and absorbing personae and voices, is less important here than the sense of his career-long psychodrama of influences reaching a point of resolution in tandem with the recovery from addiction.

The poem and the book end not just with a line in engorged upper case echoing the Sex Pistols' mocking 'God save the Queen!' but also with a sadly reiterated acceptance of mortality, 'we'll never see Christmas...' (pp.289-90). In this contrast of registers there is something of both Edgar's grim pronouncement 'Ripeness is all' and Gloucester's mournful reply, 'And that's true too'. In the decision to include both elements, to end on an oscillation between rebellious major assertion and elegiac minor disquiet, we see MacSweeney's particular restless genius. His unique position in British poetry, unsettled and unsettling, can only be provisionally located between all given states of mind, the socio-cultural territories of north and south and the simplistic oppositions between mainstream and experiment which continue to bedevil – or rather to be-demon – contemporary poetics.

TERRY KELLY

Not Dark Yet: Barry MacSweeney, Bob Dylan and the Jesus Christ Almighty

They sang 'Danny Boy' at his funeral and the Lord's Prayer.
   – Bob Dylan, *Foot of Pride*

Christmas Day, 1994. My dad's dying in hospital and the family has spent the day trying to shore-up Mam, who's not fooled for a second by our buoyant festive patter. Dad's illness has cast a shadow over the festivities and when we drop mam off, the house echoes with his absence. By nine o'clock, I'm more than ready for a drink. I grab a lager from the fridge and collapse into a chair. The phone rings. At first, I think it's Mam again, perhaps tearful again, saying she's lonely again, saying she wants someone to 'come round' again. Mam's sad mantra was as familiar as a tinselly carol that cold Christmas. But it wasn't Mam, it was Barry MacSweeney, poetic lone wolf of contemporary British verse, charismatic Geordie working-class cultural hero, devotee of J.H. Prynne and Newcastle United, legendary nocturnal telephonemeister and, when drunk, a monumental pain in the arse. And drunk Barry was, shouting some darkly ironic festive greeting down the telephone before demanding the title of a Bob Dylan song – any song, any period – with which he would duly *regale me on that cruel Yule. Great. The end of the perfect Christmas Day*, I thought: *Dad dying in hospital, my heartbroken mam in emotional bits and Geordie literary maverick Barry MacSweeney, high on red wine, demanding Bob Dylan song titles like some demented festive busker.* I tensed up, aware of the dregs of a dreary Christmas Day ebbing away as my glass of lager grew warmer in my hand. I let out a slow, calibrated sigh, considered telling Barry Patrick Mac-Sweeney to fuck right off, then remembered what day it was. Sympathy, or its pale shadow, broke through for just a split-second.

I imagined Barry alone in his rather nondescript house in Denton Burn, Newcastle, surrounded by half-empty wine bottles and left-field, slightly musty poetry collections and forgotten literary mags, watching Bruce Willis bandage his bloody feet for the thousandth time in a scuffed video of *Die Hard*, whose script Barry seemed to have memorised. Wilting to the inevitable, I leave Barry hanging on the line, while I hunted out a copy of Dylan's *Lyrics*. But it's getting late, I'm grieving for Dad in advance and the thought of Barry slurring his way through all 91 lines of 'Sad-Eyed Lady of the Lowlands' filled me with horror. What I needed was something from Dylan's country music sabbatical, so I seized on 'Sign on the Window' from Dylan's 1970 album, *New Morning*. A perfect choice, I thought: just three shortish verses of plaintive, blue collar poetry and a lovely, evocative bridge, about the rain on Main Street and Dylan hoping that 'it don't sleeeeet'. Surely the sozzled Santa of Denton Burn would race through this lesser-known number from the vast back catalogue of His Bobness. But Barry had other ideas, transforming the country haiku into an elongated Geordie dirge: 'Sign...on the...wind-ow says 'Lone-ly' / Sign...on...the...door said 'No Comp-a-ny All-ow-ed'. The lager felt like a flaming brandy in my clammy palm.

Barry MacSweeney and Bob Dylan went back a long way. While still days away from his 25th birthday, a stick-thin Dylan, looking like a rock 'n' roll alien with Daliesque hair, appeared at the Odeon Cinema, Newcastle, on Saturday, May 21, 1966. Backed by The Hawks (a largely unknown rough and tumble bar band from Canada, later to enter rock mythology as The Band), Dylan opened with his usual acoustic set, before being joined in the second half by lead guitarist Robbie Robertson, Rick Danko on bass, Richard Manuel on piano, temping drummer Mickey Jones, and the inscrutable musical genius Garth Hudson on organ. In the Newcastle audience that spring night was 17-year-old cub reporter and Dylan fanatic Barry MacSweeney. Although he worked for the Newcastle *Evening Chronicle*, Barry's review would appear in the *Chronicle*'s sister paper, the *Sunday Sun*, the following day. Barry's enthusiastic, teenage critique is still the only review of Dylan's appearance on Tyneside on his iconic 1966 tour, which proved one of the most confrontational in rock history, with the singer systematically booed throughout most of his European itinerary for allegedly "betraying" his folk roots and embracing rock n' roll, Dylan's alleged apostasy reaching an infamous climax when a fan screamed 'Judas!' at the Minnesota bard during his concert at Manchester Free Trade Hall. Ever the contrarian, Barry welcomed electric Dylan with glee, in a review headlined 'A New-Look Bob Dylan Electrifies':

> Bob Dylan, in whatever musical category, is an electrifying performer. That was revealed at last night's concert at the Odeon Cinema, Newcastle. The first half was devoted to folksy numbers and the new, cool-looking Dylan, in black suit *and boots to match*, with his barbed wire haircut, was excellent. He sang some of his more established numbers, like 'She Belongs To Me,' the unforgettable 'Mr Tambourine Man' and 'Desolation Row.' His 'Visions of Johanna' and 'Hamlet Revisited' [sic] were poignant (unusual for Dylan) and, more often than not, tongue-in-cheek. The second half saw him backed by a five-piece beat group, and for my money this was the most exciting half with, for a finale, the immortal 'Like A Rolling Stone.'

Barry's was the only detailed evidence of Dylan's Newcastle gig for another 39 years, until the release of the Martin Scorsese documentary, *No Direction Home*, in 2005. A DVD of the movie included a glorious extra: previously unseen footage of Dylan performing 'Like A Rolling Stone' in front of teenage poet and rock music obsessive Barry MacSweeney. Seeing Dylan's incendiary performance for the first time immediately made me think of Barry sitting in the cavernous Odeon Cinema four decades before, surrounded by grumpy folk fans in Aran jumpers and peeved undergraduates, muttering discontentedly about their former folk protest hero "selling out" to the pop charts. Reviewing *No Direction Home* in the UK Dylan magazine, *The Bridge*, I wrote how 'Barry would have loved seeing the footage in all its crystal clear, DVD glory, with the sound of those raw Geordie voices ringing around Dylan's ears as he dives into the limo. The performance is the high point of *No Direction Home* footage. Amphetamine fog on the Tyne'. When I interviewed Barry in 1998 about the confrontational gig and his review, he recalled:

> It was vitriolic spite. And it was so loud, it was astounding. I remember thinking: This is it. Some athletes talk of getting "zoned" when they hit their peak. It felt just like that. Dylan and Robbie Robertson had their guitars really close to each other, just getting off on the riffs, like they were shagging each other, Robertson grinning from ear to ear.

Whether real or imagined – Barry being prone to flights of fancy – he also recalled afterwards blagging his way into the Turk's Head hotel, in High Bridge, Newcastle, where Dylan and the Hawks were staying. He babbled about liking Rimbaud and about seeing Allen Ginsberg at the Morden Tower to a taciturn Dylan, who apparently ignored the young Newcastle poet before ordering some English tea.

I purposely italicised '*and boots to match*' in Barry's critique. A dandy from an early age, Barry was also something of a shoe fetishist. One of the first things to catch his eye about Dylan, particularly during the singer-songwriter's electric annus mirabilis of 1965-66, were his sharp suits and more particularly, his black suede boots. Dylan's hip footwear would inspire a MacSweeney magazine (which failed to materialise) and later Barry's own poetry imprint, as he explained in an interview with Eric Mottram in December 1974 (*Poetry Information*, Number 18, Winter/Spring 1977-78): 'It was going to be a magazine called the Blacksuede Boot, and have a photograph of Bob Dylan's black suede boot on the front'. In the same interview, he refers to 'completely finished' American rock stars living in lavish seclusion, and adds that 'there's only person that's survived out of that lot and that's Bob Dylan'. Several Mac-Sweeney titles would be published using the Dylan-inspired imprint, Blacksuede Boot Press, namely *The Last Bud* (1969), *Joint Effort* (with Pete Bland, in 1970), *Flames on the Beach at Viareggio* (1970), *Fools Gold* (1972), and a final hurrah with the revival of the press for Emma McGordon's *The HANGMAN and THE STARS* (2000).

Dylan, like Jim Morrison, Robert Johnson, Jerry Lee Lewis or Johnny Cash, formed part of the mytho-poetic or cultural iconography of Barry's work. His poetry is studded with references to rock, blues and country music. *Just Twenty Two – And I Don't Mind Dyin': The Official Poetical Biography of Jim Morrison* (Curiously Strong, 1971) references not only the Lizard King of the title, but also The Who's Pete Townsend, Stevie Winwood, Keith Richards of the Rolling Stones, Eric Burdon from Tyneside band The Animals and, as initial inspiration for the song title, blues great Willie Dixon.

A child of the 1960s, music remained a vital component of Barry's literary imagination throughout his life. But Dylan was

160

there at the beginning and end of Barry's poetic adventure. In *Flames on the Beach at Viareggio*, the third Blacksuede Boot Press collection, published in 1970, we find the first Dylan reference, in a poem dated April 10, 1968, and set at Newcastle's Central Station:

You leaning from the train window
arms outstretched
      & I leaned up
          to kiss the wet cheek
      & feeling like a moving
Bob Dylan LP cover I stood on the
          bridge parapet

In his second collection, *Our Mutual Scarlet Boulevard* (Fulcrum, 1971), we find Barry quoting from 'Absolutely Sweet Marie', from Dylan's classic 1966 *Blonde on Blonde* album, in the title poem:

          no outlaw (as the man said
your position in that case contradicts itself
'to live outside the law you must be honest'

And one of several short lyrics entitled 'poem' (*Our Mutual Scarlet Boulevard*, p.76) borrows heavily from Dylan's strung-out, night-marish travelogue, 'Just Like Tom Thumb's Blues', from the equally ground-breaking 1965 album, *Highway 61 Revisited*. Where Dylan speaks of 'picking up Angel who / Just arrived here from the coast', Barry rewrites this into disjointed narrative, noting how

    Annie
has been thanked   has perhaps
returned (broken   to the coast

before truncating and slightly misquoting Dylan's original line ('and negativity don't pull you through') as 'and negativity won't pull...'.

Barry cherished many other musical heroes, especially following the explosion of punk music in the middle of the 1970s. 'Far Cliff Babylon', from 1978, makes this debt explicit (p.78):

          When
I see the Sex Pistols in my dreams I
   roll into the garden of a small
      nightmare,
    looking for holidays in the
      sun.

That final line is an allusion to a Sex Pistols track, and the shape and form of much of Barry's poetry of the late 70s and early 80s assumes a rebellious, spiky, socially aware, panoptic or cut-up aspect; almost the literary equivalent of the music produced by another contrarian, Mark E. Smith of The Fall (another Mac-Sweeney favourite). It's easy to see how and why the punk ethic appealed to Barry's bite-the-hand-that-feeds-you nature. Punk represented an erect middle finger in the face of the British establishment and Barry responded to such rebelliousness viscerally. Likewise, he harboured an almost deranged dislike of mainstream English literary culture, or what he once sneeringly referred to in 'No Mercy', an unpublished poem from 1988, as 'The world / completely Faberised'. I still remember the look of disdain on Barry's face when he gave me a lift into Newcastle city centre in 1988, after I deliberately provoked him by revealing I was off to buy a book published that very day: Larkin's *Collected Poems*. But the much-derided gentility principle of the literary mainsteam also found an echo in Barry's divided artistic nature, which was one part street punk and one part cultured aesthete. So while his 'Wild Knitting' is ostensibly a 'State of the Nation bulletin' from 1983, and includes an epigraph from punk era troubadour Elvis Costello, the poem also conjoins 'Sex Pistols & Sibelius' (p.137), and Dylan is again referenced in the poem's closing lines (p.138):

Ravaged
in the corn, strong men
belittled by doubt

Here, Barry alludes to both 'Shelter From the Storm', from Dylan's iconic, marital break-up album, 1975's *Blood On the Tracks*, and 'Where Are You Tonight? (Journey Through Dark Heat)' from *Street Legal* in 1978.

Musical heroes became part of Barry's highly personalised literary myth-kitty. The perfect example of this is *Hellhound Memos* (The Many Press, 1993). Yoking the life of legendary Delta blues singer Robert Johnson (1911-38), with the drugged-up urban wastelands and squalid materialism of Britain in the early 1990s, plus his own battle with the bottle, Barry revels in the kind of schizoid, apocalyptic poetic tropes which would later find fuller expression in *The Book of Demons* (1997). The pamphlet's opening poem is the equivalent of a gruesome greeting from a deranged nightclub bouncer (p.186):

162

Weak-kneed sunk in my blueness, my sun
your sun. My fuck-up, your fuck-up.
My rain, your rain.

All aboard and welcome.

Hellhound Memos coincided with Barry's flirtation – unlikely as it seems for the once avowed atheist – with Born Again Christian evangelism. There are at least two references to Christ routing the money lenders in the temple and several moments where the poems echo to the sound of a kind of rich Christian pastoralism: 'And where, under this heaven, is my Mary?'

There was arguably always something of the severe fundamentalist or condemnatory Calvinist in both Barry's personal and poetic nature, and this came increasingly to the fore in his later work. He was particularly drawn to Dylan's so-called 'Born Again phase' (roughly, 1979 to 1981, encompassing the albums *Slow Train Coming, Saved* and *Shot of Love*), responding to the clearcut morality of the songs and their stark, End Times philosophy. The third poem in *Hellhound Memos* (beginning 'Me the multiplex moron...') perfectly captures this flinty moral certitude: 'I come down like slate-grey rain. That's all. No God available'. (p.187). In these poems we also find the beginnings in the later poetry of what can almost be termed the "fetishisation" of Jesus, who is from now on usually accorded the trademark MacSweeney definite article, as in the description of 'the ruby heart of the Jesus Christ Almighty'.

But Barry's musical obsessions continued to bubble to the surface. So we find The King ('where's your Elvis lipcurl now?', p.187), Hoagy Carmichael punningly transformed into 'bogey Carmichael', Bob Dylan again, Johnny Cash's classic 'Orange Blossom Special' in lower case form, and, of course, the mesmeric but ghostly figure of Robert Johnson himself, whose classic track 'Hellhound On My Trail' inspires both the collection's title and provides its epigraph. Johnson even shares top billing with the Son of God – and the troubled bard of Denton Burn: 'I was at Dunton roundabout / shaking hands with Robert Johnson and the Jesus Christ Almighty' (p.190). Officially, Johnson died of syphilis, outside Greenwood, Mississippi, but probably perished after being poisoned, on August 16, 1938. The blues myth about Johnson selling his soul at the crossroads to acquire his mesmeric musical gift is fully

163

exploited by Barry, who places himself alongside Johnson in Newcastle city centre (p.192):

Red and deep blood running at the Gallowgate crossroads
where Robert Johnson Anne Sexton Barry MacSweeney
hoy fury late chemist kitchen sink rota dead shrimp blues
onto the Olympia...

The late chemist rota is a staple element of regional newspapers, reflecting Barry's journalistic background, while 'Dead Shrimp Blues' was recorded by Johnson in San Antonio, Texas, on November 27, 1936. These lines are also notable for their inclusion of the American poet Anne Sexton, whom MacSweeney invokes as the archetypal doomed poet-martyr, placing her alongside Robert Johnson, Dylan, Johnny Cash, or 'The Killer'. Sexton, who took her own life on October 4, 1974, appears as a kind of surrogate tragic rock singer in 'Anne Sexton Blues' from *The Book of Demons* (p.263):

Woke up this morning
              in Newcastle Wyoming
Atlanta Northumberland
on the glory grain plateaux of Texas
Anne Sexton all around my bed.

While often voicing an antipathy for modern poetry's most famous suicidal poet, Sylvia Plath (perhaps a result of her mainstream literary reputation, or her marriage to the similarly 'Faberised' Ted Hughes), Barry seemed drawn towards the rather melodramatic and doomed figure of Sexton, whose name is meant to carry the same charismatic weight as Dylan or Cash or The King, and whose book titles contain a fated, MacSweeneyesque echo: *The Awful Rowing Toward God, The Book of Folly, The Death Notebooks.*

In his own blurb for *The Book of Demons*, Barry makes the Blakean distinction between *Pearl* as the product of 'pure lyrical innocence' and the 'book of hard relentless experience' that is *The Book of Demons.* While there is occasionally some poetic overlap between the two sequences, it's certainly true that *Demons* is the more worldly-wise and variously populated of the two books. While centrally concerned with Barry's battle with booze and the demonic impulses released as a result of that struggle, the sequence is also populated by Barry's fairly consistent musical dramatis personae, plus the Venerable Bede: 'and all of the saints – Bede, Bob, Sexton,

Messrs Rotten, Johnson, / Presley and Cash – abandoned me' ('Free Pet With Every Cage', p.221). These figures are supplemented with walk-on parts for Jerry Lee Lewis, country singer George Jones, folk and blues great Huddie Ledbetter (better known as Lead Belly), 'Blind Willie Milton' (a neat conjunction of the great poet and Blind Willie McTell), Muddy Waters, and even a deranged version of French singer Maurice Chevalier: 'And the leaves in the trees seem to whisper Louise because they're nuts Tom' ('From John Bunyan to Johnny Rotten', p.288).

With very few exceptions, Barry leaned towards musical heroes distinguished by both greatness and by lives lived *in extremis*, with Elvis Presley (or 'the Memphis Flash') and Jerry Lee Lewis being perfect examples. The mythology of blues or rock music seemed to appeal to Barry. The often dark nomenclature of rock or country music sated Barry's appetite for what can be called aesthetic melodrama, attracting him to such sobriquets as 'the Man in Black' (Johnny Cash) and 'the Killer' (Jerry Lee Lewis). Similarly, he felt an affinity for female singers like Tammy Wynette or Dusty Springfield, whose lives and material seemed touched by tragedy, or infused with a defining musical melancholia.

Bob Dylan features at various points throughout *The Book of Demons*. Often, Dylan's song titles or lyrics are alluded to in an almost unconscious fashion, as though Barry has absorbed the words of a song and filtered or transformed them via his nightmarish poetic vision. Thus, the poem 'Angel Showing Lead Shot Damage', contains the following lines (p.230): 'And one last gargle before the screws / are twisted in'. The lines echo Dylan's apocalyptic 1983 track, 'Foot of Pride': 'Say one more stupid thing to me before the final nail is driven in', and Barry uses the selfsame Dylan quotation as an epigraph to an unpublished poem called 'Pearl's Prayer Hits The Classifieds', which is a dry-run for 'Sweet Jesus: Pearl's Prayer'.

Barry was often drawn towards the Christian fundamentalism evidenced in Dylan's first and quite startling 'Born Again' album, *Slow Train Coming*, released in 1979. So 'Strap Down In Snowville' both quotes from Dylan's severe hymn to self-censure, 'Gonna Change My Way of Thinking' ('Stripes on your shoulders, stripes on your back & on your hands', p.268), before cross-referencing 'Daddy Wants To Murder Me' from elsewhere in the collection:

'Strips & stripes & little books & daddy's tearing flaring point of view'. More explicit still is this verbatim quotation from Dylan's epic song 'Isis' (from *Desire*, 1975): 'What / drives me to you is what drives me / insane' ('Demons In My Pocket', p.239). This poem also includes an allusion to the classic track 'Dark Was the Night (Cold Was the Ground)', a song sent into space on board Voyager One in 1977, as performed by fundamentalist Christian and blues great Blind Willie Johnson (1897-1945), another artist whom Barry co-opted into his highly personal musical, literary and mythological pantheon. Often, folk or blues music lines are submerged or transmuted within a poem, as in this echo of Pete Seeger's mid-1950s civil rights anthem, 'Where Have All the Flowers Gone?': 'O, SAS, where are you now? / Gone to an alcohol oasis every one' ('Demons Swarm Upon Our Man And Tell The World He's Lost', p.245). *The Book of Demons* also alludes three times to the Dylan track, 'I and I', from the 1983 album *Infidels*, which itself sounds like the title of an unpublished MacSweeney poetry collection. The song's chorus appealed to Barry's taste for moral or philosophical despair:

I and I
In creation where one's nature neither honours nor forgives
I and I
One says to the other, no man sees my face and lives

The Bob Dylan references, allusions and straight quotations accelerate in Barry's later work. In *Horses In Boiling Blood* (Equipage, 2004), Barry's posthumously published and freewheeling adaptations of Apollinaire, he declares: 'My tongue has not yet flicked along the holes of a harmonica / I don't want gunnes I want Bob Dylan and Emmylou Harris' ('Troubled Are These Times'). Elsewhere in the book, he references the apocalyptic, post-Born Again nature of much of Dylan's work, relating how 'I looked forward to the End Times just like Bob' ('The Vows'), and the brilliantly panoramic 'The Man who walks' opens with a reference to *The Basement Tapes* track 'Open the Door, Homer', which Dylan recorded in the autumn of 1967 with The Band: 'Open the door Richard I'm rocked by continual weeping'. In December 1998, Barry sent me a small batch of poems stapled together and bearing a highly pointed epigraph from the Dylan track 'Man in the Long Black Coat', from *Oh Mercy* (1989): 'Every man's conscience is vile and depraved'. The selection contained an uncollected poem called 'Fog, Amphetamines, Pearl', which is a condensed version of the lines 'Till she sees finally that she's like all the rest / With her fog, her amphetamines and her pearls', from 'Just Like a Woman' (*Blonde on Blonde*, 1966). The poem begins with an allusion to another classic track from the same album, 'Visions of Johanna': in Barry's poem, we hear Dylan's 'How can I explain? / Oh, it's so hard to get on' dovetail with the famous line from Elizabeth Barrett Browning's *Sonnets From the Portuguese*:

> How can I explain how much I love you?
> Let me count the many ways we walk
> down from the hush

The Dylan track 'Love Sick' (from *Time Out Of Mind*, 1997) had its Blakean title repeatedly alluded to and brooded over in the later poetry. It appears in the unpublished 'Letter to Pearl', which revisits old territory in childhood before sounding this disconsolate note of lost love:

> there is only one wonderful smell on the earth and into the earth
> and it is your urine pouring in the ground fast and quick after milk
> I love it I love you I'm love sick I love you when shall we meet again

Then there is the late and uncollected selection of poems which was given the collective title 'Sick of Love', opening with 'Ode: Sick of Love', dating from December 1998, which namechecks Pearl, Anne Sexton, and the female blues singer Memphis Minnie, before alluding to Robert Johnson again: 'I need the Gallowgate crossroads I need the bus / I need the contract for the 12-bar blues'. The similarly late and decidedly offbeat *Postcards From Hitler* (Writers Forum, 1998) refers to 'my beautiful Italian 1966 blacksuede boots'. Barry never lost his ability to pluck a Dylan line or title from his musical memory-bank and employ it as a poetic springboard. Thus, the poem 'Clouds Unbounded By Laws' (written on February 5, 2000, and published in *Tears in the Fence*, Number 28, Spring 2001), adapts its title from an obscure song called 'Lay Down Your Weary Tune', which Dylan recorded on October 24, 1963, during the sessions for *The Times They Are a-Changin'* album and performed only *once*, at Carnegie Hall, two days later. The Dylan verse which sparked Barry's imagination reads:

I stood unwound beneath the skies
And clouds unbound by laws
The cryin' rain like a trumpet sang
And asked for no applause

A MacSweeney sonnet written on November 6, 1998, even employs a verbatim Dylan quote about seeing the great Buddy Holly at Duluth Armory, in Duluth, Minnesota, on January 31, 1959. It was to be Holly's third-last concert. Three days later, after playing his final show at the Surf Ballroom, in Clear Lake, Iowa, the 22-year-old rock icon died when his plane crashed into a cornfield. Barry's title captures the sense of artistic connection Dylan clearly felt with Holly: 'I Was Three Foot From Buddy Holly And He Looked At Me'. At such times, Barry's work is stimulated by eavesdropping on rock mythology. Barry was both a self-elegist and a self-mythologist, forging poetic gold from often the most base metal. It's not unkind but accurate to suggest he was a *creative liar*, his poetry often inhabiting an alternative reality, where Robert Johnson or Bob Dylan or Memphis Minnie or Blind Willie Johnson breathed the same air as The Boy from the Green Cabaret.

I spoke to Barry for the last time on Monday, May 9, 2000: the day he died. As usual, he rang me at work, wanting to talk, and ignoring the clock. As we say on Tyneside, he had a drink on him and was keen to chide me for giving him some alleged duff information about a new Dylan album, *The Best of Bob Dylan – Volume 2*, released just the day before. *Why*, Barry wanted to know, *did you tell me that the album was a double and that it contained a second CD, with some live Dylan tracks, when there's only one CD?* Although we never had a cross word, I could be as sarcastic as Barry, when he was out of order, but I was simply polite during that final conversation, patiently explaining that the live tracks were contained inside the jewel case, *on the other side of the other CD*. There was a long silence and then a Homer Simpson-like 'D'oh!' sound on the other end of the line, before Barry thanked me and rang off, presumably to play his final Dylan tracks: live versions of 'Blowin' In the Wind' and the epic 'Highlands'. On May 17, I listened as the poet J.H. Prynne emerged from his Salinger-like seclusion to deliver the oration at Barry's funeral at John Knox Church, in West Denton, Newcastle. Barry cherished

Prynne, often calling him 'England's greatest poet', and he would have loved to have heard his old friend talk about their early adventures on a motorcycle. Prynne called Barry 'a complete original' and – in a wonderfully apt and strangely tender phrase – 'bat-eared'. Apart from 'Jerusalem', 'When I Survey the Wondrous Cross' and 'How Great Thou Art', another kind of hymn rang out at the service – a recording of Bob Dylan's 'Slow Train': 'There's a slow, slow train comin' up around the bend'.

S.J. LITHERLAND

Barry MacSweeney: A Life In Headlines

Barry MacSweeney believed himself polarised between two selves:
the tender-hearted Bar of borage blue eyes and the blade-mouthed
abuser of himself and others. In *Pearl* and *The Book of Demons*
the two appear apart – one in childhood, the other in adult
experience of pain and failure – but so strongly did they live
together that in a single day Barry could change from one to the
other several times. Between the two was another Barry:
intelligent, sharp, watchful, witty and critical; one who disliked
both the constant appeasement of Bar and the bullying of the
demon Barry. Other identities yet were lurking, including one
rarely glimpsed: a superior, malicious orchestrator of mayhem who
enjoyed the deliberate destruction of hopes and schemes. This self
was the hidden master of ceremonies over Barry's life – probably
the most powerful figure in his lexicon – representing the
authority of addiction and father of his ills.

Barry's life was determined by his extraordinary enthusiasms,
fears, and powerful emotions. His world was full of peaks and
consequently he dreaded the troughs. When the latter approached
it was a signal that an exit was required to return to the levelling
ground zero of his drinker's retreat, which he labelled The Dark
Room or The Ravaged Corner (his second bedroom). His energy
was a tonic, whether it was spent on shopping for a desirable pair
of shoes – he was always very exact: *Grensons* – or recounting his
latest poem during a 4 a.m. phone call to a friend. His despair
was no less self-dramatising. There was a moment in my house
when he seemed to be derailing into madness: 'Can't you see it?
It's printed on my forehead in blue ink,' he told me, shouting: 'I

AM THE NIGHTMARE!' 'No, I can't,' I replied, peering at his head. 'There's nothing on your forehead.' I could see the mad genie dissolving back into the bottle as he took this in. He was smart enough to remember the line and use it in 'Sweeno, Sweeno'.

Barry heightened all his experiences into the language of poetry crossed with the journo's headline; in this way the romance and drama of the newsroom entered his poetics. As news editor he would conduct the clamour of news-gathering, visualising stories pitched into print with attention-seeking titles. He was also a natural reporter, loving the chase and bagging the story. Outside of work, his life was often a continuation of this theme: taking on authority, campaigning; on his lips was always a plan to reform something or other, whether it was rubbish collection or the salvation of Swan Hunter's Shipyard. He carried around the excitement of the newsroom, which is in itself an addiction: the heady rush before a deadline, the low afterwards.

As poet and journalist Barry married the demands of the selves in his head. He was the proud possessor of a photograph of himself at work posing with his typewriter, onto which a fellow reporter had pasted the headline: The World's Biggest Bastard. Hanging behind him is a symbolic cane. The banter of the newsroom, the quips and the comradeship, suited his mischievous sharp tongue and honed the badinage he used in his poems. Zeal and cynicism sit together comfortably at a newsdesk.

His attachment to titles is obvious in the attention he gave to his own name. At the age of 16 he changed his surname McSweeney to MacSweeney because he felt it looked more "Irish". He told me he also wanted to distance himself from his father who had left home: a small name change, but meaningful to the teenager who already had visions of himself as a disaffected trendsetter in the style of James Dean. Barry's ability to invent titles added to the romance of his role-play. He was the self-proclaimed Prince of Sparty Lea who had a double, a dark vengeful doppelgänger, Mr Negative Endless or Mr Nobody. Barry was an expert on his own failings, even his delusions, as he was on his successes and his genius with language. His work is scattered with pithy epithets and laconic humour which leaven *The Book of Demons* with wit and political savvy: Mr Starched White Coat with Himmler clip-board (male nurse) the Great United Quelldom (UK), ICI Bone

171

Marrow City (Middlesbrough). This is not untypical of his take on life. Humour, like romanticism, could be used to transform his travails into something bearable and dignified.

*

Barry took his politics from the 17th century: Republican, Ranter, Leveller. Like Milton and Gerrard Winstanley, who settled the first communist society of Diggers on George's Hill, Barry gave the lie to the notion that parliamentarians only wear the garb of plain language. In Winstanley (Author of *The Law of Freedom* and *Light Shining in Buckinghamshire*) Barry found a common tongue in biblical admonishment: THIS IS THE FILTHY DREAMER AND THE CLOUD WITHOUT RAIN. It could be a line from *The Book of Demons*. This legacy of dissent was vital to Blake's visionary poems and to Walt Whitman's *Leaves of Grass*. Both poets were in the pantheon of Barry's influences and help to explain the Millenarian turns of phrase in his language. Barry also carried in his head the imagery of non-conformist Christianity of his upbringing, which he mimics in his poem 'Tom In The Market Square Outside Boots' (p.281):

> and a spanking new sign on the unused chapel
> Carpenter Wants Joiners.

The Levellers themselves looked back to the Lollards, Wycliffe, *Piers Plowman* and the Peasant Revolt. Hence 'hanging from the greenwood tree' became a recurring motif in Barry's conjuring of past times, alongside his mock-mediaeval spelling and his allusions to Chatterton's endeavours to flatter an age by imitation. In turn the mediaeval poets, especially the anonymous poet of *Gawain and The Green Knight* and *Pearl*, were using the alliterative language of the sagas, the plaiting of context, with the Anglo-Saxon practice of word-kenning to avoid repetition. Pound was another major influence with his admiration for the parataxis of early English poetry, its energy and rhythms. Barry was also deeply versed in Ruskin and Morris, the 19th-century protagonists who dreamt of a commonwealth utopia inspired by pre-industrial England, and he found a soulmate in Shelley, with his cornucopia of rich language, who employed adjectives with the abandonment of a sensualist but with the heart of a stern rebel (and one who could write 'Julian and Maddalo' to mock his predilections).

*

But what of Barry as a young Mod, with his button-down shirts and his penchant for Modernism in literature and Expressionism in painting? In 1968 Parisian students built barricades and tore up cobbles. Barry swore that he was there in a Wordsworthian moment of bliss. He was 20. Around him were the forces to propel him into a lifetime of rebellious energy and departure from safe ground into revolutionary syntax. 'It was a great discovery to realise I could let go of the left hand margin,' he once told me. The Beats, rock 'n' roll, and American Expressionists like Jackson Pollock, had taken off into uncharted regions of Bohemianism: tearing up rules in a post-war declaration of the individual. It was heady, anarchic, fast-living stuff that Barry claimed for himself.

But he was astute enough to lash himself to a job. When Barry became a cub reporter journalists were still a maverick bunch, and colourful characters were prized and protected. It was 'a living' that provided a pay packet but not at the expense of freedom. This freedom – ordained by the news editor – was called 'off the diary' when reporters were expected to live on their wits and nose down stories. The only iron law was the Deadline. Barry's poem 'Wild Knitting' is constantly swinging back to his hours in the newsroom where 'Deadlines / bang me & the phone is hell' (p.136) and he dreams of

> Not living off choirboy
> sex probe with vicar/ disturbing revelations
> that/ workshy teenager who/ stage struck sex
> queen vowed today / all the page three rumour
> gang!

A sense of drama was rarely absent from Barry's wardrobe. Barry strutted his stuff, usually in black suits (he confessed he had nine) and graceful swinging coats. Even on ready-made clothes he bestowed loving labels: My Italian Silk or My French Leather Blouson – such garments were never referred to simply as jackets. A single spot on them would necessitate another journey to the cleaners. He had obsessional purchases: black T-shirts at one time, often kept in unopened bags. His shirts were immaculately ironed each day by Barry on his early watch, about 5 a.m. before he inspected his herb garden. Somehow his treasured shoes were always polished. His appearance at readings would emphasise his love of fashion. I have a memory of Barry reading in Durham in the late 70s dressed in a trendy fair–isle tank top. His hair and glasses always followed the latest styles. Even when nearly bald, he favoured certain haircuts. He would often curtly ring me to recite a list of the clothes he was about to wear: '…loafers with the beef roll …' 'Fine.' Sometimes I had no idea what he was talking about. He would ring off happy.

He was a dandy who had to witness his own fall into The Dark Room, transformed into the nemesis of the abandoned self, living amidst bottles, cursing and crying. This circle of hell was shared with demons dressed in large overcoats and homburg hats and of course shiny shoes. Their coats were lined with rustling bats. At their head was a dwarf with no eyes and no cranium who became The Demon with Mouth of Flashing Blades. The demons' job was to taunt and jeer: manifestations of Barry's abusive tongue turned on himself.

To turn this direst of spectacles into poetry was Barry's great achievement, his riposte, his glorious turning of the tables on the demons as detractors. He wrote them into the script, he gave them starring roles. Having survived numerous periods in de-tox and rehab, he became accustomed to periods of sobriety which gave him the edge he needed, his self-knowledge sharpened. He had built his armoury of language to make his assault. His romantic nom–de–plumes such as Ranter or Finnbar couldn't do the job, so he became Sweeno, Zero Hero, Sweeney Furioso, Anti-Lazarus Ludlunatic lolltongue Lollard, reversing his former poetic roles into anti-heroes, to somehow regain, through the epic grandeur of his language, his pride.

*

Barry in life adopted roles and accents as it suited in his various crusades as a Dashing White Knight. He had the mesmeric power of a confidence trickster. On the phone to one hapless salesman of a faulty watch (the strap had broken) he became a News Agency chappie with a *Daily Telegraph* accent. He asked the salesman to imagine him at Newcastle Airport at dawn summoned to interview some VIP. But at the crucial moment the watch had fallen off his wrist! The salesman invited Barry to his store to choose a watch of his liking as replacement – 'the most expensive in the shop'. Barry acquired one that was waterproof, very flashy and had digital pins he never mastered. On another occasion he came to my daughter's rescue when dumped rubbish from a building site spilled onto the street outside the church in which she was due to be married. The builders laughed in my face when I appealed to them to clean it up. Barry rang the Managing Director of the multi-national company employing the builders. In a no-nonsense professional tone he said he intended to do a story for the papers: 'Which would you prefer: Hard-hearted firm ruins Bride's Day or Kind company saves Bride from Tears? We could do a picture of you and the Bride-to-be in hard hats smiling together?' The MD chose the latter of course and I have the clipping of my daughter and the MD in hard hats in front of the purpose-built fence speedily erected around the tidied site.

He was no less effective against bureaucracy. My son Ben was once unfairly harried by Lewisham Council. The persecution continued until Barry rode to the rescue. He blitzed the Chief Executive's office with faxes. The whole department was in an uproar. We even had our own 'Deep Throat' who rang at midnight to confess that it had been a set-up. 'Where's this going now?' he asked Barry rhetorically and gave his own reply: 'In the bin.' Barry's sense of theatre was catching, or maybe they had all been watching late night TV.

*

As a public reader of his work, Barry was blessed with a lyrical voice emphasised by his lilting Geordie accent. Many of his heroes were rock stars and country and western singers such as Jim Morrison, Johnny Cash and Dusty Springfield. Like them he lived inside the lyric and shared the experience without any sense of embarrassment. There was no curtain between his life, work and performance.

His capacity for creating and staging roles was at its greatest when taking on personae for his poetry. He took the memory of his childhood friend Pearl and absorbed her into his psyche until he became both the mute little girl and the boy teacher who would rescue her from illiteracy. The poem is often seen as an idyll of lost innocence but it is also a transposition of his suffering into the voice of the child afflicted with a roofless mouth. The Pearl role is one of empathy and possession. How much of it is dramatised, how much heightened or invented can only be guessed at. *Pearl* is a poem of childhood, of a beloved landscape, and of current grief.

A very different figure was Guillaume Apollinaire, summoned from the dead to become Barry's companion, confidante, and muse. Barry started translating Apollinaire in 1997 after we visited Paris together, and by 1998 he had written an entire book of 'collaborations' called *Horses in Boiling Blood*. Barry created an amalgam of himself and the French poet, interweaving his poetry with Apollinaire's in an act of modernist homage that was part guesswork, part blithe imagination, and part translation. He drew parallels with Apollinaire's life in the trenches and his own lapses into addiction. The poems fuse into marvellous imagery and extraordinary paratactical juxtapositions linking France with Northumberland, and have a tender, wild humour the poets shared.

*

Barry's love of language was compulsive: his mind never stopped storing words, images and phrases for future use. He would jot down found notices, instructions on labels, remarks from conversation and phrases from books into lists of possible titles. 'Free Pet with Every Cage' came from a sign propped in the window of a closing-down pet shop in Durham. He would often interrupt someone speaking by suddenly exclaiming: 'That's a great title!' When Barry worked on the subs' table, his mind was intent on writing clever headlines. Outside of the industry it is not appreciated how the subs enjoy the creativity allowed to them of writing headlines: it is not the reporter who puts the title on his work. But how did all of these Barrys conspire to write his poetic diction, which was so different from a journalist's straight-talking prose? As a newshound Barry was trained to deliver the word in simple striking sentences using the odd phrase to add "colour". This is an excerpt from his column 'Mouth of the Tyne' (*South Shields Gazette*, 1994):

> This petition, the one that was handed to John Major's flunkey today, is vitally important to Tyneside.
>
> Unless you are a fully paid-up member of the Let's Roll Over and Die Party (stacks of members, still growing), you will know how vitally important this petition is.
>
> This petition is plain and simple: it is a plea from the good folk of Tyneside, who generally do not vote for the Conservative Party, with its twisters and sex maniacs, to save the greatest shipbuilder in the history of the world – Swan Hunter.
>
> The petition asks that this Government, this Conservative Government, with its sacked ministers and failed Cabinet members, and more to be flung on the scrapheap of history in the next reshuffle, awards (a rich word, that) Swan's the order to refit the Royal Fleet Auxiliary troop landing ship Sir Bedivere.

Compare this with an extract from 'John Bunyan to Johnny Rotten' (p.284-85):

> This place, Tom, *was* a nation, making trains and ships and cranes, transporting unlikeables like us to the lands of boomerangs and redrock. Our chainbroken fingers & hands acquainted with hunger & slavering slavery kept together the hulks on the Thames, we were the true breath of the nightforest noosehang land.
>
> Tom, do you remember when lightly but enough to hear I knocked for you at midnight, starres our only light, if starres there were? God help us Tom we enjoyed it, one more Tory burned from his bed.
>
> We stood together with tightly-bridled panting steeds among pooked sheaves laughing until the sunne of togetherness warmed our roof-burning brand-throwing shoulders.
>
> How strong it was Tom, our amusement, as the red-coated militia arrived, long before they drove down the miners in the villages. We blessed Jesus the first Chartist for saving the bairns and the wife.
>
> But the port-soaked Tory was dead, Tom,
>
> and we sang our hymns with clean hearts.
>
> Tom, nothing has changed except everything.

The poet and the newspaperman lived inside his head with all the other multi-personalities. They co-existed and influenced each other. Poems such as 'Liz Hard I' and 'Liz Hard II' and 'Jury Vet' explode into capital letter headlines amidst the clutter of staccato language. The tone has the breezy frenzy of the tabloid journalist coupled with his graceful poetic diction and luminous lists of artefacts. They're tumbling through his mind at breakneck speed, where Old English contractions blend with Punk-like aggression, all of them thrown down on the page with teasing syncopation. What distinguishes the poet from the journalist is the addition of grace. Some sportsmen are renowned for their graceful execution like David Beckham with the curving ball and Ian Bell with his strokeplay. They stand apart from their heartier team-mates and bring beauty to sport. Barry brought beauty of this kind to his poetic line.

The deepest self I knew, at the core of him, was a shy man who might blush easily, a studious type concerned with his library, his record collection, his herb garden and his interest in rare plants. As a child Barry was a train spotter, and he remained a cataloguer. A powerful sense of structure was never missing in his poetry no matter how free the surface. He was always planning sequences and books, interlacing and rearranging them in an obsessive way. This inner self was inhibited by natural reserve and his northern post-war upbringing in a family overshadowed by chapel and church.

Perhaps he found in alcohol the Alice-in-Wonderland door he could open into another world. He told me that when he started drinking at 16 it was like falling in love. There is an innocence at the heart of Barry's poetry. When he refers to himself as Bar (his lifelong nickname) he is indicating a child-like soul within, gentle and prelapsarian. His adult experiences taught Barry daring, verve, intellect, and the multiplying of his more theatrical selves. Something akin to a metamorphosis may have occurred: the awkward shell of shyness dropping away.

Unlike poets who wish to control their voice, Barry gave his voices freedom or licence even. His poetry has a naturalness, an ability to change tone, voice and mood within a single sentence, for example, in this line from 'Don't Leave Me': 'The blitzblack / BirminghamCoventry merle sharpens its cornyellow on the shedend' (p.296). The references in the first part of the sentence are to the Coventry Blitz remembered by his Birmingham-born partner (myself); followed by 'merle': French/archaic word for blackbird; 'cornyellow': colour of blackbird's beak; and 'shedend': a prosaic image, with assonance emphasised by joining the words together. The mood and tone are at variance, and there is both affection and a sense of danger – a row is in the offing. Another line: 'War between ourselves, despite creamteas, you keep abandoning me' (p.297). The switch from note of attrition to the humour of 'creamteas' is to use the sense of the ridiculous in a plea-bargain.

Even extravagant switches are handled with grace and authority: the writing is so multi-layered that thoughts interject, assert, dissent and wander copiously. Their intertwining voices provide an under-composition upon which he can lay further embellishments of inverted or invented syntax, wild punning and word play, kennings, mock-mediaeval spelling, interspersed with jocular vernacular and jokes and capital letters: the whole spiel of the word addict.

The dark twin of the peaceable innocent Bar emerges as counterpoint. This self turns words into weapons: a destructive, scathing voice, often shocking and domineering, who figures in the poetry in many forms, inside and outside his head, goading, sneering, and cynical. In earlier poems it prompts many asides. In 'The Last Bud' it announces its kingdom of darkness (p.19):

> [...] Ahead of me
> is brilliant darkness, and the king
> of night. This is a signed resignation;
> I am finished with your kingdom of light.

Barry's remorse following abusive episodes was deep and profound, for example, 'Finnbar's Lament' is an anguished apologia which stands against the cursing of 'Wild Knitting'. When Barry brought together *Pearl* and *The Book of Demons* into one book of innocence and experience, he was demonstrating a truth about himself learnt from periods of sobriety. In 'Sweeno, Sweeno' he begins by describing the dichotomy within: 'Sweeno is two people – at least...' and continues (p.270):

> But really the truth is less poetic and palatable. This is the acid
> bath boy, the angel with hissing meat right off the bone. Strong
>
> tongued with viper juice, bamboo snake in jungle of his own
> green many-fingered making. Mocker and mucker-up of true
>
> love which dwells in a strong house...

The sparring between the light and the dark intensified with the arrival of the demons in hallucinations and dreams during treatment for alcoholism in 1994. My daughter Rachel had been drawing sketches of demons for her painting *The Temptation of St Anthony*. When he saw them Barry told her: 'These are my demons.' Barry's first demon poem was written while recovering at Durham County Hospital in October of that year. He had permission to walk around the city and found a small office with a typewriter he could borrow. He wrote 'Ode to Beauty Strength and Joy and In Memory of the Demons' without changing a word. The first half of the poem introduces the terrifying head demon (p.218):

> [...] This demon, this gem-hard
> hearted agent of my worst nightmare, this MC with spuriously
> disguised gesture, this orchestrator of ultimate hatred,
> the man with no eyes, no cranium, no brow no hair.
> He will always be known as the Demon with the Mouth of Rustling
> Knives, and the meshing and unmeshing blades
> are right in your face.

That Barry's torturer was also a demonisation of his father can be conjectured. The complicated axis of father and son examined in 'Daddy Wants to Murder Me' confirms that the murder to be committed in that poem is the revenge of the son. The head demon and his troupe dominated Barry's poetry until they were finally burnt out in 1998. The last poem in which they appeared was 'Don't Leave Me' (p.300):

> They have returned & are burning their shadows in movie
> Expressionist fervour: all of those bats – pipistrelles – rustling
> between their overcoated breastblades moving their huge coats
> in terrifying unison. They have a demand in their hands. They
> want me to be part of the torture along the blood-riven waveband.
> They want me me to play a part in their play of the actually dead.
> They now want my liver to explode in a shower of hot bloody starres.
> They want me to die in vain, they want me to fax my useless expiration
> to the head demon at the top of the stairs. [...]

The 'wave-band' refers to screaming heard on a radio inside Barry's head during visions of the demons.

Barry protected himself from the horrors of alcoholism with the gallows humour journalists tend to develop in a world of "sob stories". *The Book of Demons* uses black humour throughout, so much so that a fellow poet Ric Caddel wondered if Barry actually revelled in his addiction. As this wasn't the case in life, what does the work reveal? How did Barry transpose his shocking experience of mental anguish and strictures of health – he was always breaking his limbs (another feature of alcoholism) – into a gorgeous array of language, a peacock's tail of display?

Barry often said he longed to switch off his addiction. Instead he had the grinding necessity of rehab and relapses. He grieved for his lost life, his curtailed existence, the closing down of his parameters and the likelihood of premature death. But the showman inside him was banging the drum to get up and start each day. In *The Book of Demons* Barry became a self-healer, a shaman, a word wizard who mocked his own illness. This wiser self was allied with the ever-present news-gatherer enjoying the dynamics of having a great story and in league with his muse, the Booze – no longer as a lover, but a clear-eyed ex-lover.

Durham, 2006-07

NOTES ON CONTRIBUTORS

Paul Batchelor was born in Northumberland. At Newcastle University, he wrote an AHRC-funded PhD on Barry MacSweeney's poetry. For the past five years he has made a living as a freelance writer and teacher. He reviews poetry for the *Guardian* and the *Times Literary Supplement*. His first full-length collection of poems was *The Sinking Road* (Bloodaxe Books, 2008). He has received an Eric Gregory Award from the Society of Authors, the Andrew Waterhouse Award, the Arthur Welton Award from the Authors Foundation, the Times Stephen Spender Prize for Translation, and the Edwin Morgan International Poetry Competition. www.paulbatchelor.co.uk.

Andrew Duncan grew up in Loughborough and now lives in Nottingham. He studied Modern Languages and then Anglo-Saxon, Norse, and Celtic at Cambridge, before working in industry for nine years, and then for the Stock Exchange, writing software, for three. His books of poetry include *Cut Memories and False Commands* (Reality Street, 1991), *Sound Surface* (Five Eyes of Wiwaxia, 1993), Alien Skies (Equipage, 1993), *Pauper Estate* (Shearsman, 2000), *Switching and Main Exchange* (Shearsman, 2000), and *Anxiety Before Entering a Room: Selected Poems 1977-1999* (Salt, 2001). Irritated by the lack of recording of modern British poetry, he began a project which includes *The Failure of Conservatism in Modern British Poetry* (Salt, 2003), *Secrets of Nature: Origins of the Underground* (Salt, 2004), *Centre and Periphery in Modern British Poetry* (Liverpool University Press, 2005), *The Council of Heresy* (Shearsman, 2009), and *The Long 1950s* (Shearsman, 2011).

W.N. Herbert is Professor of Poetry and Creative Writing at Newcastle University. He writes poetry and libretti, and is also an essayist, reviewer and translator. He is mostly published by Bloodaxe Books. His recent publications include a collection of poems in two parallel volumes, *Omnesia* (Bloodaxe Books, 2013); an anthology of contemporary Chinese poetry in translation, *Jade Ladder* (Bloodaxe Books, 2012; co-edited with Yang Lian); and the libretto of the opera *AntiMidas* (music by Evangelia Rigaki) for the Beckett Theatre, Dublin.

Matthew Jarvis is the Anthony Dyson Fellow in Poetry in the School of Cultural Studies at the University of Wales Trinity Saint David. He also works on the Leverhulme Trust-funded research project 'Devolved Voices: Welsh Poetry in English since 1997' in the Department of English & Creative Writing at Aberystwyth University. The author of numerous essays and reviews, Matthew's volumes *Welsh Environments in Contemporary Poetry* (2008) and *Ruth Bidgood* (2012) are both published by the University of Wales Press. A volume of his new and selected essays will be published by Parthian Books.

Terry Kelly was born in Jarrow in 1958, and works as a journalist in South Tyneside. He gained degrees from Sunderland University and Newcastle University. He worked with Barry MacSweeney at the *Shields Gazette* for several years, and helped MacSweeney select and edit *Hellhound Memos* (The Many Press, 1993), eventually sharing the collection's dedication with Nicholas Johnson. He writes and reviews regularly for *The London Magazine*, *About Larkin*, the Journal of The Philip Larkin Society, and *The Bridge*, the Tyneside-based Bob Dylan magazine (www.two-riders.co.uk).

S.J. Litherland was born and bred in Warwickshire has lived in Durham since 1965. Her sixth poetry collection, *The Absolute Bonus of Rain* (Flambard, 2010), revisits a forgotten England. *The Homage* (Iron, 2006) was inspired by the final troubled season of former England cricket captain Nasser Hussain. *The Work of the Wind* (Flambard, 2006) charts her turbulent relationship with Barry MacSweeney. Other collections include *The Apple Exchange* (Flambard, 1999), *Flowers of Fever* (Iron, 1992), and *The Long Interval* (Bloodaxe Books, 1986). Her work has appeared in several anthologies, including *New Women Poets* (Bloodaxe Books, 1990) and Forward Book of Poetry 2001. 'Bad Light' from *The Homage* was selected for sports anthology *Not Just a Game* (Five Leaves Press, 2006) and broadcast on Radio 3 in the *Words and Music* series. She has won two Northern Writers' Awards: in 1993 and 2000. Her poems have been commended twice in the National Poetry Competition: 'Songster', in 2003, and 'Springtime of the Nations', in 2012.

Peter Riley studied at Pembroke College, Cambridge, and the universities of Keele and Sussex. He has taught at the University of Odense (Denmark) and from 1975 to 2008 he lived as a freelance writer and poetry bookseller. He has now retired. His publications include *Passing Measures*, *Alstonefield* and *The Glacial Stairway* (all from Carcanet), and *The Day's Final Balance: Uncollected Writings 1965-2006* and *The Llyn Writings* (both Shearsman).

William Walton Rowe is Professor of Poetics at Birkbeck College. He is the founder of the Contemporary Poetics Research Centre, Birkbeck College, a member of the Veer Books editorial group, and founder-editor of *Pores*, a journal of poetics research www.pores.bbk.ac.uk. His recent poetry collections include *The Earth Has Been Destroyed* (Veer, 2009) and *Nation* (forthcoming from Klinamen). He edited *The Salt Companion to Bill Griffiths* (Salt, 2007) and wrote *Three Lyric Poets: Lee Harwood, Barry MacSweeney, Chris Torrance* (Northcote House Publishers, 2009). He has translated many Latin American poets, including Raúl Zurita's *INRI* (Marick Press, 2009), and Antonio Cisneros's *A Cruise to the Galapagos Islands* (forthcoming from Shearsman). He is a fellow of the British Academy, and Doctor Honoris Causa of the Catholic University of Peru. Currently, he is working on *The Books of Bill Griffiths*, an introduction to Griffiths's poetry, and translating the poetry of César Vallejo.

Harriet Tarlo is a poet and academic who lives in Holmfirth, West Yorkshire. Her poetry publications include *Love/Land* (REM Press, 2003), *Poems 1990-2003* (Shearsman Books, 2004) and *Nab* (Etruscan Books, 2005). She also writes academic essays on modernist and contemporary poetry with particular attention to gender and landscape and environment. Essays in books appear in critical volumes published by Edinburgh University Press, Salt, Palgrave and Rodopi. Recent critical and creative work appears in *Pilot, Jacket, Rampike, English* and the *Journal of Ecocriticism (JoE)*. Harriet Tarlo edited a special feature on 'Women and Eco-Poetics' for *How2* Vol 3, No 2 (http:// www.asu.edu/pipercwcenter/how2journal//vol_3_no_2/index.html) and *The Ground Aslant: An Anthology of Radical Landscape Poetry* for Shearsman Books in 2011. She is currently preparing a new collection of poetry with the same press. She is Course Leader for the M.A. Writing at Sheffield Hallam University.

John Wilkinson is an English poet and Professor of Practice in the Arts at the University of Chicago. His latest book is *Reckitt's Blue* (Seagull Books, 2013), and Salt is preparing a selected edition of his earlier volumes. He has published a collection of essays, *The Lyric Touch* (Salt, 2007), and several subsequent essays, chiefly on New York School poets. He has loved Barry MacSweeney's writing since he bought a newly-published *Just Twenty Two and I Don't Mind Dyin'* as a student (it came in a sleeve like a 7" single).

NOTES

HARRIET TARLO

1   There is glorious proof of this in the full version of *Hellhound Memos* in which the protagonist twice meets 'Anne Sexton, Robert Johnson, Barry MacSweeney at the crossroads' (11, and see 19).

2   Eric Mottram, 'MacSweeney/Pickard/Smith: Poets from North-East England interviewed by Eric Mottram', *Poetry Information*, No. 18 (Winter/Spring 1977-78), p.32.

3   William Walton Rowe, *Three Lyric Poets: Harwood, Torrance, MacSweeney* (Tavistock: Northcote House Publishers, 2009), p.80.

4   Mottram, p.24.

5   Marianne Morris, 'The Abused become the Abusers: the Poetry of Barry MacSweeney', *Quid*, 14 October 2004 http://www.barquepress.com/quid14.pdf, pages unnumbered.

6   Jennifer Keith, ''Pre-Romanticism' and the ends of eighteenth-century poetry', *The Cambridge Companion to Eighteenth-Century Poetry*, ed. John Sitter (Cambridge: Cambridge University Press, 2001), p.286.

7   Keith, p.280.

8   John Wilkinson, 'A Single Striking Soviet: The Poetry of Barry MacSweeney', *The Lyric Touch: Essays on the Poetry of Excess* (Cambridge: Salt, 2007), p.83.

9   Where possible, I shall reference *Wolf Tongue*, as it is the most accessible volume of MacSweeney's work. However, where poems and sequences were originally published as single books, I shall give their original dates and italicise them.

10 Mottram, p.25.

11 Clive Bush, 'Parts in the Weal of Kynde', *Out of Dissent: A Study of Five Contemporary British Poets* (London: Talus, 1997), p.313.

12 Andrew Crozier, 'Barry MacSweeney: Tyneside poet who lived out the myth of exemplary failure', *Guardian*, Thursday 18 May 2000, http://www.guardian.co.uk/news/2000/may/18/guardianobituaries

13 See *Wolf Tongue*, pp.28, 40, 68, 83.

14 Peter Barry, 'Barry MacSweeney *Hellhound Memos*', from 'Writing the Inner City', in *Contemporary British Poetry and the City* (Manchester: Manchester University Press, 2000), p.25.

15 Matthew Jarvis, 'Barry MacSweeney's Moorland Romance', *Culture, Creativity and Environment: New Environmentalist Criticism*, ed. Fiona Becket and Terry Gifford (Amsterdam and New York: Rodopi, 2007), p.181.

16 Jarvis, p.186.

17 Jarvis, p.187.

18 Jarvis, pp.189-191.

19 Jarvis, pp.195-6.

20 Jarvis, pp.193-4.

21 Jarvis, pp.191–2.

22 I am surmising here from the powerful presence of this viaduct which rises above the poet's lover's house in Durham City and which also has wires running above it. See also 'Up a Height and Raining' for a further reference to kisses under the 'vast viaduct' (p.279).

23 See *Wolf Tongue*, pp.198, 202, 209.

24 Barry MacSweeney, *Hellhound Memos* (London: Many Press, 1993), p.16.

25 *Hellhound Memos*, p.26.

26 Rebecca A. Smith, 'Barry MacSweeney and the Bunting Influence: A key figure in his literary universe?' *Jacket* 35 (2008) http://jacketmagazine.com/35/smith-macsweeney.shtml p.20.

27 Smith, p.17.

28 Smith, p.18.

29 Smith, p.19.

30 Mottram, p.30.

31 Mottram, p.39.

32 Barry MacSweeney, *Black Torch* (London: London Pride Editions, 1978), p.7.

33 *Black Torch*, p.24.

34 *Black Torch*, p.52.

35 *Black Torch*, pp.67–8.

36 See Morris for an account of this meeting and a convincing reading of its relevance.

37 I have found no evidence that MacSweeney related to Stein, but to me, 'Liz Hard' is a brutal negative reversal of the celebratory and hopeful feminine principle of Gertrude Stein's modernist text, *Lifting Belly*. Both poems of course share the ability to shape shift through endless meanings via repetition of a single phrase.

38 Morris, pages unnumbered.

39 *Black Torch*, p.34.

40 Mottram, p.35.

41 John Bunyan, *Grace Abounding and The Life and Death of Mr Badman* (London: J.M. Dent & Sons Ltd, 1928), p.140.

42 *Hellhound Memos*, p.19.

43 Mottram, p.39.

44 Wilkinson, p.79.

45 Mottram, p.30.

46 A.D. Harvey, *English Poetry in a Changing Society 1780–1825* (London: Allison & Busby, 1980), p.37.

47 Arthur Johnston, *Enchanted Ground: The Study of Medieval Romance in the Eighteenth Century* (London: The Athlone Press, 1964), p.3.

48 Keith, p.278.

49 Harvey, p.37.

50 John Keats, *The Complete Poems*, ed. John Barnard (Harmondsworth: Penguin, 1977), p.189.

51 Harold Bloom, *The Visionary Company: A Reading of English Romantic Poetry*

(Ithaca and London: Cornell University Press, 1971), p.370.

52 Barry MacSweeney, *Elegy for January* (London: Menard Press, 1970), p.24.

53 *Letters of John Keats*, ed., Robert Gittings (Oxford: Oxford University Press, 1970), p.325.

54 *Elegy for January*, p.24.

55 The letter cited by MacSweeney is dated a year after his walking tour of the North of England in 1818, during which his letters reveal his intense interest in working people and their dialect.

56 Mottram, p.33.

57 Mottram, p.39.

58 See *Elegy for January*, pp.13-15, 22; and Mottram, p.32.

59 Paul Batchelor, 'Morphic Cubism: The Strange Case of Gwilliam Mad MacSweeney', *Modern Poetry in Translation* 3:3 (2005), p.131.

60 Wilkinson, p.77.

61 Mottram, p.33 and see Jonathan Williams, 'Some Jazz from the Baz: The Bunting-Williams Letters', *The Star You Steer By: Basil Bunting and British Modernism*, ed. James McGonigal and Richard Price (Amsterdam and Atlanta: Rodopi, 2000), p.262.

62 The copy of *Black Torch* held in the Newcastle University's MacSweeney Archive includes MacSweeney's own notes giving the meaning of North-East words, perhaps a plan for a future annotated edition or emulating Bunting's glossary for *Briggflatts*.

63 Keith, p.278.

64 Keith, p.279.

65 Keith, pp.279-80.

66 Bush, p.320.

67 John Sears, 'Out of Control' (review of *Wolf Tongue*), www.popmatters.com/books/reviews/w/wolf-tongue.shtml

68 Peter Manson, 'Barry MacSweeney *Hellhound Memos*', originally published in *Object Permanence* 1 (January 1994), http://www.petermanson.com/Macsweeney.htm

69 Mottram, p.33.

70 Gordon Burn, 'Message in a Bottle', *Guardian*, 1 June 2000, http://www.guardian.co.uk/books/2000/jun/01/poetry.features

71 Sears, np.

72 Mottram, p.34.

73 Thomas Chatterton, *The Poetical Works of Thomas Chatterton* (London and Newcastle-on-Tyne: Walter Scott, 1885), p.274.

74 Percy Bysshe Shelley, *The Poetical Works of Percy Bysshe Shelley* (London and New York: Frederick Warne, 1888), p.330.

75 Bloom, p.166.

76 William Wordsworth, *The Poems, Volume One*, ed. John O. Hayden (Harmondsworth: Penguin, 1977), p.553.

77 *Elegy for January*, p.22.

78 *Elegy for January*, p.27.

79 *Elegy for January*, p.31.

80 It should be noted that there is an alternative theory about Chatterton that he died after mistakenly taking too large a dose of arsenic as a treatment for syphilis, a theory which MacSweeney chooses to ignore.

81 *Elegy for January*, pp.7, 11, 22.

82 *Elegy for January*, p.23.

83 Rowe, p.81.

84 Rowe, p.83.

85 *Elegy for January*, p.23.

86 *Elegy for January*, pp.31–32.

87 *Elegy for January*, p.21.

88 Keats, p.348.

89 Mottram, p.33.

MATTHEW JARVIS

1 'Northumberland', *Encyclopædia Britannica*, 2008, *Encyclopædia Britannica Online*, 6 May 2008, http://search.eb.com/eb/article-9056270

2 Val Plumwood, *Environmental Culture: The Ecological Crisis of Reason* (London: Routledge, 2002), p.4.

3 Nicholas Johnson, 'Barry MacSweeney – An Appreciation', *Pores*, 1 (October 2001), 14 May 2008, http://www.pores.bbk.ac.uk/1/Nicholas%20 Johnson,%20%20'Barry%20 MacSweeney%20-%20An%20Appreciation'. htm. Sparty Lea – or Spartylea on Ordnance Survey maps – is at NGR (National Grid Reference) NY 855 485.

4 For the classical Orpheus myth, and its subsequent development in English literature, see Geoffrey Miles, ed., *Classical Mythology in English Literature: A Critical Anthology* (London: Routledge, 1999), ch. 4. For the impact of Orpheus's music on inanimate forms see, for example, Ovid's *Metamorphoses*, which recounts that 'On the top of a certain hill was a level stretch of open ground, covered with green turf. There was no shelter from the sun, but when the divinely-born poet seated himself there and struck his melodious strings, shady trees moved to the spot'; when Orpheus has finished singing, Ovid observes: 'By such songs as these the Thracian poet was drawing the woods and rocks to follow him'. See Ovid, *Metamorphoses*, tr. Mary M. Innes (Harmondsworth: Penguin, 1955), pp.227 and 246.

5 Johnson, 'Barry MacSweeney – An Appreciation'. For the year of the 'Sparty Lea Poetry Festival', see 'The Barry MacSweeney Collection', Newcastle University, 14 May 2008, http://www.ncl.ac.uk/elll/research/ literature/macsweeney/

6 See Austin Woolrych, 'ranters', in John Cannon, ed., *The Oxford Companion to British History* (Oxford: Oxford University Press, 1997), p.790.

7 Plumwood, *Environmental Culture*, p.97.

8 The Cheviot is just inside Northumberland itself, at NGR NT 905 205.

9 For Killhope Law – some two-and-a-half miles west of Allenheads and a

little over three to the south-west of Sparty Lea – see NGR NY 819 448.

10 See Austin Woolrych, 'Levellers', in Cannon, ed., *Oxford Companion*, pp. 572-73: p.572.

11 See the entry on 'Lollardy' in F. L. Cross, ed., *The Oxford Dictionary of the Christian Church*, revised 3rd edn, ed. E.A. Livingstone (Oxford: Oxford University Press, 2005), pp.999-1000.

12 See the entry on 'Luddites' in Margaret Drabble, ed., *The Oxford Companion to English Literature*, revised 5th edn (Oxford: Oxford University Press, 1995), pp.601-02.

13 See Andrew Prescott, 'Tyler, Walter [Wat] (d. 1381)', *Oxford Dictionary of National Biography* (Oxford University Press, 2004), 13 December 2012 http://www.oxforddnb.com/view/article/27942. Of course, the reference to 'Man of Kent' also echoes MacSweeney's personal history. As the biographical note in the original volume of *Ranter* indicates, MacSweeney had, by the mid-1980s, 'worked as a journalist on newspapers in Newcastle, Cumberland, London, Kent and County Durham': see Barry MacSweeney, *Ranter* (Nottingham: Slow Dancer, 1985), p.44.

14 See David Rollason and R. B. Dobson, 'Cuthbert [St Cuthbert] (*c*.635–687)', *Oxford Dictionary of National Biography*, (Oxford University Press, 2004), 14 May 2008, http://www.oxforddnb.com/view/article/6976.

15 For Halfdan and his military activity in the North East, see 'Halfdan', *Encyclopædia Britannica*, 2008, *Encyclopædia Britannica Online*, 14 May 2008, http://search.eb.com/eb/article-9038884 and Marios Costambeys, 'Halfdan (*d*. 877)', Oxford Dictionary of National Biography, Oxford University Press, 2004, 14 May 2008, http://www.oxforddnb.com/view/article/49260 – both of which note his presence on the Tyne – and David Rollason, *Northumbria, 500-1100: Creation and Destruction of a Kingdom* (Cambridge: Cambridge University Press, 2003), p.245, which indicates the threat his army posed to the religious community at Lindisfarne. In my discussion, I use the conventional form 'Halfdan', rather than MacSweeney's 'Halfden'.

16 In the era of Halfdan's military activities, as Lynda Rollason explains, Bamburgh was a 'citadel of the Anglo-Saxon kings of Bernicia': Lynda Rollason, 'Bamburgh castle', in Cannon, ed., *Oxford Companion*, p.78. However, as Marios Costambeys observes, 'The area occupied [by Halfdan] seems to have been broadly the old kingdom of Deira, centred on York; the northern part of Northumbria, Bernicia, remained in the hands of English rulers' ('Halfdan [*d*. 877]').

17 See 'Hadrian', in Simon Hornblower and Antony Spawforth, eds, *The Oxford Classical Dictionary*, 3rd edn (Oxford: Oxford University Press, 1996), pp.662-63: p.663.

18 I take 'Allendale' here to refer not to Allendale Town itself (NGR NY 835 555) but to the valley area of the River East Allen in general – which includes, for example, the Allendale Common (NGR NY 853 508) that is found to the immediate north-east of Sparty Lea (and some way upstream from Allendale Town) as well as the Allendale Common (NGR NY 831

455) that lies just west of Allenheads and rises up towards Killhope Law.

19 Lawrence Buell, *Writing for an Endangered World: Literature, Culture, and Environment in the U.S. and Beyond* (Cambridge, MA: Belknap, 2001), p.297, n. 1.

20 Matthew Jarvis, 'Barry MacSweeney's Moorland Romance', in Fiona Becket and Terry Gifford, eds, *Culture, Creativity and Environment: New Environmentalist Criticism* (Amsterdam: Rodopi, 2007), pp.181-96: p.189.

21 Plumwood, *Environmental Culture*, p.97.

22 Plumwood, p.4.

23 See *Pearl*, lines 160 and 159, in Malcolm Andrew and Ronald Waldren, eds, *The Poems of the Pearl Manuscript*, revised edition (n.p.: University of Exeter, 1987), p.62.

24 The Northumberland village of Blanchland (NGR NY 965 505) and the nearby Blanchland Moor (NGR NY 955 535) are around seven miles east-north-east of Sparty Lea as the crow flies.

25 Leo Marx, *The Machine in the Garden: Technology and the Pastoral Ideal in America* (Oxford: Oxford University Press, 1964), p.25. MacSweeney's image of hard hats in heather is, I would suggest, an interesting parallel to Marx's own eponymous image of *The Machine in the Garden*.

ANDREW DUNCAN

1 'MacSweeney/Pickard/Smith: Poets from North-East England interviewed by Eric Mottram', *Poetry Information* No. 18 (Winter/Spring 1977-78), p.39.

2 Barry MacSweeney, *Black Torch* (London: London Pride Editions, 1978), p.58.

3 *Black Torch*, p.17.

4 Victor Turner, quoted in Alan Macfarlane, *The Justice and the Mare's Ale* (Oxford: Blackwell, 1981), p.24.

5 The General Strike of 1926 began as a miners' strike, which went on for six months and was the classic strike in British history.

6 See Andrew Duncan, 'The mythical history of Northumbria; or, feathered slave to unreasonable demands: on Barry MacSweeney (1948-2000)', *Poetry Salzburg Review* No.1 (spring, 2001), pp.128-141, collected in Andrew Duncan, *The Council of Heresy: A Primer of Poetry in a Balkanised Terrain* (Exeter: Shearsman Books, 2009), pp.125-141. See also Andrew Duncan, *Origins of the Underground: British Poetry between Apocryphon and Incident Light* (Cambridge: Salt Publishing, 2008).

7 *Black Torch*, p.16.

8 *Black Torch*, p.33.

9 *Black Torch*, pp.9-10.

10 *Black Torch*, p.67

11 L.C. Knights, *Drama and Society in the Age of Jonson* (first pub. 1937, this edn., London: Methuen & Co. Ltd., 1977), p.323.

12 Knights, p.324.

13 Richard Mulcaster, quoted in Knights, p.329

14 Neville Williams, 'The Tudors', in A.G. Dickens, ed., *Courts of Europe: Politics, Patronage and Royalty 1400-1800* (London: Thames & Hudson, 1977), pp.147-68.

15 See Frank Musgrove, *The North of England: A History from Roman Times to the Present* (London: Wiley-Blackwell, 1990).

16 *Black Torch*, p.39

17 'Gweith Argoet Llwyfein', Llyfr Taliesin XXXV, See National Library of Wales, Peniarth Ms. 2, f. 28 v., http://digidol.llgc.org.uk/METS/LLT 00001/frames?div=67&subdiv=0&locale=en&mode=reference [accessed 30 December 2012].

18 The Battle of Argoed Llwyfain', translated by Tony Conran in Tony Conran, ed., *Welsh Verse* (Bridgend: Seren, 1992), p.105.

WILLIAM WALTON ROWE

1 I am grateful to Sean Bonney and Paul Sutton for conversations which have helped me formulate a number of ideas in this essay.

2 Samuel Taylor Coleridge, *The Oxford Authors: Samuel Taylor Coleridge*, ed. H.J. Jackson (Oxford: Oxford University Press, 1985), p.318.

3 Jerome Rothenberg and Pierre Joris, *Poems for the Millennium*, Volume 1 (Berkeley: University of California Press, 1995), p.184.

4 *Poems for the Millennium*, p.182.

5 Michael McClure, *Huge Dreams* (New York: Penguin, 1999), p. 33.

6 McClure, p.30.

7 See 'Bad Blood', from *A Season in Hell*, in Arthur Rimbaud, *Complete Works, Selected Letters* (Chicago and London: University of Chicago Press, 2005), pp.265-67.

8 See Danny Hayward's denunciation of this situation in 'hardly our conjuncture', in Sean Bonney, *Four Letters Four Comments* (Scarborough: Punch Press, 2011).

JOHN WILKINSON

1 Andrew Marr, *A History of Modern Britain* (London: Macmillan, 2007), p.381.

2 Martin Amis, *Money* (London: Jonathan Cape, 1984), pp.23-24.

3 Marianne Morris, 'The Abused Become the Abusers: the Poetry of Barry MacSweeney', *Quid* 14 (Winter 2004), pages unnumbered.

4 Klaus Theweleit, *Male Fantasies, Volume One: Women, Floods, Bodies, History*, tr. Stephen Conway (Minneapolis: University of Minnesota Press, 1987), pp.74-75.

5 See Wyndham Lewis, *Time and Western Man*, ed. Paul Edwards (Santa

Barbara: Black Sparrow Press, 1993).

6   Joan Bridgman, 'At School with Margaret Thatcher', *Contemporary Review* Volume 285, No. 1664 (September 2004), p.136.

7   Elvis Costello, 'Tramp the Dirt Down', *Spike* (Warner Brothers, 1989).

8   Martin Amis, 'Thatcher', *The War Against Cliché: Essays and Reviews 1971-2000* (London: Jonathan Cape, 2001), p.23.

9   Adam Piette, 'Barry MacSweeney, *Horses in Boiling Blood*', *Chicago Review* Volume 53, No.1 (Spring 2007), p.202.

PAUL BATCHELOR

1   Many of the ideas in this essay first took shape while I was writing my thesis, so a large debt is owed to my PhD supervisor, W.N. Herbert.

2   'Six Poems by Barry McSweeney', *Stand*, Vol. 8, No. 2 (1966), pp.6-9.

3   'MACSWEENEY / PICKARD / SMITH: Poets from North East England interviewed by Eric Mottram', *Poetry Information*, No. 18 (1978), p.30.

4   John Wilkinson, 'A Single Striking Soviet! The Poetry of Barry MacSweeney', *The Lyric Touch: Essays on the Poetry of Excess* (Cambridge: Salt, 2007), p.78.

5   See Barry MacSweeney Archive: Box 30.

6   Keith Tuma, in '*Contemporary British Poetry: Essays in Theory and Criticism*, ed. James Acheson and Romana Huk; *Out of Dissent: A Study of Five Contemporary British Poets* by Clive Bush', *Criticism*, Vol. XL, no. 2, (pp.313-322), p.320.

7   A selection of MacSweeney's work appears in *Anthology of Twentieth-Century British and Irish Poetry*, edited by Keith Tuma (New York: Oxford University Press, 2001), pp.755-59. The selection is unrepresentative of MacSweeney's work, being drawn entirely from *Hellhound Memos*, which had recently been anthologised in Iain Sinclair's anthology *Conductors of Chaos* (London: Picador, 1996). Tuma's brief introductory note contains several biographical errors and reiterates MacSweeney's indebtedness to Bunting.

8   Rebecca A. Smith, 'Barry MacSweeney and the Bunting Influence: A key figure in his literary universe?' *Jacket* 35 (2008) http://jacketmagazine.com/35/smith-macsweeney.shtml. Smith focuses for the most part on 'the popular appraisal of [MacSweeney's] work' and takes her title from a review of *Wolf Tongue* that appeared on popmatters.com; however, she also considers academic responses.

9   See 'The autobiography of Barry MacSweeney', *The Boy from the Green Cabaret Tells of His Mother*, (London: Hutchinson, 1968), pages unnumbered.

10 See 'Victory Over Darkness & The Sunne', from Barry MacSweeney, *Horses in Boiling Blood* (Cambridge: Equipage, 2004), pp28-29:
    The tidal causeway at Lindisfarne can be as untrue as you
    Just as Basil taught me all those years ago

And he said if you don't publish correctly the tidal charts
Seamen from Valparaiso and Houston will end up on the Black Middens
    dead on the rocks
Their cries echoing under the tidal sweep like the organs
of St Nicholas and St Mary's in the hearte of the city
And like St Denise in the outskirts of beloved Paris
And when the sun rises from the fjords' darkness
will only be in their death if you do not correct your tidal charts
Accuracy is all he said and also compression of language

11 'Unless a man knows bloody well what he's doing he's not going to do it very well, so a man whose thought is floppy is not likely to produce anything but a floppy poem...'. Basil Bunting, quoted in Donald Davie, *Under Briggflatts* (Manchester: Carcanet, 1989), pp.144-45.

12 Basil Bunting, 'Preface' to Tom Pickard, *High on the Walls* (London: Fulcrum, 1967), p.9.

13 Basil Bunting, '*Briggflatts*', *Complete Poems*, ed. Richard Caddel (Newcastle upon Tyne: Bloodaxe Books, 2000), p.73.

14 In a footnote, Smith concedes that the presence of the archangel Israfel in 'The Last Bud' must be an allusion to Bunting, but she does not pursue the reasons for, or the effect of, the allusion.

15 Harold Bloom, *The Anxiety of Influence: A Theory of Poetry*, 2nd edition (New York: Oxford University Press, 1997), p.15.

16 For the importance of these poets to Bunting, see Peter Makin, *Bunting: The Shaping of his Verse* (Oxford: Oxford University Press, 1992), pp.8-14.

17 W. Jackson Bate, *The Burden of the Past and the English Poet* (Cambridge: Harvard University Press, 1991), p.22.

18 William Wordsworth, 'Book VII: Residence in London', *The Prelude: a Parallel Text*, ed. J.C. Maxwell (Harmondsworth: Penguin, 1971), p.262. MacSweeney has annotated his copy of *The Prelude*, and among his many notes to this Book, he has underlined the words 'another lies at length'.

19 Victoria Forde, *The Poetry of Basil Bunting* (Newcastle upon Tyne: Bloodaxe Books, 1991), p.174.

20 For the importance of 'Out of the Cradle Endlessly Rocking' to Bunting, see 'Wordsworth and Whitman', *Basil Bunting on Poetry*, ed. Peter Makin (Baltimore: Johns Hopkins University Press, 1999), pp.71-98.

21 Walt Whitman, 'Out of the Cradle Endlessly Rocking', *Collected Poems*, ed. Francis Murphy (Harmondsworth: Penguin, 1975), p.276.

22 MacSweeney sent 'The Last Bud' to J.H. Prynne, who praised it as MacSweeney's finest poem to date in a letter on 15 May 1967. If this is the correct date, then MacSweeney must have sent Prynne an early draft of the poem. In a letter to his mother, MacSweeney dates 'The Last Bud' to September 1968, but claims to have been working on it for many months. See Archive: BM 1/2.

23 J.H. Prynne 'Love in the Air', *Poems*, 1st edn (Newcastle upon Tyne: Bloodaxe Books, 1999), p.55.

24 Basil Bunting, letter to Massimo Bacigalupo, 20.3.85, Bunting Archive.

Quoted in *Basil Bunting on Poetry*, p.206 n.38.

25 *Letters of John Keats*, ed. Robert Gittings (Oxford: Oxford University Press, 1970), p.292.

26 *Letters of John Keats*, p.325

27 *Poetry Information*, p.33.

28 Thomas Chatterton, 'Epistle to Mastre Canynge on Aella', *The Poetical Works of Thomas Chatterton: with notices of his life, history of the Rowley controversy, a selection of his letters, and notes critical and explanatory* (Cambridge: W.P. Grant, 1842), lines 17-18.

29 *Poetry Information*, p.32.

30 *Poetry Information*, p.32.

31 *Poetry Information*, p.37.

32 See *Plato on Poetry*: Ion; Republic 376e-398b9; Republic 595-608b10, ed. Penelope Murray (Cambridge: Cambridge University Press, 1996), pp.8-9.

33 J.H. Prynne, quoted in Robert Potts, 'Through the Oval Window', *Guardian*, 10 April 2004.

34 S.J. Litherland in a conversation with the author.

35 'Prynne encouraged Barry's course towards the violent and obscene poems of around 1980... Barry sent him a copy of 'Colonel B' with a note asking "Have I gone too far this time?" To which Jeremy gleefully replied, "No, not far enough!" as he would, for it was always his habit to push those under his influence to extremes, and it is this extremism rather than any particular stylistic traits which for me mark his influence on Barry.' Peter Riley, email to the author, 28 November 2005.

36 In 1971 Eric Mottram became editor of *Poetry Review*. During his time in post (1971-77) the Poetry Society was chaired by a succession of avant-garde poets, and the Presidents were Hugh MacDiarmid and Basil Bunting. At this time, the small-press scene was thriving, and MacSweeney would have felt at the centre of the poetic movement Mottram called the British Poetry Revival. On 26 March 1977, following a concerted effort by the Arts Council, in particular literature director Charles Osborne, to oust Mottram, the avant-garde poets staged a mass walkout, led by MacSweeney, who was then Chairman. For the definition of the term 'British Poetry Revival' see Eric Mottram, 'The British Poetry Revival, 1960-75', in *New British Poetries: The Scope of the Possible*, ed. Robert Hampson & Peter Barry (Manchester: Manchester University Press, 1993), pp.15-50. Peter Barry gives a detailed account of the period in *Poetry Wars: British Poetry of the 1970s and the Battle of Earls Court* (Cambridge: Salt, 2006).

37 *The Penguin Book of Contemporary British Poetry*, ed. Blake Morrison and Andrew Motion (Harmondsworth: Penguin, 1982), p.11.

38 *The New British Poetry* (London: Paladin, 1988). Ken Edwards's introduction to the section 'Some Younger Poets', p.265.

39 Bunting's list of French characteristics can be found in *Basil Bunting on Poetry*, pp.37-8.

40 'The Codex', *Basil Bunting on Poetry*, p.5.

41 Eric Mottram, 'Conversation with Basil Bunting on the Occasion of his

75th Birthday, 1975', *Poetry Information* No.19 (1978), p.5.

42 Oppositional mapping was not the preserve of High Modernist poets alone: in the 70s, Bunting's Northumbria would be joined by Geoffrey Hill's Mercia and Ted Hughes's Elmet. In his essay 'Englands of the Mind', Seamus Heaney discusses Hughes, Hill and Larkin in these terms: 'All three treat England as a region – or rather treat their region as England – in different and complementary ways. I believe they are afflicted with a sense of history that was once the peculiar affliction of the poets of other nations who were not themselves natives of England but who spoke the English language'. See Seamus Heaney, 'Englands of the Mind', *Preoccupations: Selected Prose 1968-1978* (London: Faber, 1980), p.77.

43 In 1069, a group of lords and earls, assisted by Denmark and Scotland, formed an army of Viking, Gaels and Angles, and attempted to reclaim the North from the Normans.

44 See *Basil Bunting on Poetry*, p.72.

45 Basil Bunting, *Complete Poems*, p.226.

46 Tony Lopez, 'Oppositional Englishness: National Identity in Basil Bunting's *'Briggflatts'*, *Meaning Performance* (Cambridge: Salt, 2006), p.158.

47 Basil Bunting, *Complete Poems*, p.226.

48 I am persuaded by Makin's interpretation of Cuthbert and Bloodaxe's significance to *Briggflatts*, and believe that this sort of detective work was precisely what Bunting (like Pound and MacDiarmid) wished to encourage in his followers. Whether Bunting's view of Bede was accurate is another matter. See Peter Makin, 'Appendix 3, St Cuthbert in the Hands of Bede', *Bunting: The Shaping of his Verse*, pp.331-33.

49 Lopez, p.152-3.

50 MacSweeney's primary source for information on the English Civil War was the work of Christopher Hill, in particular Hill's seminal book *The World Turned Upside Down*, which argues that England might have undergone a far more radical transformation had revolt been directed by the underground movements of popular protest, rather than by Cromwell's Protestantism. The English Revolution was Hill's preferred term for the Civil War. See Christopher Hill, *The World Turned Upside Down: Radical Ideas During the English Revolution* (Harmondsworth: Penguin, 1972).

51 Ken Smith, *Tristan Crazy* (Newcastle upon Tyne: Bloodaxe Books, 1978).

52 Colin Raw, 'The Godfather of the New Poetry', *You Again: Last Poems and Other Words* (Tarset: Bloodaxe Books, 2004).

53 Letter from Neil Astley to MacSweeney, dated 19 November 1984. Neil Astley sent me a photocopy of this letter.

54 Ken Smith, 'Fox Running', *The Poet Reclining: Selected Poems 1962-1980* (Newcastle upon Tyne: Bloodaxe Books, 1982), p.161.

55 Nicholas Johnson, 'Barry MacSweeney: an Appreciation', *Independent*, 13 May 2000.

56 Harriet Tarlo, 'Radical Landscapes: Contemporary British Poetry in the Bunting Tradition', *The Star You Steer By: Basil Bunting and British Modernism*, ed. James McGonigal and Richard Price (Amsterdam: Rodopi,

2000), pp.149-180.

57 Basil Bunting, *Complete Poems*, p.63.

58 Jeffrey Wainwright has noted how Wordsworth's faith in common, 'unpoetic' diction is frequently felt in Part One of *Briggflatts*. See 'William Wordsworth at *Briggflatts*', *Agenda: Basil Bunting Special Issue*, Vol. 16, No.1 (Spring 1978) p.39. Bunting admired the way Wordsworth 'could make the simplest words carry the most complex emotions'. See Peter Makin, p.272.

59 Bunting would connect his practice here to his love of Wordsworth: 'I should have said about Wordsworth that occasionally his stress on "thing" is remarkable. Any competent writer must know the importance of things'. Bunting, quoted in Jonathan Williams, 'An Interview with Basil Bunting', *Conjunctions*, 5 (1983), p.86.

PETER RILEY

1 This section is rewritten from a review of *The Book of Demons* published in *Poetry Quarterly Review 9*, 1998.

2 'Letters to Dewey' forms most of the booklet *Sweet Advocate* (Cambridge: Equipage, 1999).

W.N. HERBERT

1 Peter Barry, *Contemporary British Poetry and the City* (Manchester: Manchester University Press, 2000), pp. 69-70. All other references to this volume appear in the text.

2 Barry MacSweeney, *The Boy from the Green Cabaret Tells of His Mother* (London: Hutchinson, 1968). Charles Cros is an eccentric choice of figure to be translating, famous as much for his near-invention of the phonogram as for his poetry, which is best-known in the English-speaking world for the comic piece 'The Kippered Herring'. Several lines in Cros's poem would seem oddly appropriate to the oscillatory theme of this essay. In Edward Gorey's translation, they read:

> Since then at the end of the string, long, long, long
> A salt herring, dry, dry, dry
> Has been swinging slowly, slowly, slowly...

3 In the 1623 Folio text of *The Tempest*, Caliban is described in the 'Names of the Actors' as '*a saluage and deformed slaue*'.

4 Robert Sheppard, 'Poets Behaving Badly', http://jacketmagazine.com/31/sheppard-barry.html [accessed 14 June 2012].

5 Thomas Hardy, 'The Haunter', *Selected Poems*, ed. David Wright (Harmondsworth: Penguin, 1978), p.378.

6 Paul Durcan, 'Glocca Morra', *Daddy, Daddy* (Belfast: Blackstaff Press, 1990), p.160.

7 Arthur Rimbaud, 'Adieu', *Saison En Enfer*, http://www.mag4.net/Rimbaud/poesies/Adieu.html, accessed 14 June 2012. 'Let us all accept new strength, and real tenderness. And at dawn, armed with glowing patience, we will enter the cities of glory.' Arthur Rimbaud, *Complete Works*, tr. Paul Schmidt (London: Harper & Row, 1976), p.213.

8 William Shakespeare, *King Lear*, II, 3, 9-14 http://www.william-shakespeare.info/act2-script-text-king-lear.html accessed June 16th 2012

9 MacSweeney's relationship with mainstream poetry was ambiguous enough to require recourse here to the anecdotal. Occasionally, in the middle of the night, those who knew Barry would receive questionable phonecalls. He had a wry, lilting voice, capable of great intensity in readings, but in the dark those North-East tones became lugubrious and sinister as he suggested various bizarre crimes committed by or to be committed against what he saw as the poetry state. On one occasion he rang me up to discuss the feasibility of hanging drawing and quartering the lately-deceased Poet Laureate, Ted Hughes. It seems to me important to remember that voice from the darkness, by turns subversive, funny, disturbing and terribly moving, when referring, as here, to territory he shared with canonical poets.

10 Rebecca A. Smith, 'Barry MacSweeney and the Bunting Influence: A key figure in his literary universe?' *Jacket* 35 (2008), http://jacketmagazine.com/35/smith-macsweeney.shtml [accessed 14 June 2012].